The New Zealand
RESTAURANT COOKBOOK

The New Zealand
RESTAURANT COOKBOOK

Michael Guy & Digby Law

LINDON

Published by Lindon Publishing, P.O. Box 39-225,
Auckland West, Telephone 760-647

First published 1983

Copyright © 1983 by Michael Guy and Digby Law

All rights reserved. No part of this publication may be reproduced, stored in a retrieval system or transmitted in any form or by an means, electronic, photocopying, recording or otherwise, without the prior permission of the copyright owners.

ISBN 0-86470-005-9

Edited by Phillip Ridge
Typesetting by Artspec Typesetting Systems Ltd, Auckland
Design by Michael Guy and Phillip Ridge
Photography by Max Thomson, Stephen Ballantyne
and Lianne Ruscoe
Illustrations by Christine Brown/Paper Dart
Bookprint Consultants, Wellington
Crockery and cutlery from Designstore, Auckland

The art of dining well is no slight art, the pleasure not a slight pleasure.
    —Michel Montaigne, *Essays* (1580-88)

Tell me what you eat and I will tell you what you are.

The discovery of a new dish does more for the happiness of mankind than the discovery of a new star.

    —Jean-Anthelme Brillat-Savarin, *Physiologie du goût* (1825)

ACKNOWLEDGEMENTS

I would like to thank the many people who have helped create *The New Zealand Restaurant Cookbook*. Special thanks go to the 50 chefs who provided recipes and who spent so much time perfecting each dish. It is not an easy task to persuade chefs to provide their secret recipes, so their help and cooperation is doubly appreciated.

Thanks are extended to Hodder and Stoughton, publishers of Digby Law's *A Vegetable Cookbook* and *A Soup Cookbook*, for their assistance.

The support of Jane Caddy and Cathy Toohey is also appreciated.

Michael Guy

Contents

INTRODUCTION	Introduction	10
	Herbs and Spices	12
	Kitchen Equivalents	15
	General Cooking Hints	22
	Thickeners and Moisteners	23
	Cooking Methods	23
	Some Cooking Terms	25
THE RESTAURANTS	The Restaurants	27
DIGBY LAW	Introduction	159
	Entrées and Soups	160
	Vegetables and Salads	167
	Main Courses	170
	Desserts	177
INDEX	Recipe Index	180
	Restaurant Index	182

Introduction

The New Zealand Restaurant Cookbook is the first book of its type to be produced here in New Zealand. It is a unique look at the best dishes from the chefs of some of the country's finest restaurants. When the original concept for this cookbook was discussed it was decided to invite the restaurants to submit recipes for an entrée, main course and a dessert. But in the past few years there has been such a proliferation of so many different types of ethnic restaurants that eating out is no longer limited to French style cuisine, basic New Zealand or Chinese cookery. Now we have restaurants featuring the cuisine not only of France, but Italy, Korea, Japan, Vietnam, Thailand, Spain, Mexico, India, Indonesia and many other countries. Different ethnic restaurants are opening regularly throughout New Zealand. Most of the restaurants featured in this cookbook *do* present an entrée, main course and dessert, but some cuisines do not break their meal into three fairly rigid courses. The Chinese tend to eat a number of main course dishes, the Koreans with their bulgogi-style cooking dispense entirely with entrées and desserts, as do the Japanese. This is what makes this book so interesting. It offers a variety of different styles. If you want a French style meal just choose one of these and you can present an entire meal for your guests. Alternatively, you can choose one of the many other cuisines. The variation is enormous. You can choose to cook a simple whitebait fritter, attempt a more difficult mousse, or present a full Japanese meal.

Generally cookbooks tend to be the product of one particular cook who might have spent years perfecting their particular technique, whether it be Robert Carrier, Elizabeth David, Gretta Anna or Julia Childs. But the recipes in *The New Zealand Restaurant Cookbook* feature the work of a myriad of cooks and restaurateurs from those who have spent years perfecting their ideas, to the young and upcoming chefs introducing a new mainstream of inventiveness to their dishes. The cookbook also features a number of dishes from Digby Law, one of the doyens of New Zealand cooking. His recipes are an attempt to balance the strong overseas influence in the restaurant recipes, with dishes that are generic in many instances to New Zealand. His dishes feature New Zealand venison, salmon, lamb, scallops, whitebait, rabbit, the humble kumara, and even that much argued about dish — the pavlova.

New Zealand is quickly becoming much more sophisticated in its style of eating, and in the preparation and presentation of its dishes. In Europe, especially in France and Italy, the main meal of the day has long been a ritual — a drawn-out affair that is the hub of social and family life. Here in New Zealand the traditions have not been so pronounced. Meals have historically been divided into a short breakfast, a quick lunch and uninspiring dinners. But slowly, with the advent of so many more restaurants, and the availability of a much wider range of meats, seafoods, vegetables and other ingredients, our style of eating is changing. Added to this is the improvement in the standard and increasing consumption of New Zealand wine. All these add up to a greater interest in food, cooking, dining out, and making the nightly meal a more social occasion. Perhaps in the years to come, New Zealand may move even closer to the French and the Italian style of eating. In France you can visit a country restaurant on Sunday, arriving about noon; within the hour the restaurant is full, and they begin serving the meal. You don't choose from a menu. The cook has already worked out what he is going to serve, and you merely wait for it to arrive. The eating, drinking and conversation will occupy the next four hours or so. This is slowly beginning to happen here with restaurants in many areas starting to open for Sunday brunch. These innovative restaurants have stimulated public interest in cuisine and home experimentation. Delicatessens featuring exotic imported ingredients are flourishing. Cookery schools such as Julie Biuso's 'La Dolce Vita' and the Cordon Bleu school are booming, and distributors of gamefoods and the more exotic seafoods are finding an unprecedented demand.

Apart from merely presenting the recipes, *The New Zealand Restaurant Cookbook* also includes a guide to cookery terms, stocks, basic ingredients, moisteners, thickeners, wine, herbs and spices. Therefore, the book can be enjoyed by both amateur cooks and the more skilled. Bon appetit!

Michael Guy

Herbs & Spices

New Zealand's style of cooking has never been closely allied with the use of herbs, but this is slowly changing as our eating habits become more refined.

The word 'herb' means herbage or grass, and comes from the Latin *herba*. For thousands of years herbs have been used for their medicinal qualities, and even now they are still used for pharmaceutical purposes. Their seeds, roots, stems, flowers and leaves are used for culinary purposes throughout the world, according to the varying tradition of different countries. Whereas New Zealand has concentrated on mint with lamb or peas and parsley on potatoes, the Scandinavians use dill widely for their fish dishes, the Italians use oregano for their pasta, the French fennel with fish or tarragon with chicken, the English sage with pork, and the Latin American countries coriander with their famous *ceviche* or raw fish salad. The beauty of herbs is that they can be used fresh, dried or frozen, though fresh is generally preferable. Most herbs can be grown relatively easily in New Zealand. Dried herbs are stronger than fresh herbs because they have no water content. Therefore, in cooking a useful rule is for every three teaspoons of fresh herbs you only need one teaspoon of dried herbs. If you grow your own herbs, pick them when they begin to flower, tie in bunches and dry in a warm room away from sunlight or in a warm oven. Store in airtight containers in a cool, dry place. Herbs can be frozen by blanching, then plunged into iced water, drained, sealed in foil and put in the freezer, to be thawed slowly before using. Herbs do lose their perfume and flavour.

For cooking, it is best not to be too generous with the addition of herbs until you have experimented to find out their effects. Many herbs, if cooked too long or used excessively, will impart a bitter taste. It is often better to add them towards the end of preparing a dish.

Some of the recipes in this book mention *bouquet garni*, which the French use in a lot of dishes. Bouquet garni generally consists of thyme, parsley and bay leaf, tied in a piece of cheesecloth with string. The bouquet is added to sauces, stews and *court bouillon*, and is always taken out at the end of cooking. Other herbs, such as rosemary, marjoram, garlic and celery can be added to a bouquet.

THE HERBS

Sweet Basil: This very aromatic and sometimes pungent herb is excellent in stew, soups, sauces and salads. It is a native of India, but the Italians use it extensively because it is compatible with tomatoes. In New Zealand, it goes especially well with lamb. It can be used dried, preserved in oil, or fresh.

Bay: One of the ingredients of bouquet garni, it comes from the bay tree which grows around the Mediterranean. Available dried or powdered, it is used in stews, meat dishes, soups, or with white sauces.

Chervil: Chervil, with its feathery appearance, is part of the parsley family. A native of the Middle East and Southern Russia, it is best used fresh in soups, salads, omelettes and stuffings, or on grilled fish. It is one of the *fines herbes* of French cooking, and with parsley, tarragon and chives, makes a superb omelette aux fines herbes.

Coriander: This herb has its greatest use in Mexican and Latin American dishes, which are slowly becoming more popular in this country. It can be used in the mashed avocado dip called guacamole, and also in raw fish salad (*ceviche*). The Chinese call coriander Chinese parsley, while in India and Asia the seeds or roots are widely used in curries. It can also be used in chutneys, cream of celery soup, and in New Zealand coriander is excellent in a lemon sauce over venison.

Dill: Probably best known for its use in dill pickles, dill is used extensively by the Swedes, Russians and Germans, especially with fish. Dried dill can be used with soups and various sauces, as can its seeds. Fresh, it goes well with potatoes or fish salads.

Fennel: Another of the feathery herbs, similar to dill, fennel is a native of Southern Europe and is widely used in Mediterranean and Italian cooking. It can be used dried, as seeds, or fresh. The fresh bulbs are excellent in salads. The stems can be cooked as vegetables. The seeds have a licorice taste, hence the use of fennel in anisette.

Marjoram: This strong herb can be used fresh or dried in meat, fish, or vegetable dishes, in omelettes, sausages, soups or stews. You need very little, otherwise the dish might take on a bitter taste. It is very good in stuffings, while a touch can be added to a bouquet garni.

Mint: Mint is almost as popular in New Zealand as parsley. Its use with roast lamb has almost become a national tradition. There are many varieties of mint, spearmint being the most popular. It can be used with mint sauce, peas and potatoes, salads, cold summer drinks and salad dressings.

Oregano: Also known as wild marjoram, this herb is brilliant in pizzas. The Italians use it in many of their pasta sauces because it goes so well with tomatoes and cheese. Use it in meat and poultry dishes, with eggplant, bean dishes, or in marinades and basting sauces. The Greeks use the flowers of one variety of oregano, which they call rigani, to garnish their meat dishes.

Parsley: This is probably the most widely used herb in New Zealand and probably the most easily grown. There are a number of varieties, from the broad or curly-leaved, to the Hamburg and Italian parsleys. Rich in vitamins, it is most used as a garnish, but can be chopped finely for sauces, stuffings, soups, stews or fried with fish. It is one of the *fines herbes*, and is used in bouquet garni.

Rosemary: Again of Mediterranean origin, the leaves of rosemary contain oil of camphor. It is best used fresh, chopped finely and added to baked chicken, sprinkled on steak, lamb, veal or to complement fish. It can be used in salads or soups in powder form, or sprinkled in its dry form on potatoes during baking.

Sage: This northern Mediterranean herb is another of those with a strong flavour that can drown more delicate tastes if too much is used. It is best in stuffings for pork and duck, or in the Italian Saltimbocca — thin slices of veal with Parma ham cooked in butter. With casseroles and stews, it should be used with care.

Tarragon: With its slightly anise flavour, tarragon is an essential ingredient in bearnaise and hollandaise sauces. There is a French and Russian variety, with the French herb more aromatic and superior in its flavour. It is widely used in restaurants for savoury butters, soups, salads, and it can be added to roast chicken or in marinating fish and meats. It can be used fresh, dried or powdered.

Thyme: This herb is widely used in soups, stews and sauces. A number of varieties exist, including garden, wild and lemon thyme. It can be rubbed over meat before roasting, added to casseroles or poultry, used in stuffings, or added to butter to serve with potatoes or carrots.

THE SPICES

Allspice: Often called the Jamaica pepper, the allspice is the dried fruit of the pimento tree which is a native to the West Indies. Its taste is a mixture of cinnamon, nutmeg, cloves and mace. The French call this combination *quatre épices*, although ginger is often substituted for cinnamon. Allspice is used in baking, savoury dishes and for pickling, but it is good in game and poultry stuffings.

Anise: This strong and sweet-scented spice has a definite licorice flavour and it is commonly used for baking and confectionery. The French distill it to make Pernod and anisette. A drop or two of Pernod in fish soups and ragout can make a remarkable difference.

Caraway: Best known for its use in baking, although caraway flavoured cheese is widely available in delicatessens. Caraway is commonly used in Europe and Asia to add its characteristic taste to dishes.

Cardamon: Cardamon comes in green, black or white pods. Its small seeds are used in Asia and India in curry powders and sauces. It is the world's most expensive spice, after saffron, and it was once considered an aphrodisiac in France. Cardamon can also be used in its ground state in cakes or pastries, sprinkled on fruit, or in coffee.

Cayenne Pepper: This originally came from Cayenne in French Guiana. It should be used with care in curries, soups, stews, with New Zealand whitebait or oysters, in white sauce, or sprinkled on cheese dishes.

Chilli powder: Chillies belong to the capsicum family. The red pepper is made from dried ground chilli peppers, and varies from mild to very hot. It adds colour and flavour to soups, stews, meat and sauces. Commercial chilli powders often add paprika, garlic, oregano and cumin seed to the ground chilli pepper.

Cinnamon: This is a native to India and comes from the inner bark of the cinnamon tree. It is commercially available as a powder or in sticks, and has a wide range of uses: in cakes, puddings, sweets, to spice rice, fish, chicken, ham, and curries. It is popular in mulled wine or sprinkled on cream in coffee.

Cloves: This powerful aromatic flower bud is available whole or powdered. Whole it can be used for pickling, in ham and pork, for fruit dishes or in apple pie. In desserts it is generally best ground, but because it is very pungent it should be used sparingly. Clove oil is famous as a remedy for toothache.

Coriander: Strangely enough the leaves of the coriander are used as a herb and the seeds as a spice. It is sweet but tart and is often used in curries. Also excellent with lamb and pork chops, in stuffings, marinades and pickles.

Cumin: The pungent taste of cumin is similar but stronger than caraway. It is used for curries and meat dishes. The Mexicans use it with bean dishes, but it also flavours lamb and chicken dishes.

Curry powder: This is a mixture of herbs and spices, and the range of curry powders varies enormously, depending on the specific ingredients. Some commercial varieties might include up to 40 different herbs and spices, with the varying amount of hot pepper used to give the curry its particular strength.

Fenugreek: Although this plant originated in the Middle East, it is used mainly in Indian and Greek cooking. The seeds are used as a spice and the leaves as a herb.

Ginger: Available in root, powder or pickled form, ginger originally came from China. It can be used in Oriental dishes, pickles, chutneys, stewed fruits, or even with meat and fish.

Mace and Nutmeg: These both come from the nutmeg tree, a native of Southeast Asia. Mace, which is the stronger in flavour, is the dried outer layer of the kernel of the tree's fruit. Nutmeg is the dried seed of the fruit. Both have a similar flavour and smell, but nutmeg is used for sweet dishes, while mace when ground is excellent in game sauces, for pickling or marinades. It can also be used in various vegetable dishes.

Paprika: This spice originally came from Turkey. It is bright red, and has a variety of uses in many cuisines. It is a member of the capsicum family, and it adds colour and sweetness to chicken or veal dishes, cream soups, white sauces, goulash and fish.

Pepper: Pepper is one of the most widely used spices in both its white or black ground varieties or as whole peppercorns, whether green, black or white. The black peppercorns are sun-dried berries picked from the vine when green. White peppercorns are picked when ripe and the skins removed when they turn red. Black pepper is best ground when you need to use it so it does not lose its flavour. The milder white pepper is best used with lighter sauces or where black pepper would contrast too much with the dish.

Saffron: Saffron is made from the stigma of a crocus and is used for flavouring and colouring rice dishes, soups, paella, cakes or breads. It is the world's most expensive spice because 75,000 stigmas have to be hand-harvested to produce only half a kilo of saffron.

Turmeric: This Southeast Asian bright yellow spice is available powdered or as a dried root. It is used to flavour curries, mustards and pickles.

Kitchen Equivalents

BUTTER		SUGAR	
1 cup	250g	1 cup approximately	250g
1 tablespoons	15g	1 tablespoons	15g
1 dessertspoon	10g	1 dessertspoon	10g

FLOUR		OTHER	
2 cups (sifted)	250g	1000g	1kg
2 tablespoon	15g	100g	3.5oz
2 dessertspoon	10g	1000ml	1 litre

COMMON KITCHEN METRIC MEASUREMENTS

1 tablespoon	15ml
1 dessertspoon	10ml
1 teaspoon	5ml
3 teaspoons	1 tablespoon
2 teaspoons	1 dessertspoon
16 tablespoons	approximately 1 cup
1 cup	250ml
4 cups	1 litre

GRAMS TO OUNCES

When metric scales are not available use these approximate conversions.

25g - 1 oz		250g - 9 oz	
50g - 2 oz		275g - 10 oz	
75g - 3 oz		300g - 10.5 oz	
100g - 3.5 oz		325g - 11 oz	
125g - 4 oz		350g - 12 oz	
150g - 5 oz		375g - 13 oz	
175g - 6 oz		400g - 14 oz	
200g - 7 oz		425g - 15 oz	
225g - 8 oz		450g - 16 oz	

OVEN SETTING EQUIVALENTS

	FAHRENHEIT	CELSIUS	REGULO NOS.
Very Cool	225 - 275	110 - 140	¼ - 1
Cool	300 - 325	150 - 160	2 - 3
Moderate	350 - 375	180 - 190	4 - 5
Hot	400 - 450	200 - 230	6 - 8
Very Hot	475 - 500	250 - 260	9 - 10

It will be many years before all New Zealand stoves have thermostats converted to degrees celsius.

The following is a chart showing conversion from farenheit to celsius:

ELECTRIC DEGREES FARENHEIT	DEGREES CELSIUS	GAS MARK
250	120	½
275	140	1
300	150	2
325	160	3
350	180	4
375	190	5
400	200	6
425	220	7
450	230	8
475	250	9
500	260	10

Opposite: Shellfish chowder (p. 165). This richly flavoured shellfish chowder prepared by Digby Law, is an excellent winter entrée. A variety of New Zealand shellfish can be used, including mussels, pipis, oysters, toheroa or even scallops. The chowder can also be visually exciting with the addition of plump scallops or mussels in the slightly opened shell. *(Photograph by Max Thomson.)*

---

1. Chai, who rarely offers his surname, runs the August Moon in Auckland. *(Photograph by Stephen Ballantyne).*

---

2. Loaves of fresh bread baked daily at Anderson's restaurant in Hamilton. *(Photograph by Lianne Ruscoe).*

---

3. Antoine's, run by Tony and Beth Astle, has received world-wide recognition for its superb cuisine. *(Photograph by Lianne Ruscoe).*

1

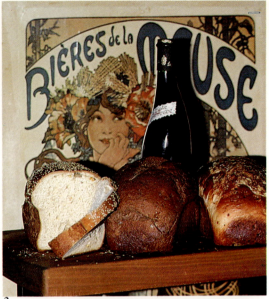

2

3

4

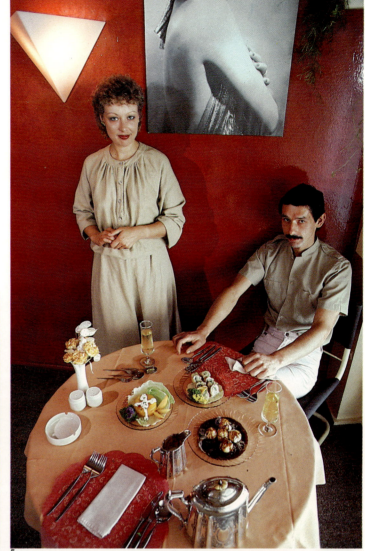

5

6

Opposite: Melanesian Fish Salad (p. 63). This stunning Melanesian fish salad, prepared by Wendy Lever of Flamingos Restaurant, uses the very popular deep sea fish orange roughy which marinates extremely well. But other fish can also be used, including snapper, to produce this typical Melanesian raw fish recipe. It should be presented imaginatively with freshly sliced fruits, flowers and leaves. *(Photograph by Max Thomson.)*

---

4. Kasey Coory, in the bar at his Bacchus restaurant in Wellington, is renowned for cooking dishes par excellence. *(Photograph by Lianne Ruscoe).*

---

5. Laurie and Judith Bartup took over what was an Auckland restaurant with a poor reputation, renamed it Bartups, and turned it into a highly successful venture. *(Photograph by Stephen Ballantyne).*

---

6. The Beachcomber seafood restaurant is situated on the waterfront at Sumner near Christchurch. At high tide the water laps around what were once the tearooms on the old Sumner pier. *(Photograph by Stephen Ballantyne).*

General cooking hints

New Zealand has a superb choice of fresh ingredients, with choice lamb and beef, excellent vegetables, fruit, and a wonderful array of seafoods and fresh fish. In fact New Zealand is a cook's paradise. Because fresh produce is so readily available, there is no excuse not to use fresh ingredients when cooking. A trout caught from the banks of Lake Taupo and cooked within the hour has an unforgettable taste; the oysters and fresh mussels eaten within a short time of harvesting are magnificent, and nothing can surpass vegetables and salad ingredients picked fresh from the garden. This availability leads to the first rule of cooking — try and make sure your ingredients are as fresh as possible. If it is necessary to obtain them well in advance of preparation put them in airtight containers in the refrigerator so that they retain their moisture and keep in good condition.

An equally important rule is to use only the finest basics of cooking. Do not try to cut corners and costs by using inferior oils, ordinary black pepper or cheap wine. Use olive oil, peanut or corn oil if vegetable oils are needed, and try and use fresh herbs from the garden if possible. It is strange that so many people only use dried herbs brought from the supermarket when herbs are so easy to grow, particularly parsley which grows so prolifically in most areas.

With wines it is a common practice to resort to using a wine barely fit to drink. But a dish will only be as good as its ingredients. If a poor wine is used, it is quite possible that the dish will be unappetizing. Larry Charman from Auckland's Meridian Restaurant recounts the story of his cooking in the kitchen of a restaurant in Provence. He was a novice cook just learning the art of French cooking. He looked around the kitchen for wine to add to his boeuf à la bourguignonne and the owner directed him to the wine generally used for cooking which turned out to be a particularly fine vintage of Bordeaux red. Wine in cooking basically adds flavour; it also tenderizes and moistens when used for marinating. When it is cooked it changes taste and loses its alcohol content. Many of the recipes in this book call for both red and white wine. Generally, there is no set rule as to whether red goes with red meats or white with white meats. White wines can be used with some red meats, while on the other hand, red wine is often added to fish dishes. Liqueurs, port, sherry, Marsala and Madeira all add unique flavours to many dishes. One recipe in this book calls for the use of Drambuie in cooking fillet steak. With alcohol in cooking there seems to be no end to imagination.

Generally, all the recipes in *The New Zealand Restaurant Cookbook* call for the use of butter. Personally, I prefer butter above margarine for cooking. To date, I still have not seen a first-class cook in New Zealand using margarine for cooking. I have been brought up using butter in cooking, and there seems to be no advantage in changing old habits. Where recipes in this book call for slow frying, put a little oil in the pan first, and then an equal amount of butter. The addition of oil will keep the butter from browning. I still prefer olive oil above others, for its richness, taste and quality. Like all ingredients, there is good oil and bad oil — olive oil is no exception. A first-pressing olive oil is preferable to a second-pressing oil, so consult your delicatessen owner as to the quality of any oil you use.

THICKENERS AND MOISTENERS

If the sauce in the dish you are preparing needs to be thickened you have two choices. Either make a *beurre manié* or use egg yolks. A *beurre manié* is made by mixing equal amounts of butter and flour and adding it bit by bit to the sauce. It can be kneaded between the fingers and dropped in piece by piece. It needs time for the flour in the *beurre manié* to cook properly. If you use eggs to thicken the sauce beat the yolk thoroughly, pour a little of the hot sauce into a third container, mix thoroughly, then add it into the main dish, and stir continuously. Do not boil or the yolk can cook and streak the dish.

Dishes can be moistened either by using stock, wine or cream, and all are called for in various recipes in this book. Beef, chicken and other stocks are commercially available everywhere, although stocks can be made so easily by boiling poultry, beef, and other meats. You can then put the stock in the freezer until you need it. These stocks are so much richer and give much more flavour to your cooking than commercial varieties. If you use wine for moistening, make sure it is a good wine. Remember, your dishes will only be as good as your ingredients, and this includes wine. These days wine is fairly cheap in New Zealand so do not skimp by using cheap flagon varieties that are barely drinkable. It will do nothing to enhance the flavour of your cooking. Cream as a moistener is another essential ingredient that does much to improve many dishes. It can be added merely to round out a dish or make a sauce. Sauce Normande is made by making a roux of butter and flour. Vegetables and herbs are boiled together to make a *bouillon* and the condensed liquid is added to the roux. Egg yolks or white wine can then be added, followed by a touch of cream, butter and lemon.

COOKING METHODS

Since the recipes in this book call for various cooking methods, an explanation of each will be helpful:

BASTING: Basting meats and poultry prevents them drying out during cooking. If you are roasting in the oven, the dish should be basted every 10 to 15 minutes, 30 minutes after beginning to cook. If you are grilling or have the meat on a spit, baste with butter or oil. You can tell when the meat is cooked by the spots of blood that appear on the surface of the meat.

BLANCHING: This is a process used to take away bitterness, remove skins, preserve whiteness in some meats or to remove excess salt from fatty bacon. The vegetable or meat is put in a saucepan of cold water, brought to boiling point, and then drained.

BOILING: So many dishes involve boiling, generally in water or flavoured water. 'Flavoured' means the addition of salt, herbs, spices, wine, butter or any variety of ingredients. Boiling is essential to the art of cooking, whether it be boiling eggs or preparing a chicken in a stock.

BRAISING: This is a mixture of sautéeing and casseroling to preserve the flavour and juices of a meat. Generally the meat is sautéed to seal in the juices and colour it. To add flavour it can be marinated beforehand with herbs, vegetables, salt, pepper and various other ingredients. After sautéeing the meat, the marinade ingredients can be placed in the casserole, the meat put on top, stock added, and the dish casseroled in the oven.

FRYING: Whether pan-frying, deep-frying or oven-frying, frying involves putting the food in very hot oil or fat. Pan-frying is the most common method used in the recipes here. Do not forget to add a little olive oil to the butter when pan-frying to prevent the butter from browning. Thin slices of meat pan fry best; the more tender the ingredient being cooked the more successful pan-frying will be. Do not cover foods being pan-fried as the steam softens the food.

If you are deep-frying, vegetable fats and salad oils are best. The cardinal rule is that the fat or oil should be clean, and hot enough to seal the outside of the food when it is dropped into the fat. This will prevent it from being greasy and help it retain its flavour.

Oven-frying is cooking in oil, or oil and butter, in a baking dish in the oven. Chicken, fish or even potatoes can be excellent when cooked using this method.

GRILLING: This is an extremely popular method of cooking in New Zealand, and can be done successfully inside or outside. Outside it can be done over the open fire or barbeque, and inside using electricity or gas. Grilling is cooking on a metal grid. Heat the grid to prevent sticking; and if the meat is thick keep it further from the heat than you would thinner cuts. Steaks, chops, poultry and even fish can be grilled successfully. Grilling can also be done by using a grill pan. If the meat is thick, grill it with a high heat to seal in the juices and then turn down the heat to allow the centre to cook more slowly. Thinner meats should be cooked at a constant high heat.

MARINATING: Marinating greatly adds to the flavour of meat and also tenderizes it. A few hours marinating meat in a mixture of wine and a little olive oil greatly enhances taste. Herbs, onions, garlic or spices can be added to the marinade. An excellent summer dish is chicken marinated in a mixture of equal parts of soy sauce and water, with garlic, ginger and herbs added, and then grilled or barbequed. Red meat can be marinated in a mixture of salt, pepper, herbs, onions, carrots, garlic, a few strips of fatty bacon, and then covered in wine for 2-3 hours to allow the added flavours to penetrate the meat. It can then be sautéed and casseroled.

POACHING: Poaching can be done with water or various other liquids. The ingredient is placed in the liquid before the liquid starts to boil. Eggs can be poached in a lot of water or fish can be poached in a shallow court bouillon.

ROASTING: Roasting can be done by placing the meat on a grid in the oven and basting it frequently. However, many modern ovens have built-in spits that turn the meat constantly to ensure even cooking. Many cuts of lamb, beef, pork and chicken can be roasted. The meat should be put in the oven at room temperature, kept on a grid in a pan so it does not sit in the juices, and basted every 10 to 15 minutes from about 30 minutes after the start of cooking, to keep it moist. If cooking lamb you can tell when it is cooked by testing it with a fork. The juices that escape should be clear or a light pink. With beef, clear liquid means it is well-cooked, pink means it is medium, and blood-red very rare.

SAUTEEING: To sauté meat or vegetables use a little olive oil, butter or a combination of these in a frypan. The meat or vegetables are then placed in the pan at a medium heat to seal in the natural juices and to colour the meat. Some cooks prefer to use bacon fat or lard for sautéeing but the recipes in this book generally use a butter-oil combination.

STEAMING: To steam you need either a double saucepan with a perforated bottom, or you can use a casserole. When using a casserole, place the ingredients in a separate dish which then sits in the water inside the larger utensil. Many Southeast Asian dishes use steaming as a method of cooking because it is simple, the food cooks quickly, it does not retain as much moisture as it would boiling, and it retains its flavour. Do not put the meats or vegetables into the pan until it is boiling and the steam rising. Make sure the pan is well sealed during cooking to prevent steam escaping and serve the steamed food hot. Meat, poultry, fish and vegetables can all be successfully steamed. Marinated meats or poultry are particularly good when steamed.

General note: Many restaurants these days use microwave ovens for some of their cooking. This book does not advocate their use, but if you need to know the equivalent preparation of some ingredients using a microwave, there are some excellent books available at bookshops.

SOME COOKING TERMS

Acidify: The addition of lemon juice or vinegar to a cooked dish or sauce.

Acidulated water: The addition of lemon juice or vinegar, mixed with water to blanch veal, chicken or sweetbreads. Lemon juice and water mixed in equal quantities will stop sliced fruits turning brown.

Aspic: The jelly made from the bones of meat, fish or poultry, in which any meat, fish, poultry, game or vegetable may be served.

Al dente: Literally 'firm to the teeth'; the correct texture of cooked pasta.

Bain-marie: This utensil consists of a saucepan standing in a larger pan filled with boiling water. It keeps liquids at simmering point and helps avoid over-cooking. A double saucepan will suffice.

Bake: Cooking breads, cakes, biscuits, pastries and pies in the oven using a dry heat.

Barbecue: Very popular in New Zealand, this method consists of cooking over a fire, on a grill or spit out in the open.

Baste: To pour liquid over food as it cooks to moisten and flavour. It usually refers to using the juices in which the dish is cooking.

Batter: The mixture from which pancakes and cakes are made, or the egg-flour-milk mixture in which seafoods may be dipped before deep-frying.

Beat: Mixing, with a hand or electric utensil, to make the ingredients smooth.

Blanch: To heat in boiling water or steam to loosen outer skins of tomatoes and such; to whiten chicken, veal or sweetbreads; to remove bitter flavours; to prepare fruits and vegetables for preserving, canning or freezing.

Blend: The thorough mixing of ingredients.

Boil: To bring liquids to boiling point, when bubbles rise and break over the liquid surface.

Bone: The removal of bones from meat, fish, poultry or game.

Bouillon: Clear soup, stock or broth made from poultry, beef, veal and vegetables, strained before using.

Bouquet garni: A mixture of herbs tied in cheesecloth and added to a dish during cooking. It is removed at the end of cooking.

Bread: To coat or roll in breadcrumbs for cooking.

Broil: Cooking by direct heat over charcoal, gas or electricity.

Caramelize: Melting sugar until it becomes a syrup by stirring continuously in a saucepan.

Chill: To put in the refrigerator or freezer until cold, not frozen.

Chop: To cut into small pieces.

Clarify: The addition of slightly-beaten egg whites and crushed egg shells to stock or broth to make it clear. The mixture must be brought to the boil, cooked and strained.

Cool: To stand at room temperature until cool. Do not put in the refrigerator.

Court-bouillon: Water with the additon of bay leaf, celery stalks, onion, carrots, salt and freshly ground pepper, wine, stock, olive oil, garlic etc, in which meat, poultry or fish is cooked to give added flavour.

Cream: To blend ingredients such as butter and sugar until soft and creamy.

Crimp: To pinch together the edges of pastry to seal before cooking.

Crôuton: Bread slices minus the crusts, diced, and sautéed in oil or butter until crisp.

Deep-fry: or *French-fry:* To cook in deep hot fat until crisp.

Dice: To cut into small even cubes.

Disjoint: To cut meat at the joint to produce edible-sized pieces.

Dissolve: To melt a dry ingredient with liquid.

Dust: To sprinkle flour, sugar or seasonings evenly over food.

Farcie: To stuff with ingredients.

Fillet: A special cut of lamb, beef, pork, game, poultry or fish, or the cutting of these to be used in cooking.

Flake: To break into small pieces.

Flame or flambé: To pour alcohol over a dish or ingredients and ignite.

Fold in: To gently fold other ingredients into a light, fluffy mixture so that the air is retained.

Fricassée: A form of braising where the meat or poultry is cooked in fat until golden and then put in a sauce.

Fry: To cook in fat, oil or butter in a frying pan.

Garnish or garniture: Addition of trimmings, often just for decorative purposes, to a dish after it has been cooked or prepared.

Glaze: To coat various foods, pastries, meats, poultry with syrup of aspic.

Grate: To reduce to small particles using a grater.

Gratin or au gratin: To brown food in the oven until crisp and golden.

Grease: To smear with butter, margarine, oil or fat.

Grill: To cook over an open fire or with gas or electricity.

Julienne: To cut vegetables into fine strips.

Knead: To work dough into a suitable consistency.

Lard: Pork fat after being melted.

Marinade: A special mixture of liquids, herbs, spices and similar, cooked or uncooked, to add flavour or soften food. To marinate is to have the food steeped in the marinade for a particular length of time.

Mask: To cover cooked food with a sauce.

Mince: To cut or chop into very small pieces.

Oven-fry: To cook meat and such in the oven, leaving it uncovered, and basting it with fat.

Parboil: To partially cook by boiling or pre-cooking.

Peel: Removing the outside skin of fruit or vegetable.

Papillote or en papilotte: To cook food enclosed in foil or oiled paper.

Poach: To cook by placing in liquid that is not quite boiling.

Pit: To remove the stone, pit or seed from fruit.

Purée: To reduce to a smooth soft texture by using a sieve or food processor.

Reduce: To cook a liquid or sauce uncovered over a high heat until it evaporates to a desired consistency, in order to improve or increase flavour or appearance.

Roast: To cook meat in an oven or over a fire.

Roux: The mixing of butter and flour at a low heat. Once cooked it should absorb six times its own weight.

Sauté: To lightly fry ingredients in a little oil or fat, taking care not to burn by stirring frequently or shaking the pan.

Scald: To heat just below boiling point.

Sear: To seal the surface of meat over a high heat to prevent juices from escaping.

Sift: To put through a fine sieve.

Simmer: To cook something not quite to boiling point with the bubbles occasionally breaking the surface.

Skewer: Either defines the metal or wooden 'brochette' used to skewer, or the process of keeping meat or poultry in shape with a skewer.

Soft peak: Used to describe cream when it has been lightly beaten so it retains a 'soft peak'.

Steam: To cook food over boiling water or stock.

Stir: To blend ingredients with a spoon, using a circular motion.

Whisk: To beat rapidly with a whisk, or by electric appliances to increase air content and volume.

Zest: The finely grated rind of orange or lemon.

THE RESTAURANTS

The east coast city of Tauranga has developed remarkably in the past few years, and along with the population increase has come a marked increase in the quality of its restaurants. One of the finest is Altons, situated on the main road into the city centre. It is an unobtrusive single storey restaurant opened three years ago by Tony and Alison Breeds. The combination of their christian names solved the argument of what to call the restaurant.

Altons is the culmination of Alison's travels overseas, where she did a Cordon Bleu course, before returning to New Zealand to team up with Tony, who had trained and freelanced in restaurants in this country. They decided to adopt a wide approach to their cooking, embracing many different nationalities but owing allegiance only to those ingredients available in each season; serving everything only when it was fresh. It was a mixture of unusual cuisines: the homely, the classic and the creative. The concept seems to have been well accepted, judging by Altons' reputation. The restaurant itself is reasonably small, with dining on three levels with creates privacy and makes it a more interesting space. There is an abundance of fresh, green plants set off against pink walls on which hang old framed prints and china plates. Tables are set with lace cloths and fresh flowers, and Tony and Alison go to the trouble of making home-made chocolates for the end of the meal. Diners are given crudités at the start of each meal — all part of the art of running a good restaurant.

Altons,
316 Cameron Road, Tauranga.
Telephone 87-360. BYO.

ENTREES

Kidneys Turbigo
Mango prawns with horseradish mayonnaise
Mushrooms Alton
Calamari, sautéed with onion, garlic and parsley
Banana and bacon rolls

MAIN COURSES

Chicken breast stuffed with plums and spinach
Pork Dijonnaise
Veal escalopes with rum and orange sauce
Baked noisettes of lamb
Seafood Newberg
Oven baked fish with fresh fruit and hazelnuts

DESSERTS

Blueberry Chantilly
Crème caramel
Bananas Caribbean
Poached figs with orange cream cheese.

MUSHROOMS ALTON

2 TABLESPOONS BUTTER
1 ONION
4 SLICES BACON, CHOPPED
400G BUTTON MUSHROOMS, SLICED AND TRIMMED
1 CLOVE GARLIC, CRUSHED
1 TEASPOON LEMON JUICE
100G BEANSPROUTS
1 TABLESPOON CHOPPED PARSLEY

Heat the butter in a sauté pan and add the onion and chopped bacon. Cook until the bacon is nearly crisp, and then add the mushrooms, garlic and lemon juice. Sauté over a medium heat for 3-5 minutes, stirring constantly. Add the beansprouts and parsley and cook for a further minute. Serve immediately. **Serves 4-6.**

FISH FILLETS WITH TAMARILLO SAUCE

4 FILLETS FRESH FISH
100G CASHEW NUTS, COARSELY CHOPPED
½ CUP DRY WHITE WINE
Sauce:
6 TAMARILLOS, PULPED
¼ CUP WATER
2 TABLESPOONS RAW SUGAR
¼ CUP CREAM
LEMON TWISTS, CHOPPED PARSLEY, FENNEL SPRIGS FOR GARNISH

Press the chopped cashew nuts into the fish fillets. Place the fish in a buttered baking dish, and add the white wine. Cover with foil and bake in a pre-heated 190°C oven for 20-25 minutes.
To make the sauce: Cook the tamarillo pulp and sugar in the water for 5 minutes. Place this in the blender for 15 seconds and then put the mixture through a sieve. Add the cream. Simmer the mixture until it has a creamy consistency.
Pour the sauce over the fish just before serving, and garnish with lemon twists, chopped parsley and sprigs of fennel. **Serves 4-6.**

MIDDLE EASTERN SALAD

250G DRIED APRICOTS
250G DRIED FIGS
125G PITTED PRUNES
125G RAISINS
100G ALMONDS, SLICED
60G PINENUTS
1 TABLESPOON ROSEWATER
1 TABLESPOON ORANGE FLOWER WATER
50G RAW SUGAR
CREAM, YOGHURT FOR GARNISH

Wash the apricots, dried figs, prunes and raisins and place in a large bowl. Add the almonds and pinenuts. Pour in the rose and flower water — available from chemists. Add the sugar to taste and cover with water. Let the fruits marinate for at least 48 hours. Serve in glass bowls, and garnish with either cream or yoghurt. **Serves 6-8.**

Anderson's is as much an institution as a restaurant in Hamilton, after more than a decade as one of that city's finest eating houses. Its medieval Banquet Hall — complete with live performances — was the first of its type in New Zealand. The restaurant itself has been decorated with an olde English bar, antique cash register, stained glass, hunting prints and posters, silver candelabra, a set of 1892 Encyclopaedia Britannica, old hogshead barrels, candles and fine crystal — all giving the place a relaxed and interesting atmosphere. Distinctly different in its furnishings is the Music Room which seats up to 18 diners. So called because of the old zither, double bass, trumpet and drum on the walls, the room is further enhanced by an old stag head.

Anderson's chef, Rex Anderson, has cooked there for more than 5 years, creating some excellent dishes; and in 1980 he attended the Hotelympia competition in London. Anderson's other chefs have also been with the restaurant for a number of years, possibly explaining why the restaurant has such a strong core of regulars. Dishes are all individually prepared, the menu changes every 6 weeks and the cuisine tends towards the unusual. However, there is the standard fare, such as the French onion soup and the crêpes, which has been a feature of the restaurant for a long time. Under the direction of the restaurant's owner, Greg Ball, an excellent wine cellar has been built, featuring some impressive wines. This in turn, has proved popular with Hamilton's theatre-goers, keen to enjoy their meals and sample the restaurant's wines in relaxed, convivial surroundings, before going to the Founder's Theatre.

Anderson's,
104 London Street, Hamilton.
Telephone 395-957. Licensed.

ENTREES

Cocktail grapes stuffed with cream cheese, onion and celery
Smoked eel fillets with toasted rye bread
French onion soup
Australian scallops in garlic cream sauce, in the shell with croûtons
Raw mushroom salad

MAIN COURSES

Pacific Crêpe — with fish, shrimps, scallops and oysters
Medallions of pork fillet with pear slices and Grand Marnier
Lamb cutlets with fennel in a herb and wine sauce
Chicken pieces with Black Doris plums in port
Moules à la Marinière
Duckling with mangoes
Entrecôte de Boeuf with French mustard
Fish poached in white wine, with asparagus and tomato

DESSERTS

Deep fried ice cream balls and hot caramel sauce
Profiteroles
Fraises au chocolat
Coffee liqueur cheesecake
Devil's chocolate cake

KIWIFRUIT COCKTAIL

1 EGG	SALT AND PEPPER	1KG SHRIMPS
1 TABLESPOON VINEGAR	½ CUP SOYA BEAN OIL	LEMON AND WATERCRESS FOR GARNISH
1 CLOVE GARLIC, DICED	1 KIWIFRUIT	

Prepare a mayonnaise by whisking the egg, vinegar, garlic and salt and pepper to taste. When the mixture is light and fluffy, gradually add the soya bean oil until the mayonnaise is creamy. Purée the kiwifruit and add to the mayonnaise, mixing well. Next add the shrimps, and stir until they are well coated with the mayonnaise. Serve in a lettuce-lined cocktail dish and decorate with a lemon wedge and watercress. For variation and colour add a crab claw to the cocktail. **Serves 6.**

PHEASANT WITH WINE AND CHERRY SAUCE

2 PHEASANTS	*Wine and cherry sauce:*	⅓ CUP CHERRY GLAZE
SALT AND FRESHLY GROUND PEPPER	6 TABLESPOONS REDCURRANT JELLY	SALT AND FRESHLY GROUND PEPPER
MIXED HERBS	3 CUPS RED WINE	2 TABLESPOONS CORNFLOUR
200G FRESH CHERRIES	1 TABLESPOON GROUND JUNIPER BERRIES	

Place the pheasants in a roasting tray, half filled with water, and season with salt, pepper and mixed herbs. Cover the tray with aluminium foil and place in a 200°C oven for 1 hour. Remove the pheasants from the oven and allow to cool before breaking the birds lengthwise into halves and placing them in a clean roasting pan.

To make the sauce: In a saucepan, add the redcurrant jelly, red wine, juniper berries, cherry glaze and salt and pepper to taste. Gradually bring to the boil and when boiling thicken with the cornflour dissolve in a little water. Spoon the sauce over the birds and cook for a further 1¼ hour at 180°C. Ten minutes before serving add the fresh cherries to the dish. **Serves 4.**

GRAND PANACHE

1 FRESH PINEAPPLE	1 PUNNET STRAWBERRIES	¼ CUP COINTREAU OR KIRSCH
1 BUNCH OF GRAPES	2 TABLESPOONS SUGAR	1 BOTTLE MOSELLE, CHILLED

Cut the pineapple into bite-size pieces. In a shallow bowl mix the pineapple, grapes and strawberries. Sprinkle the sugar over the fruit and add the Cointreau or Kirsch. Chill the mixture in the refrigerator for 3-4 hours. Just before serving, pour the moselle over the fruit. Serve in long-stemmed champagne glasses, and decorate with frosted grapes. **Serves 4.**

Antoine's and Tony Astle are definitely climbing towards legend status amongst New Zealand restaurants. Since 1973, when Antoine's opened in Parnell Village, the reputations of both the restaurant and its owner-cook have spread both throughout the country and overseas.

The slight and bearded Tony Astle started out in the world of food after seeing Graeme Kerr on television. He wrote to Kerr and the Galloping Gourmet arranged for Tony to work with Madame Louise at the then magnificent Le Normandie in Wellington, where he started as a waiter before moving into the kitchen. It was there he met Des Britten, who went off to open his Coachman Restaurant. Tony soon followed to work at the Coachman for five years before moving to Christchurch to run a dairy and to work in a few of that city's then dreadful restaurants, before returning to the Coachman. But marriage meant the decision to travel with his wife, Beth, to England where they arrived to promptly spend all their money on one enormously expensive meal at the Café Royale. To keep body and soul together they began the first of a series of jobs in hotels in England, before returning to New Zealand in 1973. Antoine's was opened in partnership with an old friend, Roger Coles, who has since gone but who helped restore the old building from its dilapidated state. They managed to get a licence and opened as one of the first classical French restaurants in Auckland, with dinner-suited waiters and elegant surroundings down to silver napkin rings and twisted brass candlesticks. Over the years Antoine's has been lauded in *American Gourmet* and a myriad of other overseas publications, which have spread the reputation of Tony Astle and Antoine's dishes abroad.

Antoine's,
333 Parnell Road, Parnell, Auckland.
Telephone 798-756. Licensed.

ENTREES

Seafood chowder topped with pastry and baked
Sliced raw beef marinated in cognac and lemon
Boned leg of chicken stuffed with mushrooms, spinach and pork terrine
Chilled lamb brains on smoked cod roe with spinach mayonnaise
Camembert and smoked eel in phyllo

MAIN COURSES

Fresh fish fillets stuffed with lettuce and shrimp mousse
Pork fillet stuffed with lamb brains
Rack of lamb coated in herbs with mint flavoured Bearnaise
Boned half chicken stuffed with spinach and blue vein cheese
Chateaubriant with a redcurrant and Madeira sauce
Roast duckling with kiwifruit and Cumberland sauce

DESSERTS

Fresh fruit salad with liqueur and cream
White chocolate mousse on a fruit purée
Rich lemon roll with Grand Marnier and cream
Meringue filled with chocolate Bavarian cream and hot caramel sauce

HAM AND BLUE CHEESE MOUSSE

1 TABLESPOON GELATINE	250G LEAN HAM CHUNKS, COOKED	2 EGG WHITES
2 TABLESPOONS COLD WATER	4 FRESH MINT LEAVES	WHITE PEPPER
1 CUP CHICKEN STOCK	1 CLOVE GARLIC, CRUSHED	JULIENNE OF HAM, MAYONNAISE,
125G BLUE CHEESE	9 TABLESPOONS CREAM	FRESH MINT FOR GARNISH

Sprinkle the gelatine over the cold water in a small bowl and let it soften for 5 minutes. In a large bowl stir the gelatine into the stock over heat until it dissolves. Blend the blue cheese, ham, mint and garlic in a food processor until smooth, and add this to the cool gelatine mixture and combine well. Beat the cream to soft peaks in a chilled bowl and fold into the ham and cheese mixture.

In another bowl beat the egg whites to soft peaks and carefully fold into the other mixture, adding pepper to taste. Either set in a mould or individual ramekins for 3 hours. Pipe mayonnaise on top, sprinkle with Juliennes of ham and decorate with mint leaves. **Serves 6.**

CHICKEN LEGS STUFFED WITH CAMEMBERT

4 BONED CHICKEN LEGS	Sauce:	JULIENNE OF CARROT, COURGETTE,
2 ROUNDS CAMEMBERT	1 SMALL ONION, FINELY CHOPPED	GREEN PEPPER, FINELY SLICED
JUICE OF 3 LEMONS	¼ CUP WHITE VERMOUTH	
150ML CREAM	¼ CUP WHITE WINE	
SALT AND PEPPER		

Stuff the chicken legs with camembert and fold the skin around so the cheese does not escape when cooking. Flour the legs and slowly cook in oil until cooked and evenly browned. Place in an ovenproof dish and keep warm in the oven.
To make the sauce: Using the pan juices, fry the onion, making sure not to brown. Add the vermouth, white wine and lemon juice, reducing by three-quarters, before adding the cream. Reduce by a quarter and then add the vegetables, and salt and pepper to taste. Pour the sauce over the chicken, bring to boil, sprinkle with parsley and serve. **Serves 2.**

MARQUISE AU CHOCOLAT
with coffee flavoured custard

60G CHOCOLATE	225ML CREAM	Custard:
4 EGG YOLKS	25G ICING SUGAR	3 EGG YOLKS
100G CASTOR SUGAR	½ CUP STRONG COFFEE	60G SUGAR
130G UNSALTED SOFT BUTTER	SPONGE FINGERS	1 TABLESPOON INSTANT COFFEE
60G COCOA		225ML MILK

Melt the chocolate over simmering water. Beat the egg yolks and castor sugar until they are very thick and the castor sugar has dissolved. Add the melted chocolate. Beat the butter and cocoa until thoroughly blended, and combine the two mixtures. Lightly whip the cream to soft peaks, add the icing sugar and combine with the chocolate mixture.

Line an oiled mould with sponge fingers that have been dipped on only one side into the coffee. The dipped side should face outside. Pour the mixture into the mould and set in the refrigerator.
To make the custard: Beat the egg yolks, sugar and instant coffee together. Boil the milk and add to the mixture. Over a *bain-marie* whisk the custard until the mixture coats the back of a spoon. Do not boil or the custard will curdle. Let cool before serving. **Serves 4.**

The August Moon is a mixture of both Chinese and Malaysian cuisine. The Chinese is the less common Peking cuisine, while the Malaysian is the rich and spicy fare, whose excellent curries and dishes are similar in style to Chinese, Indonesian and even Indian cooking.

The Peking dishes include barbecued Peking duck and Beggars's Chicken — chicken stuffed with special spices before being wrapped in lotus leaves and then covered in mud before being cooked.

The August Moon — so named after the Ancient Chinese Moon Goddess of fertility, abundance of food, and successful harvests — is actually owned by a Malaysian-Chinese, Chai, with his wife Angela acting as hostess. Chai's grounding in Chinese cooking came from his mother, an expert in Chinese-Malaysian cooking. Before taking over the August Moon Chai did a degree at Canterbury University, graduating as an analytical chemist and then working for eight years as an analyst in a laboratory. With the restaurant he is slowly introducing a number of different dishes to make it even more interesting. It is a large restaurant, seating 120 guests under a ceiling of teak dragon tiles with Chinese hanging lamps, teak handcarved chairs, a beautiful lacquered dividing screen, separate bar area, and five original paintings by Professor Wu, a well-known Taiwanese artist who specializes in calligraphy.

August Moon,
Cnr Albert and Victoria Streets, Auckland
Telephone 34-141. Licensed.

ENTREES

Hot and sour soup
Malaysian satay with spiced hot peanut sauce
Malaysian style fried chicken's wings
Gong Bo prawns
Bird nest soup

MAIN COURSES

Paper wrapped chicken
Crayfish in garlic and black been sauce
Crispy skin roast pork Malaysian style
Szechuan chicken, beef, pork and prawns
Malaysian curry
Crispy skin chicken with spiced salt
Peking duck
Sizzling beef

DESSERTS

August Moon moon cakes

GONG HO PRAWNS

10-15 PRAWNS
2 EGG YOLKS
CORNFLOUR
SOYA BEAN OIL FOR DEEP FRYING
½ ONION, THINLY SLICED

1 TABLESPOON SOYA OIL
2 CLOVES GARLIC, FINELY CHOPPED
2 TEASPOONS SUGAR
1 TABLESPOON VINEGAR
3 DROPS CHILLI OIL

SALT AND MONOSODIUM GLUTAMATE FOR SEASONING
¼ CUP CHICKEN STOCK
½ TEASPOON SESAME SEED OIL
½ CUP CASHEWS DEEP FRIED

Remove the spinal canals from the prawns. Dip the prawns in the egg yolk and dust in cornflour before deep-frying in the soya bean oil at a medium to high heat for 1 minute.

Lightly fry the onion slices for ½ minute and spread the onions on a serving plate.

Heat a wok to medium heat, and add the tablespoon of soya oil, garlic, sugar, vinegar, chilli oil, salt and monosodium glutamate to taste. Add the chicken stock and prawns and toss or stir quickly over high heat. Add the sesame seed oil and cashew nuts and then serve on the onion decorated plate. **Serves 4.**

CURRY CHICKEN MALAYSIAN STYLE

½ LARGE CHICKEN, CUT INTO PIECES
1 TABLESPOON MILD CURRY POWDER

1½ TABLESPOONS HOT CURRY POWDER
1 POTATO, QUARTERED
1 ONION, QUARTERED

3 TABLESPOONS COOKING OIL
½ CUP WATER
2 TABLESPOONS COCONUT MILK
1 TEASPOON SALT

Marinate the chicken pieces in the curry powder for ½ hour. Deep fry the potato. Lightly fry the onion in the oil over a medium heat in a pot, and then add the chicken pieces, stirring lightly until the flesh shrinks. Add the water and bring to the boil, before simmering for 2 minutes. Add the coconut milk and salt to taste. Let stand for a few hours if time allows so that the sauce marinates the chicken. Preheat to serve. **Serves 4.**

BRAISED SOY SAUCE CHICKEN

1 MEDIUM-SIZED CHICKEN
300ML COLD WATER
300ML SOY SAUCE

2 TABLESPOONS RICE WINE OR DRY SHERRY
5 SLICES FRESH GINGER ROOT

1 WHOLE ANISE
5 TEASPOONS SUGAR
1 TEASPOON SESAME SEED OIL

Wash the chicken under cold water and dry thoroughly. Add all the ingredients except the sugar and the sesame seed oil to a medium-sized stock pot and bring to the boil. Add the chicken which should be half submerged. Bring to the boil again and then reduce heat and cook for 20 minutes. Turn the chicken and cook the other side. Stir the sugar into the sauce and baste the chicken thoroughly, simmering for a further 20 minutes and basting frequently. Take the pot off the heat and let the chicken stand for 2 hours. Transfer the chicken to a chopping board, brush with sesame seed oil, cut into pieces, and reconstruct the chicken on a plate to serve. Moisten the chicken pieces with a few tablespoons of the sauce. Serve hot or cold. **Serves 4.**

Opposite: Chilled Avocado and Orange Soup (p. 71). The beauty of this dish, prepared by Jo Coulter of Auckland's Harley's Restaurant, is that it can be prepared early in the day and served much later. The addition of a swirl of sour cream and chopped fresh herbs adds visual interest. It is excellent both in summer and winter. *(Photograph by Max Thomson.)*

---

7. Ron Dunn of Auckland's Captain Crab keeps crayfish alive in a large tank in the restaurant so customers can choose their meal. *(Photograph by Stephen Ballantyne).*

---

8. Antonio Olla of Colosseo in Auckland, with chef Todd Corson, pictured in what is one of the country's busiest Italian restaurants. *(Photograph by Stephen Ballantyne).*

---

9. Vinu and Kam Patel run The Bengal Tiger Indian restaurant in Wellington, which has the only genuine Tandoor oven in the country. *(Photograph by Lianne Ruscoe).*

7

8

9

Opposite: Lamb Waiatarua (p. 172). Roast lamb is a traditional New Zealand dish. Digby Law's preparation of Lamb Waiatarua includes making deep incisions into the leg of lamb and inserting slivers of garlic, rosemary leaves and grated lemon rind. The garlic and rosemary gives the flavour and the lemon juice cuts down fattiness. *(Photograph by Max Thomson.)*

---

10. Wendy Lever and Alan Titchall, partners in Auckland's Flamingos restaurant, one of the city's most highly-regarded BYOs. *(Photograph by Lianne Ruscoe).*

---

11. Alan and Luba Perry of Waikanae's Country Life serve some excellent Russian dishes and own probably the best wine cellar in the country. *(Photograph by Lianne Ruscoe).*

---

12. Des Britten, photographed with his wife Lorraine, is probably the country's best known chef, with a television cooking series and a number of cookbooks to his credit. *(Photograph by Lianne Ruscoe).*

In 1971 the little brick-fronted building in Wellington's Courtenay Place, which now houses Bacchus, served the best fish and chips in the capital. In fact Kasey Coory, former bikie and mechanic, was so intrigued with the possibilities of the place that he took up the suggestion of a friend that they should buy the shop and expand it into a coffee bar. From these humble beginnings grew what is now a renowned restaurant, named after the Roman mythological God of the vine and its fruits, whose Bacchanalian festivals led to such excesses of celebration that they were finally suppressed by the Roman Senate.

In those early days of the 1970's Bacchus had just two tables, with Kasey's partner Ross Waters cooking, and Kasey waiter. But after only three months Ross suddenly died. Kasey decided to expand the restaurant and it quickly became one of the first of Wellington's 'underground' BYO's that were periodically raided by the police. Kasey had applied for a licence in 1972 and it was granted, but it was not until 1976 that he managed to get the money together to actually afford the license. In the meantime, armed with a myriad of cookery books, Kasey developed his now quite remarkable cooking skills. And over the years Bacchus developed into a superb silver-service restaurant, with muted elegance, dinner-suited waiters, and classical French dishes with the Coory touch; attracting many members of the capital's diplomatic corps, business people and those who like the classical approach to dining. In recent times Kasey has whittled down what was an extremely long menu to just 14 main courses, which allows him to concentrate more on the sauces and the quality of the dishes. Eating here is definitely Bacchanalian.

Bacchus,
8 Courtenay Place, Wellington.
Telephone 846-592. Licensed.

ENTREES

Fillets of smoked eel with horse radish and dill sauce
Avocado and smoked salmon, garnished with chervil and hollandaise sauce
Warm prawns with dijon piquant mayonnaise
Scallops poached in vermouth, served in a light sabayon sauce
Sauté of veal liver and mushrooms with port sauce in puff pastry
Crayfish and mushrooms served in red wine

MAIN COURSES

Roast duckling with ginger sauce and fresh fruits
Chicken in cherry brandy, served with grape sauce
Fresh crayfish salad
Fresh crayfish served with cognac butter sauce and herbs
Marinated sirloin with a red wine sauce
Tornedos of beef fillet with a tarragon bearnaise sauce
Milk fed white veal tenderloins sautéed with mushrooms, served with Madeira cream sauce.
Lamb medallions glazed with redcurrant, orange and port sauce

DESSERTS

Chocolate almond cream flavoured with Cointreau and rum
Sorbet
Grapes
Puff pastry with fruits and cream pâtisserie
Camembert

VEAL IN PASTRY

1 VEAL TENDERLOIN	Farcie:	Sauce:
SALT AND FRESHLY GROUND PEPPER	200G MUSHROOMS, SLICED	¼ CUP MADEIRA
PUFF PASTRY	50G JULIENNE HAM	300ML CREAM
1 YOLK, MIXED WITH 1 TABLESPOON WATER	50 PINE NUTS	1 TABLESPOON CHOPPED CHIVES
	100G RICE	2 DROPS LEMON JUICE
	4 TABLESPOONS GRATED GRUYERE	
	4 LEAVES FRESH SAGE	
	4 LEAVES SPINACH, JULIENNE	

To make the farcie: Gently sauté in butter the ham, then the mushrooms, then the pine nuts. Total cooking time should be 2 minutes. Allow to cool. Cook the rice in salted water and drain completely. Combine all the farcie ingredients.

Cut the fat from the veal and season. Fry the veal in hot fat to seal the juices. Place the veal on a rack in a 400°C oven and cook until rare. Allow to cool.

Place the veal on the puff pastry sheet, allowing enough pastry to wrap over and crimp. Spread the farcie over the veal. Wrap the veal in the pasty and crimp, until sealed. Make three gas holes in the top of the pastry. Brush the pastry with the egg yolk and water mixture. Place in a 400°C oven for 25-30 minutes until the pastry browns. Remove and allow to cool for 10 minutes.

To make the sauce: Reduce the Madeira by half. Add the cream and reduce until slightly thickened. Add the chives, lemon juice and salt and pepper to taste.

Cut the veal into thick slices and pour the sauce over. **Serves 4-6.**

CRAYFISH IN CHAMPAGNE

1 LIVE 500G CRAYFISH	Sauce:	SALT AND FRESHLY GROUND PEPPER
	1 BOTTLE FRENCH CHAMPAGNE	LEMON JUICE
Boullion:	300ML CREAM	CRAYFISH CORAL
1 ONION, CHOPPED	2 YOLKS, MIXED WITH 50ML CREAM	
1 CARROT, CHOPPED	½ TEASPOON FRESH THYME LEAVES	
2 STICKS CELERY, CHOPPED	⅛ TEASPOON SAFFRON	
BOUQUET GARNI		

Drown the crayfish in water. With a sharp knife split the cray through the centre from head to tail. Remove the head and gently separate the tail, leaving the flesh in the tail shell. Save the coral and legs.

Crush the head in a pot and add the boullion vegetables. Add 1 litre of cold water and simmer for 15 minutes. Strain off, pouring the liquid into another pot large enough to accommodate the tail. Simmer for 5 minutes, keeping the flesh in its tail shell. Do not allow the boullion to boil. Remove the bouquet garni.

To make the sauce: Add 1 cup champagne and ½ cup boullion to a 1-2 litre capacity pot (the remaining champagne can be drunk with the crayfish). Reduce to 4 tablespoons. Add the cream and reduce until the sauce is slightly thickened. Remove the pan from the heat and whisk. Gently cook over a low heat, stirring constantly for 1 minute. Do not allow the sauce to approach boiling point or it will curdle. Add the thyme, saffron, salt and pepper to taste, a few drops of lemon juice and the coral.

Remove the flesh from the tail shell. Pour the sauce over and garnish with cray legs. **Serves 2.**

SOUFFLE GRAND MARNIER

4 EGG YOLKS	40G GRAND MARNIER	⅛ TEASPOON CREAM OF TARTAR
½ CUP SUGAR	5 EGG WHITES	2 TABLESPOONS ICING SUGAR

Beat the egg yolks and sugar in a steel bowl until thick. Cook the mixture over simmering water until it thickens and is warm to touch. Dribble in the Grand Marnier, stirring constantly.

Float the bowl and mixture in a large bowl of iced water, stirring constantly until the sauce mixture is cool and thick.

Beat the egg whites, icing sugar and tartar to a soft peak. Mix a quarter of the egg whites with the sauce until they are well combined. Gently fold in the remaining egg whites but do not completely combine the whites and the sauce or the soufflé will not rise.

Grease a 1 litre capacity bowl with butter and coat it with sugar. Tie a greased paper collar around the bowl and pour the soufflé into the bowl. Cook in a 400°C oven for 20 minutes, or until the top browns slightly. Sprinkle with icing sugar and serve with liquid cream. **Serves 2.**

Judith Bartup's vow when she left school was not to get involved in the restaurant world. But when you are born a Littlejohn and brought up in an environment that centred around Orsini's — one of the top restaurants in Wellington — then it's not easy to find a profession a world apart from your heritage. It becomes even more difficult when your future husband works at your parents' restaurant. You are virtually guaranteed to end up running your own restaurant.

So it was with Judith and Laurie Bartup. When Phillip and Valerie Littlejohn sold Orsini's in Wellington to retire in Auckland, that retirement was extremely shortlived. They decided to open an Orsini's in Auckland and Judith and Laurie ended up moving north to help get the new venture underway. But after the new Orsini's was open and operating successfully Judith and Laurie decided it was about time they branched out on their own. During 1982 the restaurant business in Auckland was having a difficult time so they had a choice of about 100 places that were on the market. It did not take long to find what they were looking for, a BYO in the centre of the Ponsonby restaurant district. The place was all very Art Deco, with soft creams and rusty reds, sandblasted glass dividers, triangular wall lights, and large photo murals of movie stars. They renamed it Bartups with a bright neon sign, added a number of their own possesions, and with Laurie creating some excellent dishes and Judith as hostess, Bartups became a reality and the end of a vow.

Bartups,
222 Ponsonby Road, Auckland.
Telephone 767-888. BYO.

ENTREES

Smoked snapper and cod roe mousse with caviar
Whole baby flounder with sautéed almonds and bananas
Kidneys flamed in Grand Marnier on egg noodles
Mussels in the half shell with a white wine sauce
Crumbed scallops and mushrooms skewered, with a vermouth crème sauce
Jellied fruit salad with sour cream
Champagne sorbet

MAIN COURSES

Pork slices with a clear cherry sauce
Boned rolled loin of lamb roasted with garlic, served with a grape sauce
Fillet of beef with mushroom sauce
Fish of the day
Boned chicken breasts rolled with spinach and pears, with maraschino sauce
Roast duckling with orange sauce

DESSERTS

Profiteroles with frangelica and hot walnut sauce
Boysenberry ice cream
Banana fritters with an apricot rum sauce
Crêpes — Suzettes, Claudette, Ginette or Yvette

JELLY FRUIT SALAD

2 PEACHES
1 PINEAPPLE

10G GELATINE
½ CUP BOILING WATER
450ML GRAPEFRUIT JUICE

SQUEEZE OF LEMON
½ CUP SOUR CREAM

Pit and slice the peaches and peel and dice the pineapple. Melt the gelatine in the hot water and whisk in the grapefruit juice and lemon. Add the fruit and mix well before setting in individual moulds for 2-3 hours in the refrigerator. To serve, unmould on to a lettuce bed and serve with the sour cream and fresh fruit. **Serves 4.**

CHICKEN BREASTS WITH MARASCHINO SAUCE

8 BONED CHICKEN BREASTS
1 BUNCH SPINACH
2 PEARS, PEELED
OIL TO COVER BASE OF LARGE PAN
SALT AND PEPPER

2½ TABLESPOONS BRANDY
PARSLEY FOR GARNISH

Maraschino sauce:
6 SPRING ONIONS, CHOPPED
30G BUTTER
2 TABLESPOONS MARASCHINO
150ML CREAM
1 EGG YOLK
1 TEASPOON ADVOCAAT
SALT AND PEPPER TO TASTE

Lightly pound the chicken breasts. Boil the spinach until tender and then drain and trim into 5cm squares. Cut the pears into strips, approximately 4cm long by 1½cm square, and fold the spinach squares around these. Depending on the size of the chicken breasts you will need just enough spinach and pear parcels so that the flattened breasts can be wrapped around them. Secure each breast with toothpicks and sear them brown in a large pan using the cooking oil. Season. Flambé with the brandy and then place in a moderate oven for 15 minutes.

To make the sauce: Lightly sauté the spring onions in the butter. Flambé the spring onions in the Maraschino and add the cream and yolk, then simmer until thickened. Finish with Advocaat and seasoning.

Remove the toothpicks from the chicken and cut the roll into approximately 3cm slices. Serve with the Maraschino sauce and garnish with chopped parsley. **Serves 4.**

VIENNESE PROFITEROLES WITH HOT WALNUT SAUCE

30G BUTTER
105G WATER
PINCH OF SUGAR
75G PLAIN FLOUR
2 EGGS AND 1 EGG YOLK

Walnut sauce:
600ML WATER
120 WALNUTS, ROUGHLY CHOPPED
500G SOFT BROWN SUGAR

½ TEASPOON VANILLA ESSENCE
30G BUTTER
300ML CREAM

To make the basic choux pastry for the profiteroles bring the butter, water and sugar to a rolling boil in a narrow pot. When this starts rising add the flour and beat well with a wooden spoon. Add the eggs and yolk, continue beating until quite thick, then remove from the heat. Pipe the mixture into cone shapes on a flat baking sheet and cook in a pre-heated oven at 150°C. This will make approximately 20 profiteroles which should be cooled before storing.

To make the sauce: Combine the water, walnuts, sugar and essence in a pot, stir until the sugar melts and bring to the boil. Simmer until quite thick and take off the heat. Stir in butter and cool slightly before stirring in the cream. Pipe the profiteroles full of cream, and then cover these with the sauce. The sauce is also excellent on ice cream. **Serves 4.**

At the turn of the century the seaside resort of Sumner was the equivalent of England's Brighton. Visitors made the journey from Christchurch just to stroll along the pier, take a dip in the hot saltwater baths, picnic, or just visit the tearooms. They were the days when Sumner was a deepwater port where vessels docked to unload goods which were then carted off to Christchurch. But the construction of a seawall changed the sweep of the tides and the harbour silted up, to be followed years later by a storm that wrecked the pier. Sumner then reverted to being just a quiet seaside village.

In 1978 Russell Black and his Japanese wife Kumiko, drove out to Sumner and there heard that the old tearooms were for sale. Russell had been a high-country stockman before making the move to Christchurch where he met and married Kumiko. After inspecting the building, he bought the old tearooms overlooking the Sumner sands with the incoming tide swirling around. They gave the interior a nautical look with fishing nets on the ceiling and glass float balls, and began with a seafood and steak menu. But as they gained confidence Kumiko gradually added Japanese specialties such as Sukiyaki, Tempura, Yosenabe and Misudaki. The combination was so successful that Russell and Kumiko were able to open yet another restaurant — the Japanese Kurashiki restaurant in Christchurch. Russell only decided to keep the Beachcomber when Michael Cathels agreed to work there as a chef. Michael had worked in Sydney, Holland and New Zealand as an executive chef, and under his capable direction the Beachcomber has reverted to a seafood restaurant.

Beachcomber,
The Esplanade, Sumner, Christchurch.
Telephone 266-592. BYO.

ENTREES

Oysters Maraska — with diced seafood and garlic cheese
Paella — long grain rice tossed with fish and seafoods
Seafood chowder
Port Hill mushrooms with a piquant sauce
Taylor's Mistake — savoury pancake with chicken and mushrooms

MAIN COURSES

Seafood Marina — seafoods in tomato and garlic with spaghetti and grilled with cheese
Hot seafood platter with prawns, scallops, mussels and garlic
Islander king prawns — dipped in batter, coconut and fried
Boned chicken in a honey and soy sauce
Seafood Kababu — various seafoods with a butter and lemon sauce
Breakwater scallops with onions, tomatoes, spices and cream brandy
Ribeye or Porterhouse steak

DESSERTS

Apricot brandy and cream
Lemon soufflé and cream
King George parfait with Advocaat and cherry brandy

DEEP-FRIED SQUID

FRESH WHOLE SQUID	SALT AND PEPPER	BREADCRUMBS
2 CUPS FLOUR	1 EGG	OIL FOR DEEP-FRYING
	¼ CUP WATER	

Make sure the squid is fresh when you buy it. It should be quite shiny. Under running water pull the body from the head, and remove the skin. Cut the body into rounds about 1cm wide, and chop the legs into 2cm long pieces. Dust with flour, salt and pepper. Beat the egg and water, dip in the squid pieces and then roll them in breadcrumbs.

Make sure the oil is very hot before dropping the squid in for just a few minutes until brown. Do not overcook or it will become tough. Serve immediately with lemon and tartare sauce. **Serves 4.**

NEPTUNE'S TREASURE CHEST

PUFF PASTRY	4 SLICES LEMON	8 SQUID RINGS
4 FILLETS FRESH FISH	PARSLEY	4 MUSSELS
4 BAY LEAVES	12 SCALLOPS	4 OYSTERS
4 OLIVES		1 SMALL CRAYFISH

Roll out some puff pastry into 4 thin circles, each with a 20cm diameter. On one half of each of the pastry circles, place a fish fillet — groper if you can get it — a bay leaf, an olive, a slice of lemon, a sprig of parsley, 3 scallops, 2 squid rings, a mussel, an oyster and some crayfish. Fold the remaining flap over and seal together.

Place in the oven at medium heat for about 15 minutes. The raw seafoods will bake in the pastry. **Serves 4.**

CHICKEN YAKITORI

PINCH CHILLI POWDER	1 TABLESPOON WHITE WINE	1 TABLESPOON SOYA SAUCE
SALT AND GROUND PEPPER	1 CLOVE GARLIC	1 ONION
1 DESSERTSPOON SUGAR	½ TEASPOON GINGER	500G CHICKEN PIECES

Mix the ingredients, apart from the chicken and onion, together. The mixture can be left overnight to ensure a better marinade.

The chicken can be either marinated in the mixture or merely dipped before cooking. Skewer the chicken pieces, putting a piece of onion between each chicken portion to separate. Simply grill till golden brown. Any remaining sauce can be poured over the chicken once it is cooked. Serve on a bed of rice. **Serves 4.**

Indian restaurants for some reason have made little impression in the New Zealand restaurant world. Auckland has a few curry houses, but for some reason Wellington has only one Indian restaurant — the Bengal Tiger. Vinu and Kam Patel, both Indian-born, decided to settle in the capital because after London it was the city they knew best and there was no competition from other Indian restaurants. After a long search they found the fire-blackened premises of Torro's in the central city, but with a few months work they cleaned, renovated and rebuilt the first-storey restaurant into the Bengal Tiger which opened in 1981. Vinu asked a friend in London to send out a Tandoor oven so they could cook their dishes over the glowing charcoal of what was the first Tandoor oven to be used in New Zealand. The marinated and spiced chicken proved so popular that Vinu eventually began bottling his marinade to sell commercially.

Most people tend to think of Indian food as consisting only of curries. Certainly, there are regions of India, especially in the south, which have fiery vindaloo curries, but there are others where a vegetarian regime exists and the dishes tend to be much more bland. The Patel's prepare dishes that cover much of India, from the Moghul lamb and birianis of northwestern India and the seafoods of Bengal in the east, to the Madras curries of southern India. Since religion plays such a large part in Indian cooking, with the Hindus not eating beef and the Muslims pork, Vinu and Kam only prepare chicken, lamb, fish and vegetarian dishes, served with chapatis, rice and various accompaniments. These are followed by traditional Indian desserts such as the rose-flavoured sweetmeats.

Bengal Tiger,
83 Willis Street, Wellington.
Telephone 728-706. Licensed.

ENTREES

Dal soup
Puri Bataka — deep fried pastry with potatoes in sauce
Prawn Pataya — prawns in a sweet-sour sauce on deep fried pastry
Sheek Kebab — minced skewered lamb cooked over the Tandoor
Chicken wings — spiced and cooked over charcoal
Bhajees — onions fried in pea-flour batter

MAIN COURSES

Chicken or lamb vindaloo
Tandoori chicken
Chicken Khasmiri — in cream with spices and fruit
Lamb Badam Pasanda — with nuts, cream and spices
Curried whole crab
Matter Pannir — peas cooked with home-made Indian cheese
Navratan Korma — Indian vegetables with dry fruits and nuts
Masala fish

DESSERTS

Kulfi — Indian ice cream
Gulab Jambu — rose-flavoured sweetmeats
Shrikand — yoghurt with dried fruit, nuts and spices
Faluda — sago and vermicelli with rosemary, pistachios and ice cream

CHICKEN BIRIANI

250G LONG GRAIN RICE
3 TABLESPOONS OF GHEE OR OIL
250G CHICKEN, BONED

1 TEASPOON SALT
1 TEASPOON CHILLI POWDER
25G GINGER, FINELY CHOPPED

1 CUP OF WATER
TOMATOES AND CUCUMBER
  FOR GARNISH

Cook the rice as normal and leave it in a hot oven to separate the grains. Add 1 teaspoon of orange colouring if you wish to make it more visual.

Heat the oil in a pan and add the chicken which should be cut into serving pieces. At the same time add the remaining ingredients. Cook gently until the chicken is cooked and then add the rice to the pan with the heat high. Stir continuously for about 3 minutes and then serve, garnishing with tomatoes and cucumber. **Serves 4-6.**

TANDOORI CHICKEN

1½ KG WHOLE CHICKEN
1 TEASPOON CHILLI POWDER
150ML WHITE VINEGAR
1½ TEASPOONS SALT
600ML YOGHURT

4 CLOVES GARLIC
100G GINGER
2 TEASPOONS GARAM MASALA
1 TEASPOON PAPRIKA

JUICE OF 2 LEMONS
RED COLOURING
ONION AND TOMATOES
  FOR GARNISH

Skin the chicken and with a sharp knife make a number of ½ centimetre deep cuts across the flesh. Rub the chilli, vinegar and salt over the chicken. Mix the rest of the ingredients in a blender until it is a smooth sauce. Rub this over the chicken and then place the bird in the refrigerator for 12-24 hours to marinate. Place the chicken on foil paper on a baking tray and bake for 1¼ to 1½ hours at 350°F. Serve on a bed of lettuce and garnish with onion rings and tomatoes. **Serves 4.**

GULAB JAMBU

85G DRIED WHOLE FULL CREAM MILK
70G SIEVED FLOUR
70G CASTOR SUGAR

⅛ TEASPOON BAKING POWDER
500G GHEE
500G SUGAR

4 DROPS ROSE ESSENCE
500ML WATER
1 TABLESPOON MILK

Mix the dried milk with the flour, castor sugar and baking powder. You will need to progressively add water until the ingredients become a smooth dough. Divide the dough into walnut size balls, and then fry them in the ghee over a medium heat until they brown evenly.

Make a syrup with the sugar, rose essence and water. This should be brought to the boil before adding the milk. Take off the boil and remove the head from the mixture and then strain the rest of the syrup through a piece of muslin cloth and allow to cool. You can then add the balls to the syrup and serve. **Serves 4.**

There was a time in Ron Dunn's restaurant career as owner of Captain Crab when he decided he just had to have Australian mud crab on the menu. It would be a good finishing touch, he thought, to a menu that already included crayfish, tua tua, paua, mussels, king prawns, marlin, eel, caviar, oysters, scallops, whitebait, squid, Scottish herring, Moreton Bay bugs and even whole Alaskan Dungeness crab. He ordered 1000 live crabs through an Australian supplier, had them flown in to Auckland airport, and went out to have them cleared by the Department of Agriculture and Customs. Sorry, said the authorities. Only dead crabs were allowed into the country, so Ron had to spend the day drowning 1000 crabs. This tale illustrates the lengths Ron goes to make Captain Crab one of the best seafood restaurants in the country. Nestled up a flight of stairs in the middle of Newmarket, Captain Crab opened in 1979 with the idea of serving a rather remarkable array of seafoods, all prepared fairly simply, using a minimum of sauces so that the seafood would be the predominant taste. Tanks were put in the restaurant so crayfish could be kept alive, and Ron then set out to ensure a steady supply of every possible type of seafood. Captain Crab became very much a family business, with his wife Margaret as accountant, one daughter Debbie working as a waitress, and another daughter Sharon (the first deaf person in the country to complete an Auckland Technical Institute City and Guilds course) as a trainee chef in the kitchen. Strangely enough, New Zealand has always had relatively few seafood restaurants, despite a strong fishing industry and excellent fresh seafoods. This in part explains why Captain Crab is so successful. Whereas the majority of the country's restaurants compete at serving French style fare, there are a bare dozen purely seafood restaurants in New Zealand.

Captain Crab,
1 Teed Street, Newmarket, Auckland.
Telephone 504-273. Licensed.

ENTREES

Tua Tua Soup finished with cream
Seafood chowder – mussels, John Dory, prawns
Seafood pâté with prawns, scallops, John Dory and brandy
Avocado and smoked fish
Smoked silver-belly eel with toast
Smoked roe served with toast
Russian and Danish caviar
Marinated fish in lemon, limes and coconut cream
Alaskan Dungeness Crab claws deep fried in butter

MAIN COURSES

Crayfish mornay with prawns
Scallops kebab with rice
King or green prawns with varied preparations
Slipper lobster mornay or whole with butter
Mariner casserole
Poached and grilled whole salmon on rice
Australian mud crab served whole
Fresh mussels with chilli onion sauce and mornay
Paua fritters pan fried in butter

CREAM OF TUA TUA SOUP

24 FRESH TUA TUA IN THE SHELL	PEPPER AND SALT	75ML MILK
1 SMALL ONION	50ML WATER	125ML CREAM
PINCH MUSTARD		PARSLEY FOR GARNISH

Shell the tua tua and wash them in cold salted water. Put them in the blender with the onion, water, mustard and pepper and salt and mince well. Transfer the mixture to a cooking pot and add the milk and simmer for 3 minutes over a medium heat. Do not boil. Add the cream and then simmer for 2 minutes, before serving. Garnish with parsley. **Serves 4.**

WHITEBAIT FRITTERS

2 EGGS	SALT AND PEPPER TO TASTE	150G BUTTER
500 GRAMS WHITEBAIT		LEMON AND PARSLEY FOR GARNISH

Beat the eggs, and then add the whitebait and seasoning. Melt the butter in the frypan and when this is simmering drop spoonfuls of the mixture into the pan. The size of the fritters is left to personal preference. Cook approximately 3 minutes each side and then serve with lemon wedges and parsley. **Serves 4.**

CRAYFISH CAPTAIN-STYLE

4/600G FRESH LIVE CRAYFISH	300G PRAWN CUTLETS	PRAWNS, TOMATO, LEMON AND PARSLEY FOR GARNISH
500ML MORNAY SAUCE	150G MUSHROOMS	

Drown the crayfish in fresh cold water for approximately 15 to 20 minutes. Place the crayfish in a large pot and cover with cold salted water. Bring the pot to boiling point without actually boiling and then drain off the water before covering with iced water for at least 10 minutes. Split the crayfish down the centre into two halves, remove the meat and cut into bite-size pieces. Add the flesh to the mornay sauce and then add either small button mushrooms or sliced mushrooms and simmer for 3 minutes. Pan fry the prawn cutlets in butter and at the same time heat the crayfish shells in the oven. Then place the shells on individual plates on a bed of lettuce, fill the bodies with the crayfish mornay. You can decorate this by sprinkling with paprika, and garnishing with prawns, tomato, lemon and parsley. **Serves 4-6.**

Thanks to his television cookery shows, an early radio series, and some highly successful cookbooks, Des Britten is probably the best-known New Zealand *restaurateur*. In the past 18 years his Coachman Restaurant has gained an enviable reputation, and the remarkable thing is that fame has fallen lightly on Des' shoulders. The informal atmosphere of the restaurant, with its exceptionally high standards in cooking and presentation, has made the Coachman one of the country's most successful restaurants.

Des spent his childhood on his father's sheep property in Hawkes Bay but the lure of radio took him to Napier, Hamilton, Australia and back to Wellington and 2ZB. To supplement his income he began working part-time at Drago Kovac's Copper Room, but with the advent of television, cooking turned into a full-time occupation. When Madame Louise bought out Drago, Des moved to Le Normandie, but there came the day when he was fired. He and his wife Lorraine then found an old shoe storeroom above Courtenay Place, and together they transformed it into the Coachman, with tables and chairs bought cheaply from a department store cafeteria. Today, the tables still remain, but are surrounded by the warmth and elegance of soft pinks and greys, brass curtain rods, spotlit metal framed prints, antique lights, superb tulips in tall glass vases, and an impressive wine cellar. These days Des is continually experimenting, trying new dishes, and keeping a strict eye on three apprentices. He still selects produce, fish and meats from the local markets and shops each day, but there is also a new interest in life. Any spare moments he devotes to his involvement in church affairs as an Anglican deacon. Any extra food, along with soup made from the off-cuts of vegetables and meat, is taken by Des to the alcoholics at a local city mission.

Coachman,
46 Courtenay Place, Wellington.
Telephone 848-200. Licensed.

ENTREES

Paw paw, avocado and sliced mushroom caps with honey and lemon vinaigrette
Rare beef sliced with mustard and grain mayonnaise, cream and cognac
Pumpkin soup with creamed cottage cheese and strip of grilled chicken breast
Warm chicken liver salad
Seafood mousse with chilled creamed prawn purée

MAIN COURSES

Boned baby leg of lamb with minted butter sauce
Boned duckling pieces with fresh fruit sauce
Fillets of fresh fish, grilled with white wine and cream
Venison slices in a light red wine sauce
Sirloin steak — wrapped in a green peppercorn and herb crêpe, grilled with blue vein butter
Australian king prawns with fresh lime and ginger

DESSERTS

Crêpes simmered in orange juice and Grand Marnier flambéed in cognac
Chocolate soufflé
Winter fruits with a cointreau flavoured sauce
Sabayon — egg yolks, champagne and liqueurs
Trio of home-made ice creams
Quenelles of chocolate mousse with fresh orange juice

AVOCADO AND TOMATO SOUP

2 RIPE AVOCADOS
1 TEASPOON GRATED ONION
2 TABLESPOONS LEMON JUICE
3 TABLESPOONS MAYONNAISE
3 TABLESPOONS CREAM
½ TEASPOON CHOPPED CAPERS

SALT AND FRESHLY GROUND PEPPER
2 CANS TOMATO JUICE
½ TEASPOON BASIL
1 CLOVE GARLIC, CRUSHED
½ TEASPOON TARRAGON
½ CUP CHOPPED GREEN PEPPER
½ CUP SLICED CELERY

DASH OF HOT PEPPER SAUCE
1 CUCUMBER SLICE, PER PORTION
1 TOMATO SLICE, PER PORTION
2 ICE CUBES, PER PORTION
CHOPPED DILL OR PARSLEY
  FOR GARNISH

Purée the avocados. Add the grated onion, lemon juice, mayonnaise, cream, capers, salt and pepper and blend well together.

Heat the tomato juice with the basil, garlic, tarragon and seasonings. Chill well, and then add the green pepper, celery and hot pepper sauce.

Spoon the avocado purée into soup dishes and carefully spoon the tomato mixture over the avocado mixture so as not to mix. Slide a cucumber and tomato slice and two ice cubes into each dish. Sprinkle with chopped dill or parsley. **Serves 4-6.**

ROAST DUCKLING WITH ORANGE SAUCE

1 ROAST DUCKLING (1½-2KG)
SALT AND PEPPER

Sauce:
1 TABLESPOON SUGAR
1 TABLESPOON VINEGAR

275ML CHICKEN STOCK
JUICE OF THREE ORANGES
3 TABLESPOONS CORNFLOUR

To roast the duckling remove the wings at the second joint. Place these in the roasting dish and sit the duck on the wings so it does not stick while cooking. Place the duck breast-side up. Add no butter or fat. Lightly season with salt and freshly ground pepper. Seal the top of the roasting dish with aluminium foil. It must be a tight seal to keep the steam in while cooking. Roast for about 2 hours at 180°C. Remove the foil and test the drumstick by squeezing it with your thumb and first finger. If it is tender the duck is ready. If not, re-cover and roast for a further 15 minutes, or until it is tender. Remove from the oven, take off the foil and cool sufficiently before handling and boning.

To make the sauce: Combine the ingredients and heat over a medium heat, thickening with the cornflour. **Serves 4-6.**

CHOCOLATE CREAM

1 CUP SUGAR
½ CUP OF WATER
200G CHOCOLATE

1¾ CUPS CREAM, AT LEAST
  A DAY OLD

ICE CREAM
SLIVERED ALMONDS FOR GARNISH

Melt the sugar with the water. Do not overheat, just enough to dissolve the sugar. Add the broken chocolate and heat gradually until smooth. Put aside to cool and thicken. When the chocolate is cool and thick, beat the cream until it is half whipped. Using a wire whisk, beat the chocolate mixture into the cream and continue beating until thick.

Serve in a big glass with a scoop of ice cream in the bottom. It can be garnished with slivered almonds or similar. **Serves 4.**

The Coach Trail Lodge sits tucked into the hillside at Waiwera, a holiday and thermal pools resort just half an hour's drive north of Auckland. With its 14 units perched on the steep hillside, the Lodge is vaguely reminiscent of the white houses dotting the Mediterranean coastline of Greece. When Bill Glanville bought the complex some six years ago it had only been partly finished. The original idea was for own-your-own apartments, but Bill, an Englishman and former construction engineer on hydro-electric projects, decided to turn it into a lodge which would give equal importance to a restaurant and accommodation. Hotels, motels and lodges generally treat their restaurants as an afterthought, and only a few ever manage to build any sort of reputation for their food. But the Coach Trail has had an excellent reputation ever since Bill and his daughter started the Lodge. These days Bill, with Diane Anderson as his restaurant manager, and Bernard Frost as chef, present dishes specializing in game and New Zealand foods. The pheasant — that royalty of game birds — is individually cooked for the diner, and takes at least 1½ hours to prepare from the time the order is taken. There is also fresh salmon, venison, duck and rabbit which is cooked in red wine sauce with bacon, mushroom and onion and served with a pastry top in an earthenware dish. There is usually a number of special dishes each night, ranging from mussels marinated in white wine and honey to braised goat's shoulder.

Coach Trail Lodge,
Waiwera.
Telephone 0942-64-792. Licensed.

ENTREES

Chilled paw paw with Anisette
Lamb brains with a poivrade sauce
Whitebait fritters
French snails with garlic and parsley butter
Crème de Tua Tua
Smoked eel with lemon, horseradish and rye
Pâté maison

MAIN COURSES

Roast pheasant with a game sauce
Salmon baked with butter, lemon juice and almonds
Rack of lamb with banana and paw paw sauce
Venison in a spicy sauce
Duck in a passionfruit sauce
Farmhouse rabbit pie
Baked flounder with lemon butter
Tournedos with bearnaise sauce

DESSERTS

Parfait with cherry chocolate liqueur
Lemon soufflé with Curaçao
Profiteroles with minted chocolate
French Camembert or Blue Stilton

HONEY AND GINGER SCALLOPS

FLOUR
SALT AND PEPPER TO SEASON
2 TABLESPOONS BUTTER
½ CUP WHITE WINE

½ TEASPOON CRUSHED FRESH GINGER
1 TABLESPOON HONEY
1 TABLESPOON LEMON JUICE

½ TEASPOON FINELY GRATED POTATO
PAPRIKA AND CHOPPED PARSLEY FOR GARNISH

Season some flour with salt and pepper. Lightly flour the scallops with the seasoned flour. In a frypan, lightly brown both sides of the scallops in the butter. Add the wine, ginger, honey, lemon juice and grated potato. Stir the mixture until the sauce thickens. Cooking should be carried out quickly so that the scallops are only just cooked.

Serve in scallop shells and garnish with paprika and chopped parsley. **Serves 2.**

PUMPKIN SOUP

3 RASHERS BACON
2 ONIONS
FRESH SAGE, ROSEMARY, THYME
1 TABLESPOON BUTTER

1 LARGE POTATO
750G PUMPKIN
600ML CHICKEN STOCK

300ML CREAM
4 TABLESPOONS WHITE WINE
WHITE PEPPER, SALT TO SEASON
1 TABLESPOON GROUND NUTMEG

Sauté the chopped bacon, onions and herbs in the butter but do not brown. Cook the potato and pumpkin in water. Pass the bacon, onions, potato and pumpkin through a fine mincer, and then add the pumpkin water, chicken stock, and ⅔ cream. Add the wine and seasoning to taste after the soup has simmered for 5 minutes. Cook until smooth. Serve in hot dishes with a pinch of ground nutmeg and whipped cream topping. **Serves 6.**

BRAISED GOAT SADDLE

1 GOAT SADDLE
1 POTATO, DICED

Marinade:
1 LEVEL TEASPOON TUMERIC
1 CLOVE GARLIC, CRUSHED
1 CUP RED WINE
2 CARROTS, DICED

1 ONION, DICED
1 GREEN PEPPER, DICED
3 STICKS CELERY, DICED
1 CUP BEEF STOCK
SALT AND PEPPER TO TASTE

Combine the ingredients of the marinade in a large bowl. Cut 30mm incisions across the backbone of the saddle and soak the saddle in the marinade for 2 days.

Braise the meat the normal way in a covered dish — include the diced potato at this stage. Use all the ingredients of the marinade and ensure that the meat is covered with liquid all the time. After slow cooking for approximately 1½ hours, allow to cool. Remove the saddle and pour the remaining stock and vegetables through a fine sieve. Make a rich dark sauce with the sieved liquid. Pour the sauce over the saddle and reheat in a covered dish. Serve accompanied with vegetables. **Serves 4.**

Antonio Olla was just 15 years old when he began working in his parents' restaurant in Rome, and for the past 30 years restaurants have been his life and love. His move to New Zealand followed that of his brother, Sergio, who set up his Italian restaurant in Auckland's Newmarket, and that was where Antonio started work in this country. He spoke no English, but it took only a matter of months before he had a rudimentary knowledge of the language, enough for him to decide to open his own place. When he opened the tiny Colosseo in 1974 in what was then a fairly disreputable part of the city, it was basically a pizzeria serving lasagna, cannelloni and the usual Italian dishes. Since then, however, Colosseo has turned into one of the more interesting Italian BYOs, specializing in veal and other dishes characteristic of the restaurants in which Antonio worked when he was living in Rome. Night after night the restaurant is packed with regular diners enjoying veal, chicken, seafood and pasta dishes, supplemented by crisp Italian salads covered with an excellent olive oil dressing. Out in the kitchen Antonio and Todd Corson work over the gas stoves cooking the veal quickly over a high heat to keep it tender and adding the variety of ingredients that make up the sauces. These days they find people are getting more adventurous in their eating habits, eating less pasta dishes and trying more seafoods, poultry and meats. It is probably a trend, Antonio believes, similar to that in Italy when the large Italian family with six or more children were served pasta in the wake of the war years, because it was cheap, filling and had plenty of carbohydrate. These days other foods are available cheaply, so old eating habits are changing. Antonio's only major criticism is the lack of different seafoods and other ingredients in New Zealand. Whereas in Italy some half-dozen varieties of squid are available, here there is only one.

Colosseo,
368 Karangahape Road, Auckland.
Telephone 771-694. BYO.

ENTREES

Antipasto with Italian salami
Lasagne Verde or Rossa
Cannelloni
Spaghetti Pescatora
Tagliatelle
Ravioli

MAIN COURSES

Bocconcini – veal stuffed with ham and cheese
Firenze – veal with mustard and anchovies in wine
Spiedini – shish kebabs of of veal, bacon and bayleaf
Pollo – chicken in wine with herbs, olives and capers
Cozze Marinare – mussel in tomatoes, wine and herbs
Gypsy chicken
Pasta of spaghetti, lasagne, cannelloni, ravioli or tagliatelli
Veneziano – veal in port wine, fennel and herbs

DESSERTS

Zabaglione
Home-made cassata
Fragole – strawberries in season
Ricotta – cottage cheese with liqueur
Fruit salad of fresh fruits

VEAL SALTIMBOCCA

16 PIECES FILLET VEAL	3 TABLESPOONS BUTTER	GARLIC POWDER
16 STRIPS BACON, 4CM LONG	3 TABLESPOONS OLIVE OIL	¼ TEASPOON SAGE
16 BAYLEAVES	FLOUR	½ CUP RED WINE
	SALT AND PEPPER	

Cut the veal to ½cm thicknesses and tenderize. Cut the bacon into strips not longer than the width of the veal. Place one strip of bacon on top of each piece of veal, and top each piece of bacon with a bayleaf, again not bigger than the veal. Secure by passing a toothpick through one end of the bayleaf, through the bacon, into the meat at an angle, and bring it back up through the bacon and the bayleaf so that the toothpick lies horizontally.

Melt the butter and oil in a large heavy frypan at a high heat so that it is bubbling but not burning. Flour the veal and add to the pan. Season with salt, pepper, a little garlic powder to taste, and the sage. When one side of the veal is cooked turn it over and cook the second side. When cooked splash the wine around the outer rim of the frypan so the wine partly evaporates with the high heat but also partly mixes with the other juices. The temperature must be high so that the wine does not cool the veal and make it soggy. When serving pour the pan juices over the meat. **Serves 4.**

VEAL VENEZIANO

½KG FILLET VEAL	2 TEASPOONS FENNEL SEED	½ CUP PORT WINE
25G BUTTER	2 BAYLEAVES	HOT WATER
1 CLOVE GARLIC, FINELY CHOPPED	2 TEASPOONS PARSLEY, FINELY CHOPPED	FLOUR
4 TEASPOONS BEEF STOCK		SALT AND PEPPER TO SEASON
2 TEASPOONS LEMON JUICE		

Have your butcher prepare the veal by cutting it into 16 ½cm thick pieces which you can then tenderize.

Melt the butter in a large frypan. Add the garlic, stock, lemon juice, fennel seed, bayleaf and parsley. Stir in the port before adding enough hot water to just cover the veal when added. Bring to the boil, stirring constantly.

Flour the veal. Add the veal to the pan, season, and let simmer for about 30 seconds before turning over the veal. Shake the pan occasionally so it does not stick to the bottom. Cook for another 30 seconds until the sauce evaporates slightly and thickens, and then serve. **Serves 4.**

ZABAGLIONE

2 LARGE EGGS	1 TABLESPOON MARSALA WINE	GROUND NUTMEG OR CINNAMON FOR GARNISH
3 TABLESPOONS WHITE SUGAR	1 TABLESPOON BRANDY	

Add the ingredients to a thin plastic mixing bowl that will not crack with heat. Put the bowl in a pan of hot water on the element and slowly heat. At the same time mix the ingredients, using an electric mixer, until smooth and creamy but firm. Pour the mixture into four tall serving glasses, sprinkle with nutmeg or cinnamon, and serve warm. It can be further garnished with cherries, strawberries or similar. **Serves 4.**

Country Life is found in the middle of nowhere at Waikanae — 56 kilometres from Wellington. It was originally a main highway tearoom in 1949 but in 1977 Alan and Luba Perry and Bill and Eileen Harrington moved from Wellington and turned it into a licensed restaurant — not unlike a country lodge. Complete with surrounding rose garden, stone fireplace, wooden colonial chairs, floral table-cloths, fresh flowers and prints of New Zealand, the restaurant offers both excellent food and the nation's most comprehensive wine list. Running Country Life was the perfect foil for the Perry's. It gave Luba, who started cooking as a young girl in Russia, the chance to extend her culinary art, and it gave Alan the chance to offer his fine wine collection for sale. His interest in wines started many years ago, but only became an extensive collection in 1959 when he went to a Christchurch wholesaler with the intention of spending £100 on a few bottles of fine vintage. Instead he spent more than £2000. Now his collection includes 150 types of wine including a 1904 Château Palmer, a 1929 Château Haut-Brion and a 1949 Château D'yquem — as well as many local wines which he does not offer until they have matured. His love of wine is illustrated by the fact the wine list includes a detailed description of the regions where the various wines originate. Indeed it is not uncommon for people to spend more on wine than on food when dining at this restaurant. Nevertheless, Luba's cooking is excellent, especially her Siberian-style meat filled dumplings. Coupled with Alan's wine knowledge and Luba's nightly wanderings through the restaurant chatting to diners, a journey to Country Life is extremely worthwhile.

Country Life,
Highway 1, Waikanae.
Telephone (0583) 6353. Licensed.

ENTREES

Pel'Meni — Siberian meat-filled dumplings with yoghurt sauce
Escargots à la bourguignonne
South Pacific bouillabaisse
Sautéed lambs brains in lemon butter with capers
Farmed green mussels in white wine and herb sauce
Tomatoes stuffed with scallops and shrimps, with mayonnaise and topped with king prawns

MAIN COURSES

Rack of lamb with honey and almonds
Roast duckling with Cointreau and kumquats
Fondue bourguignonne
Veal Marsala — white veal with a sweet Sicilian wine
Steak Luba — thin slices of prime fillet with tomatoes, shallots, white wine and spices
Fish of the day grilled with maître d'hotel butter
Crêpes filled with Tasman Bay scallops

DESSERTS

Home-made from the trolley

PEL'MENI — SIBERIAN MEAT-FILLED DUMPLINGS

1 EGG	SALT AND PEPPER	1 SMALL ONION, DICED
2½ TABLESPOONS COLD WATER	200G GROUND BEEF	1 LITRE SALTED WATER OR STOCK
FLOUR	200G GROUND LEAN PORK OR VEAL	

To make the pastry: Mix the egg, water, flour and salt into a stiff dough and let stand for half an hour. Roll the pastry out into thin, 50mm diameter circles.

Mix the ground beef, pork and onion, and add 1-2 tablespoons cold water and season. Put a little of this filling on each pastry circle, crimp the edges forming a plump semi-circle, and join the two tapering ends, pinching them to make them stick. They are preferable if made quite small; do not put in too much filling, allow for a little space between the meat and the dough for the juices to collect. Make about 12 pel'meni per person.

The pel'meni can be prepared in advance and kept in the refrigerator but they must not touch each other.

To serve: Drop the pel'meni into the boiling salted water, two at a time, and simmer for 10 minutes or until they float to the surface. Serve immediately with either melted butter or sour cream. Alternatively, they may be dropped into boiling stock and served with the stock as a delicious soup.

OLD-FASHIONED CHICKEN AND RICE PIE

SOUR CREAM PASTRY OR PUFF PASTRY	¼ TEASPOON NUTMEG	1 TABLESPOON BUTTER
1 CHICKEN	½ CUP CREAM	3 TABLESPOONS SOUR CREAM
1 LARGE CLOVE GARLIC, PEELED	1 TABLESPOON CHOPPED PARSLEY	5 HARD-BOILED EGGS, FINELY CHOPPED
2 ONIONS, PEELED AND THINLY SLICED	1 TEASPOON LEMON JUICE	1 EGG YOLK, BEATEN UP WITH 1½ TABLESPOONS CREAM
1 SMALL STICK CELERY WITH LEAVES	200G LONG GRAIN RICE	
	PEPPER AND SALT	
	200G FRESH MUSHROOMS, THINLY SLICED	

Prepare the pastry. Boil the chicken with the garlic, onions and celery. Remove the chicken, take the meat off the bones and slice. Pour out ¼ litre of the stock, add nutmeg and cream, simmer and reduce by about half, add parsley, lemon juice and the sliced chicken and cool.

Put the rice into ½ litre of stock. bring to the boil, stir occasionally and then simmer until done. Season with pepper and salt.

Fry the mushrooms in the butter, add the sour cream and simmer gently until done.

Roll out three-quarters of the pastry — 6mm thick — and transfer to a lightly-greased baking dish. Layer with rice, leaving the edges of the pastry free. Put half of the chopped eggs on the rice, cover with half the chicken and then half the mushrooms. Repeat the layers, and then end with a layer of rice.

Roll out the remaining pastry, again about 6mm thick, cover the dish and pinch together the edges of the bottom and the top pastry to seal them. Cut out a 25mm hole from the middle of the top pastry. Brush the pastry with the egg yolk and cream mixture and bake in the centre of the oven at about 200°C for 15 minutes. Reduce to 170°C and bake for a further 30-40 minutes, until the crust is golden brown. Serve immediately. **Serves 6.**

ROCK MELON WITH GINGER

200ML WATER OR WHITE WINE	100G SUGAR	6 SMALL CUBES OF PRESERVED GINGER
1 SMALL PIECE OF FRESH GINGER	2 MEDIUM ROCK MELONS	2 TABLESPOONS LEMON JUICE

Gently boil the water (or wine) with the fresh ginger and sugar until reduced by half. Remove the ginger and discard. Leave the syrup to cool.

Meanwhile, clean the melons and cut into any small shaped pieces, or scoop out balls. Cut the preserved ginger thinly and mix with the melon pieces, the cooled syrup and the lemon juice.

Chill and serve with cream or ice cream. **Serves 4.**

Restaurants generally have a habit of specializing in entrées and main courses, while desserts tend to become an afterthought. Perhaps it is also the tendency of cookery training to treat desserts as such, for it is the practice of large hotels to have apprentice cooks specialize in only a few facets of cooking, to the almost total neglect of baking and desserts. 95 Filleul is one of those few restaurants in New Zealand where the desserts are an integral part of the meal. Run by Alex and Sue Cameron, it has developed into one of the South Island's best BYO's.

Alex, born in Scotland, began taking an interest in cooking when he was just seven years old, and when he left school he did a diploma in cookery, and a certificate in bakery and cookery, in Wales. After that he worked in the British Merchant Navy, ending up in New Zealand in 1972 where he worked in the kitchens of various hotels. But disillusionment finally set in with this style of cooking. He met and married Sue who was a primary school teacher and together they decided to open a bakery in Wellington. From there they bought a small lunchtime BYO in Wellington called Chlöe, where Sue began developing her bakery and desserts skills under Alex's watchful expertise. At the same time they made a habit of eating at all the major restaurants in the capital, gathering ideas which whetted their appetite to have a restaurant that was not as limited as Chlöe. Sue had gone to school in Dunedin, so when 95 Filleul came up for sale they grabbed the opportunity. The size and style of the place gave Alex and second chef Andrae McLaughlin flexibility to develop their cooking skills, while Sue prepared the desserts which Alex decorated. Filleul's dessert trolley and menu dessert are now desserts *par excellence*.

95 Filleul,
95 Filleul Street, Dunedin.
Telephone 777-233. BYO.

ENTREES

Asparagus pâté
Terrine Guerard
Scallops and mussels in Pernod sauce
Marinated chicken pieces
Suppli with Mozarella cheese filling

MAIN COURSES

Fresh fish with Marsala, cream and almond sauce
Boned breast of chicken with brie and apricot sauce
Noisettes des Tournelles with Soubise purée
Loin of pork with spinach purée, prunes and pinenuts
Rib eye steak with garlic butter
Jambon de Saulieu

DESSERTS

Chocolate Marquise
Cassata Filleul
Apricot Dacquoise
Chocolate mousse
From the Trolley

CHEESE SOUFFLE

1 LARGE EGG
1½ TABLESPOONS MALT BEER
2 TABLESPOONS STRONG CHEDDAR CHEESE
½ TEASPOON FLOUR

Butter individual soufflé dishes (9cm wide by 5cm deep). Whisk the egg for 5 minutes or until thick. Bring the beer to the boil and add the cheese. Melt slowly. Add the flour off the heat and mix well before blending in the beaten egg. Fill the soufflé dish to 1 cm from the top, and bake for 10 minutes at 215°C, turning down to 200°C after 2 minutes. Do not overbake, although the soufflé needs a high heat for a lift at the start of cooking. **Per portion.**

PAUPIETTES OF PORK

8 PRUNES, SOAKED OVERNIGHT
3 APPLES, PEELED
1 TABLESPOON SUGAR
8 LARGE SLICES LEG PORK
1½ CUPS BREADCRUMBS
8 PICKLED WALNUTS
FLOUR
2 EGGS, BEATEN
½ CUP DESSICATED COCONUT
2 TABLESPOONS CLARIFIED BUTTER
2 TABLESPOONS BRANDY
300ML CREAM
1 TABLESPOON CHICKEN STOCK
MARJORAM FOR GARNISH

Cook the prunes in the water they have been soaking in overnight. Once cooked, remove the stones, and add 1 chopped apple and the sugar. Cook for 5 minutes. Remove from the heat and beat with a wooden spoon until blended. Leave to cool.

Cut the pork slices into 16 equal rectangles. Add enough breadcrumbs to the prune mixture to ensure a slightly firm consistency. Put 1 teaspoon of prune stuffing and half a pickled walnut on each pork slice and roll up into uniform paupiettes. Chill the paupiettes in the freezer to enable them to firm.

Dip the paupiettes in flour, the beaten eggs, the remaining breadcrumbs and the dessicated coconut. Deep fry until golden brown, then finish by baking in a hot (210°C) oven for 15 minutes.

Cut the remaining apples into 16 wedges. Flame the wedges in the clarified butter and the brandy. Add the cream and the chicken stock and reduce slightly.

Pour the cream sauce onto each plate and arrange the paupiettes to form a cross with the apple wedges between each paupiette. Garnish with a sprig of marjoram in the centre. **Serves 4.**

CHOCOLATE HAZELNUT TORTE

Meringue:
8 EGG WHITES
1½ CUPS CASTOR SUGAR
100G GROUND HAZELNUTS
50G BUTTER, MELTED
½ CUP SIFTED FLOUR

Brandy cream:
300ML CREAM
3 TABLESPOONS CASTOR SUGAR
1 TABLESPOON BRANDY
1 DESSERTSPOON CHICORY COFFEE ESSENCE

Chocolate cream
300ML CREAM
3 TABLESPOONS CASTOR SUGAR
3 TABLESPOONS COCOA
1 TEASPOON VANILLA

Raspberry purée:
250G FROZEN RASPBERRIES
250G SUGAR

To make the meringue: Cover three baking trays with non-stick baking paper and mark a 40cm by 30cm rectangle on each sheet.

Beat the egg whites till firm, gradually beat in the sugar, until dissolved. Fold in the nuts, melted butter and sifted flour. Divide the mixture evenly between the trays and spread with a pallet knife. Bake at 160°C for 30-45 minutes until crisp. Allow to cool.
To make the cream: Whisk the ingredients for each cream filling until thick.
To make the puree: Strain the juice from the raspberries and simmer for a further 3 minutes.

To decorate the torte: Spread a thin layer of raspberry purée, followed by ½ brandy cream on the first hazelnut sheet. Place the second hazelnut sheet on top and repeat the process. Place the third hazelnut sheet on top and spread ⅓ or more of the chocolate cream on top, using a pallet knife dipped in hot water. Leave to set in the refrigerator for ½ hour.

Cut the torte into desired shapes and decorate with the remaining chocolate cream using a piping bag. **Serves 4.**

Flamingos is one of those highly successful restaurants with a reputation that spreads like wildfire. Such reputations don't come easily. They are a product of hard-working owners, first-class food and presentation, personality, interesting surroundings and good luck.

Wendy Lever, the chef, and her husband Alan Titchall, originally met in Sydney while Wendy was working at a French restaurant. In those days Alan's forte was more in film scripting than restaurants. Both were New Zealanders and so they made the normal trip back to visit family and friends. It just happened that they were taken to Flamingos for dinner and it was mentioned that the owners wanted to sell. That was enough; they decided on the spot they would buy the restaurant. There was little to change; the menu was similar to Wendy's style of cooking. Likewise, the black and white tiled floor, white trellises, pink and white tablecloths, ritz palms, ceiling fan and a fireplace for winter gave Flamingos a Mediterranean feel that they decided to keep. Another reason for retaining it was the fact it was a retaurant unique to Auckland. But changes were gradually introduced. These were probably inevitable since Alan and Wendy made it a habit to visit other restaurants on their nights off to try different styles of cooking, talk with other restaurant owners, and keep abreast with developments. Wendy's constant experimentation with new ideas and dishes brought regular change to the menu, while Alan looked after the restaurant, introducing excellent music such as Sarah Vaughan, Betty Carter and Billie Holliday, and adding little touches like offering a glass of port to end a meal. Their intense interest in making the restaurant their way of life is all part of Flamingos' success.

Flamingos,
242 Jervois Road, Herne Bay, Auckland.
Telephone 765-899. BYO.

ENTREES

Florida Fizz Cocktail
Iced tomato and cantaloupe bisque
Sâté Manis with hot peanut sauce
Russian Blini – yeast pancakes with sour cream and caviar
Smoked Mussel Salad – with Green Goddess dressing
Venison Feuillette – with blackcurrant purée

MAIN COURSES

Orange roughy fillets with Galliano and almonds
Barbequed pork spareribs
Chicken phyllo – with cream cheese, paw paw and nuts with a paw paw sauce
Melanesian seafood salad
Beef fillet with crab and cognac sauce

DESSERTS

Glazed fruit basket with cream and liqueur
Passionfruit mousse with kiwifruit coulis
Dark chocolate cake with fresh fruits and orange liqueur
South Pacific Exotic Delight – nut and fruit ice cream with a plum purée
Cheese 'n fruit platter

VENISON FEUILLETTE

¼ KG LEAN, TRIMMED VENISON STEAK
2 ONIONS, COARSELY CHOPPED
1 CLOVE GARLIC
2 TABLESPOONS OIL
HALF BOTTLE IRISH STOUT

1 TABLESPOON WORCESTERSHIRE SAUCE
1 TABLESPOON BLACKCURRANT JAM
MIXED HERBS
2 SHEETS PHYLLO PASTRY

Blackcurrant purée:
4 TABLESPOONS BLACKCURRANT JAM
½ CUP LEMON JUICE
1 TEASPOON HERBS
¼ TEASPOON PEPPER
1 TEASPOON VINEGAR
1 TABLESPOON ARROWROOT

Cut the venison steak into 2cm cubes, flour and season. In a medium-sized saucepan brown the onions and garlic in the oil, and then add the venison. After browning, add the Stout, Worcestershire sauce, blackcurrant jam and a liberal sprinkling of mixed herbs. Leave to simmer uncovered. Cooking time varies with the cut of meat but between 1 and 2½ hours should be sufficient. But do not overcook or the venison might become very dry. The cubes should be tender enough to fall apart easily in the mouth. Spread the cooked mixture to cool in a shallow dish. If it needs thickening spoon off the surplus gravy.

Spread out the phyllo sheets, and spoon large tablespoons of venison into one corner. Brush the edges with melted butter and carefully wrap the pastry into a parcel. If preparing in advance keep the parcels under a moist towel. Bake these in the oven at a medium temperature for 10-15 minutes until the pastry is brown.

To make the blackcurrant purée: Melt the ingredients over a low heat in a small saucepan. Spoon the purée over the baked pastry. Serve. **Serves 6.**

MELANESIAN FISH SALAD

2 WHITE FISH FILLETS
LEMON JUICE
1 RED PEPPER
1 GREEN PEPPER

3 TOMATOES, QUARTERED AND SEEDED
1 ONION, FINELY CHOPPED
1 TEASPOON CUMIN

¼ CUP FRESHLY GRATED GINGER
420G COCONUT MILK
FRESH FRUIT FOR GARNISH

Cut the fish fillets (orange roughy if possible) into long strips, and place in an enamel or plastic container, covering completely with freshly squeezed lemon juice. Orange roughy will take 2 hours to marinate, but other 'thick' fish including snapper will take 24 hours. Drain well. Add the strips of peppers, the tomatoes, onion, cumin, ginger and coconut milk, and mix by hand. Season to taste with salt.

Serve on a bed of lettuce or ginger leaves and garnish with freshly sliced fruit flowers or leaves. **Per portion.**

FRUIT BASKETS

Brandy Snaps:
150G BUTTER
6 TABLESPOONS GOLDEN SYRUP
⅞ CUP CASTOR SUGAR

2 TEASPOONS GINGER
1 CUP FLOUR

Garnishing:
ICE CREAM
FRUIT, FRESHLY SLICED
CREAM
LIQUEUR

To make the brandy snaps: Melt the ingredients in a saucepan. Place one tablespoon of the mixture at a time onto a non-stick oven tray. The mixture has to be runny — if it is not add more butter. Cook in a medium oven for 7-8 minutes. As the mixture cools prise off the sheets with a plastic slice. Drape each sheet over the bottom of a well-greased glass and pinch in the sides to form the basket and allow to set. If cooked in advance, store in an airtight container.

Place the basket on a small leaf with one scoop of ice cream in the bottom. Layer with freshly sliced fruits, a layer of cream, more fruit, and finally a small dab of cream and a dash of liqueur. Serve at once. **Serves 6.**

Fraser's is part of the old Shamrock Hotel complex in Thorndon, Wellington, where on St Patrick's Day the chefs prepare a large green cake shaped like a cloverleaf, while staff dispense green beer in the courtyard throughout the day. In the evening Wellington's Irish community wildly celebrates at Fraser's. The rest of the year is not nearly as chaotic. Fraser's returns to its normal role as a lunch and dinner BYO with dishes that lean towards a French-English cusine.

Before it became a restaurant the building housing Fraser's was the old Galatea Family Hotel. It was situated about a mile from its present site, and it was about to be knocked down to make way for a high-rise building when Rex Nichols, who specialises in restoring old buildings, discovered it. He moved it lock, stock and barrel, began renovations and decided he wanted a British-style restaurant in the building. At the same time James Holdich had arrived from England with his New Zealand wife Patricia. They noticed a sign saying a restaurant would be contained in the Shamrock building so James promptly rang Rex and it was agreed James would set up and run Fraser's. James had been running hotels and restaurants in South Wales so he was reasonably *au fait* with setting up a restaurant from scratch. They decided to keep with the colonial look, with antique lamps, prints of early Wellington, and an old bar mirror advertising Scotch whisky. But there were the added refinements of white German porcelain and fine silver contrasting with a regal blue and white colour scheme.

Fraser's now has a strong following among local Thorndon residents, but the building has become widely known due to its being designated a 'place of interest' by the Historic Places Trust.

Fraser's,
Tinakori Road, Wellington.
Telephone 730-342. BYO.

ENTREES

Avocado pear filled with shrimps and pineapple in mayonnaise sauce
Smoked eel fillets with horseradish sauce
Soup of the day
Snails with garlic and parsley butter
Chicken livers sautéed with bacon and mushrooms
Grilled seafood kebab served on creamed spinach
Crumbed sweetbreads with tartare sauce

MAIN COURSES

Whole South Island salmon, meuniére style with toasted almonds
Pork Normandy flamed in calvados with cream sauce
Fillet steak topped with crayfish, asparagus spears and hollandaise sauce
Supreme of chicken with apricot sauce

DESSERTS

Selection from the trolley
Selection of New Zealand and imported cheeses

MUSSELS FRASER

24 FRESH MUSSELS IN SHELL	SPRIG FRESH THYME	Sauce:
2 CUPS WHITE WINE	100G BUTTER	FISH VELOUTE
1 CUP WATER	2 CLOVES GARLIC, CHOPPED	2 TABLESPOONS HOLLANDAISE
1 ONION, CHOPPED	1 TABLESPOON CHOPPED PARSLEY	PEPPER FOR SEASONING
6 PEPPERCORNS	2 FILLETS GROPER	
1 BAYLEAF	BREADCRUMBS	
	OIL FOR DEEP FRYING	

Poach the mussels in their shells until they open in a poaching liquor of the wine, water, onion, peppercorns, bayleaf and thyme. Once cooked, remove the mussels from their shells, trim off the beards, tongues and eyes and fill each mussel with garlic butter made by melting the butter and add the garlic and parsley.

Thinly slice the groper fillets into 8cm lengths and wrap one fillet around each mussel. Crumb with breadcrumbs and deep fry in hot oil.

To make the sauce: Heat the fish velouté thickened with white roux, add the hollandaise sauce and seasoning.

Serve the mussels in the shell on a bed of cream of spinach. **Serves 6.**

SUPREME OF CHICKEN
with sherry, cream and pineapple

1 LARGE CHICKEN BREAST	1 CARROT, GRATED	½ TEASPOON PAPRIKA
½ TEASPOON SALT	2 LEEKS, THINLY SLICED	½ TEASPOON CHILLI POWDER
1 TABLESPOON SOY SAUCE	1 TEASPOON CORNFLOUR	2 TABLESPOONS DRY SHERRY
4 TABLESPOONS OIL	2 SLICED FRESH PINEAPPLE, CHOPPED	½ TEASPOON SUGAR

Rub the salt into the chicken breast and sprinkle the soy sauce over the chicken. Cut the breast into thin strips. Heat the oil in a pan and fry the chicken strips for 3 minutes. Flour the grated carrot in the cornflour, and add the carrot and leeks to the pan and heat for a further 2 minutes.

Flour the pineapple in the cornflour. Add the pineapple, paprika and chilli powder to the pan. Place the lid on the pan and cook for 12 minutes before adding the sherry and sugar. Serve on a bed of rice. **Per portion.**

PORK LOIN WITH MUSHROOM AND PARSLEY STUFFING

4 DOUBLE BONED LOIN PORK CHOPS	¼ TEASPOON CAYENNE PEPPER	1 CLOVE GARLIC, CRUSHED
1 TABLESPOON CHOPPED FRESH PARSLEY	¼ TEASPOON BLACK PEPPER	75G MUSHROOMS, FINELY CHOPPED
½ CUP WHITE BREADCRUMBS, FRESH	½ TEASPOON SALT	1 TABLESPOON VEGETABLE OIL
	2 TABLESPOONS BUTTER	75G MAITRE D'HOTEL BUTTER, SLICED
	1 SMALL ONION, FINELY CHOPPED	

Preheat the oven to 170°C. Place the pork flat on a board and cut horizontal slits into the cutlets. Mix the parsley, breadcrumbs, cayenne, black pepper and salt. In a small saucepan melt the butter over a moderate heat, add the onion and garlic and cook for 3 minutes, stirring occasionally. Remove the pan from the heat, and stir in the mushrooms to blend. Blend the two mixtures and then spoon the stuffing into the incisions, closing with cocktail sticks.

Place the pork in an ovenproof casserole and brush the pork with the oil. Cover the casserole, place in their centre of the oven, and cook for 1 hour. Uncover the dish and cook for a further 30 minutes. Remove the pork from the casserole dish and take out the cocktail sticks. Place the pork on a serving dish. Finish with slices of the maître d'hotel butter and serve. **Serves 4.**

Ian Fraser was the national sales manager for one of the country's biggest travel companies when he first came across the idea of opening Fraser's Place, one of the country's few deli-restaurants. He had been travelling for 6½ years before he discovered delicatessens in both Hawaii and California where you could have lunch or dinner, and then pick up the odd pot of pâté, some cheese, French bread and other goods to stock up at home. It was a casual way of eating that he thought would do well in Auckland, so he threw in his well-paid and secure position, and went on the hunt for suitable premises, which he finally found at the bottom end of Auckland's trendy Parnell Road. He built a delicatessen in the front of the ground floor, and behind this he put in bar-style seating for local office workers who wanted to have a hurried lunch. Upstairs he put in a Piaf room with pictures of the legendary singer, lots of greenery, ceiling fan and flower boxes in the windows; a tiny Graffiti Room, in which he covered the walls with hundreds of pieces of graffiti; and a Conversation Room, so called because of the unusual prints on the walls. He then added his collection of another 46 prints by various artists to decorate the place, plus a 250 tape collection so he could feature a lunchtime concert each day with music from Randy Crawford to Louis Armstrong. The blackboard menu means the dishes can be changed daily, and a lot of the dishes centre around the foods sold in the delicatessen. Added to some superb salads are dishes centred around venison, turkey, fresh fish and seafoods, and spicy Eastern fare — a formula that has proved to be highly successful.

Fraser's Place,
116 Parnell Road, Parnell, Auckland.
Telephone 774-080. BYO.

ENTREES

Mulligatawny soup
Mushroom quiche
Salmon crème

MAIN COURSES

Chilli con carne
Turkey breast and fruit platter with cranberry sauce
Jungfrau venison
Coppa and paw paw
Presentation salads

DESSERTS

Lemon cheesecake
Plum torte
Fresh fruits and cheese

SALMON CREME

220G RED OR PINK SALMON
250G CREAM CHEESE
1 PACKET ONION SOUP
1 DESSERTSPOON CHOPPED PARSLEY
1 TABLESPOON LEMON JUICE
SALT AND PEPPER TO TASTE
75G CHOPPED NUTS

This is a simple but easily prepared pâté for an entrée or just a snack with a drink.

Drain the salmon and remove the backbone. Combine all the ingredients thoroughly, except the chopped nuts. Shape into a log and roll in the nuts before chilling. Serve chilled. **Serves 4.**

MULLIGATAWNY SOUP

½ KG CHUCK STEAK, DICED
1 TABLESPOON CRACKED PEPPER
1 TEASPOON GROUND CINNAMON
2½ LITRES WATER
SALT
BUTTER
3 ONIONS, DICED
2 APPLES, PEELED AND DICED
2 CARROTS, DICED
3 STICKS CELERY, DICED
3 LARGE TOMATOES, RIPE
3 MEDIUM POTATOES, PEELED AND DICED
1 LARGE TABLESPOON MADRAS CURRY
½ TEASPOON GROUND CHILLI POWDER
PINCH TURMERIC
½ TEASPOON GROUND GINGER
JUICE OF 1 LEMON
300ML COCONUT MILK (OPTIONAL)

Put the chuck steak, ground pepper, cinnamon and salt into a pot with the water. Bring to the boil and then simmer for 1½ hours.

In a separate pot, fry the onions, and then add the apples, carrrots, celery, tomatoes and potatoes — tossing regularly. After 10 minutes add the curry powder, chilli, turmeric, ginger and lemon juice. Mix well, stirring regularly. After 15-20 minutes add the chuck steak and stock. Simmer for an additional 2 hours, adding the coconut milk if desired. Finally put the soup, including the steak, through the blender. Reheat and serve. This soup freezes well. **Serves at least 10.**

SUMMERTIME TURKEY AND FRUIT PLATTER

PRESSED TURKEY BREAST
WHOLE STRAWBERRIES AND RASPBERRIES
WHOLE CHERRIES
WATERMELON, DICED
ROCK MELON, SLICED
PAW PAW, SLICED
APRICOTS, PLUMS, NECTARINES, HALVED
BANANA, SLICED
ORANGE SEGMENTS
CRANBERRY SAUCE

This is not so much a recipe but an arrangement for a light summer dish. However, in winter, available fruit such as pineapple, paw paw, grape and bananas can be used. All you need is a large serving plate. Use the sliced rockmelon as the base which is then covered with the various fruits and turkey as decoratively as possible. The pressed breast of turkey, imported from America, and available from delicatessens, is the best to use because of its flavour. It is not dry, and there is no wastage. Serve with the cranberry sauce.

The tendency these days is for many restaurants to cut down their menus to just a few entrées, possibly six main courses and four or so desserts. But Brian King, chef and part-owner of Gainsborough House, refuses to bow to this new convention. Instead, he presents 19 entrées, 26 main courses, plus specials and desserts. His theory is that the licensed Gainsborough House attracts a lot of top company executives who regularly entertain, sometimes three times a week. A short menu, he feels, would soon become boring to such patrons.

Brian runs Gainsborough in partnership with John Marshall and Keith McDonnell. Gainsborough House is a 65-year-old Tudor style building with leaded windows, so named after the eighteenth century English artist Thomas Gainsborough. Gainsborough prints, including the famous 'The Blue Boy', adorn the restaurant, adding to the traditional air created by tapestry-covered chairs, wooden panelling, and fine crystal and silver. With his cooking, Brian relies mainly on his own ideas and he vows he never reads a cookbook. He left those behind when he finished his apprenticeship and ever since has relied on experimentation to present what he terms an 'international' menu and style of cooking. He hangs all his meat for three weeks, which he believes is imperative to improve texture and flavour, and once a year, when the Hamilton Agricultural Show is held at Mystery Creek, he manages to obtain the superb Murray Grey beef for the menu. The flavour of that meat is comparable to Japan's famous Kobe beef, sadly unobtainable in this country.

Gainsborough House,
61 Ulster Street, Hamilton.
Telephone 394-172. Licensed.

ENTREES

Seafood platter
Smoked eel with seafood sauce
Oysters, natural or mornay
Chicken breasts in chopped nuts and almonds
Fresh fish bearnaise
Pâté maison

MAIN COURSES

Crayfish tossed in butter, garlic and shallots
Scallops with a white wine sauce
Fresh fish in almond butter
Hazelnut chicken flambéed with Frangelico
Cranberry pork
Entrecôte Chasseur
Châteaubriant with bearnaise
Lamb Maharani

DESSERTS

Tia Maria ice cream gâteau
Kiwifruit ice cream
Profiteroles
Cheese and fruit platter

GAINSBOROUGH SCALLOPS

24 SCALLOPS
½ LARGE ONION, CHOPPED
125G PACKET ALMONDS
25G BUTTER
100ML WHITE WINE

JUICE OF 3 SMALL LEMONS
2 TABLESPOONS TOMATO PUREE
SALT AND PEPPER

White sauce:
25G BUTTER
25G FLOUR
½ LITRE MILK
SALT AND PEPPER

Sauté the scallops, onion and almonds in the butter until half cooked. Add the white wine, lemon juice and tomato purée. Simmer for 1 minute.
To make the white sauce: Melt the butter slowly. Add the flour and gently cook for 2 minutes. Heat the milk and gradually add it to the mixture until thick and smooth. Season to taste.
Add the white sauce to the scallop dish and gently cook for 2-3 minutes. Season to taste. **Serves 4.**

HAZELNUT CHICKEN

8 BONELESS CHICKEN BREASTS
SALT AND PEPPER
50G BUTTER

1 SMALL ONION, CHOPPED
4 LARGE KIWIFRUIT, PEELED AND CHOPPED

125G HAZELNUTS, CHOPPED
200ML FRANGELICO HAZELNUT LIQUEUR

Flatten the chicken breasts and season. Melt the butter in a frypan and sauté the onion and the chicken breasts until nearly cooked. Add the kiwifruit and hazelnuts, and cook for 2 minutes over a low heat. Add the liqueur and reduce by half.
When serving, spoon the kiwifruit, nuts and onions on top of the breasts, topped with some of the cooking liquid. **Serves 4.**

TIA MARIA ICE CREAM GATEAU

50G BUTTER, MELTED
1 PACKET MALT BISCUITS, CRUSHED

2 LITRES VANILLA ICE CREAM
2 TABLESPOONS COFFEE ESSENCE

200ML CREAM, LIGHTLY WHIPPED
TIA MARIA

Mix the melted butter and the malt biscuits. Place the mixture into an 18cm round cake tin. Bake at 180°C for 15 minutes. Chill until completely cold.
Mix the coffee essence and the cream, beat the ice cream until smooth, then add the ice cream to the cream. Use a spoon to slowly fold the two mixtures together. Add Tia Maria to taste, then pour the mixture onto the chilled base. Freeze, but do not defrost and then refreeze. **Serves 6-8.**

Harley's is one of those rare restaurants that opens without much ado, but within a very short time becomes an institution. The effervescent duo behind Harley's are Jo Coulter and Helen Brabazon, who originally met as nurses in one of the scrub rooms at Auckland Hospital. They became good friends and in 1977 decided to go to London to continue working as nurses. Even in those early days they were talking about opening their own restaurant in Auckland, and with this in mind Jo applied for the Cordon Bleu cookery course in London. It was from Helen's work in a Harley Street clinic that the name was to emerge.

They returned to New Zealand in 1981, fired with enthusiasm, Jo with her Cordon Bleu certificate, virtually penniless, but very determined. Eventually they found an old warehouse in Anzac Avenue which was once the country's first aircraft factory, but which was now in a pitiful state of disrepair. Starting from a bare shell they installed walls, put in plumbing, built a kitchen, painted myriads of coats of marine red paint on the walls and Ceramco blue on the ceiling, hung a variety of spotlit prints, added an old piano, carpeted the place, and set the tables with fine Rosenthal china and crystal glasses. They also added their personal touch with a painting of Helen's, and Jo's collection of ornamental ducks. The result was a modern and relaxed restaurant. While Jo went into the kitchen, Helen handled the customers.

Shortly after they opened in March of 1982, they were given a five-star rating as Auckland's best BYO by *Metro* magazine. Since then they have not looked back going from strength to strength with rarely an empty table in the 60-seat restaurant.

Harley's,
25 Anzac Avenue, Auckland.
Telephone 735-801. BYO.

ENTREES

Tarragon chicken in phyllo with lemon sauce
Marinated raw fish, smoked mussels and prawns in spiced coconut milk served in a clam shell
Avocado with sour cream, caviar and vinaigrette
Blue cheese and mushroom soup
Harley's cocktail — Pureed ice fruit, cream and white rum
Special salad — Smoked eel, mushroom, fetta cheese, and grapes
Prune, lychee and bacon kebabs

MAIN COURSES

Chicken breasts — stuffed with ginger and cream cheese with apricot sauce
Lamb cutlets with minted kiwifruit sauce
Brie and asparagus wrapped in a yeast crêpe
Crayfish — panfried in butter
Pork fillet slices with a light mustard, brandy and cream sauce with pickled walnuts
Fillet with a grain mustard
Orange roughy fillets panfried in lemon and butter

DESSERTS

Bultard sour cream pie served hot with meringue topping and icecream
Fresh mango sorbet
Brandy snap basket filled with Drambuie and coconut icecream
Fresh fruit in Cointreau and champagne
Macadamia coffee cream with chocolate flakes

CHILLED AVOCADO AND ORANGE SOUP

3 MEDIUM-SIZED AVOCADOS
1 CARTON NATURAL YOGHURT
2 CUPS FRESHLY SQUEEZED ORANGE JUICE
SALT AND FRESHLY GROUND PEPPER
300ML MILK
SOUR CREAM AND CHOPPED FRESH HERBS FOR GARNISH

Blend the avocados and yoghurt in a liquidizer. Add the orange juice, salt and pepper. Thin down with milk. Chill and serve with a swirl of sour cream and chopped fresh herbs. **Serves 4.**

FRESH ASPARAGUS AND BRIE PARCELS

600ML MILK
1 CUP FLOUR
2 TABLESPOONS OIL
2 TABLETS OF DRIED YEAST
3 EGGS
1 TEASPOON SUGAR
2 ROUNDS BRIE
1 KG ASPARAGUS
SALT AND FRESHLY GROUND PEPPER

To make yeast crêpes: Blend milk, flour, oil, eggs, sugar and yeast in a liquidizer. Leave the mixture for 2 hours, then blend again.

This mixture will make about 16 crêpes. As they are cooked they should be stacked with greaseproof paper between each crêpe to prevent sticking. In the middle of each crêpe pile thick slices of Brie and spears of cooked asparagus. Add salt and pepper to taste, sprinkle with grated cheese, and then fold into 100mm² parcels before heating in an ovenproof dish. **Serves 4.**

TOOT SWEET

2 CUPS BROWN SUGAR
1 CUP FLOUR
600ML MILK
3 EGGS
225G BUTTER
SWEET SHORT PASTRY
1 CUP CASTOR SUGAR

Heat the brown sugar, flour and milk in a saucepan. When glutinous blend with the egg yolks in a liquidizer. Add the butter, blend thoroughly and pour into a prepared blindly-baked sweet short pastry case.

Whip the egg whites until stiff, gradually mixing in the castor sugar. Spread the meringue mixture over the top of the pie and bake at 150°C for 1 hour or until set. Serve with vanilla ice cream. **Serves 4.**

Opposite: Silver beet salad (p. 168). Silver beet grows so widely throughout New Zealand that many people consider it an inferior vegetable. But it makes an excellent salad, according to Digby Law, especially when prepared with bacon, almonds and cream cheese. Young silver beet leaves are best used in salads, as the older leaves can be tough. *(Photograph by Max Thomson.)*

---

13. Helen Brabazon and her partner-chef Jo Coulter of Harley's, named by *Metro* magazine for two consecutive years as Auckland's best BYO. *(Photograph by Stephen Ballantyne).*

---

14. Harland Harland-Baker and his wife Diana own the world-renowned Huka Lodge on the banks of the Waikato River near Lake Taupo. *(Photograph by Lianne Ruscoe).*

---

15. Gainsborough House in Hamilton was built early this century in the Tudor style by a local milliner. It is now one of the city's best known restaurants. *(Photograph by Lianne Ruscoe).*

---

16. Ian Fraser runs Fraser's Place in Auckland's Parnell, a restaurant-deli specializing in presentation salads, soups and excellent venison and turkey. *(Photograph by Lianne Ruscoe).*

13

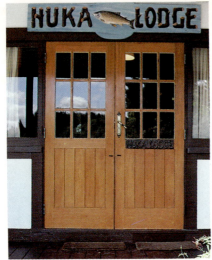

14

15

16

17

18

19

75

Opposite: Trout baked with herbs (p. 174). In New Zealand the sale of trout is illegal, but farmed salmon is becoming more plentiful although still quite expensive. To prepare this dish, as prepared by Digby Law, you will either have to catch your own trout or buy a salmon. With this dish, lemon, parsley and thyme is stuffed into the trout before cooking. It can be served hot but is preferable served cold. *(Photograph by Max Thomson.)*

---

17. Remiro and Fay Breselin, with their Italian chef Franco Zanotto, at their renowned Il Casino in Wellington, which features innovative Italian cuisine in luxurious surroundings. *(Photograph by Stephen Ballantyne).*

---

18. The stylish interior of Robert Clark's Korean Barbecue restaurant in Auckland. The Korean bulgogi style of cooking means patrons cook their own meals at the table over a bulgogi dome. *(Photograph by Stephen Ballantyne).*

---

19. The country's top Japanese restaurant, Kurashiki in Christchurch, is owned by Russell Black and his wife Kumiko, pictured with their chefs and staff. *(Photograph by Stephen Ballantyne).*

Huka Lodge is famous both as a fishing lodge on the banks of the Waikato River and for its cuisine which has a strong leaning towards game dishes. Decades ago Alan Pye opened the Lodge as a fishing retreat but it soon attracted visiting royalty and heads of state who came lured by tales of the beauty of the Lodge, its food and style. These days Harland Harland-Baker, his wife Diana, and brother and sister-in-law Charles and Diane Baker, share the running of the Lodge. Guests, a large number from overseas, spend their days fishing and hunting and a lot of the game finds its way to the table. These include venison, trout, wild boar, opossum, bush turkey, wild hare or rabbit, and duck. Vegetables are fresh from the Lodge garden, and the fruit for the desserts comes from their own fruit trees. Eating is done in style, with guests at two long tables to promote conversation. Fresh river water is served in chilled pewter goblets, while fine cutlery and crystal is used in the five course dinner. Dinner is as dinner should be, very European, with four or five hours devoted to the ritual. When the food comes to the table it is fairly simply prepared with no masking of natural flavours. The roast lamb has a hint of garlic and is served with wild river mint; the smoked marlin is served 'au naturel'; the paua fritters are merely served with a slice of lemon, and the home-made pies are cooked with fruit from the backyard, a crusty pastry and fresh runny cream. It's straightforward cuisine, simple in preparation, but excellent in taste, texture and presentation. Judging by the international reputation of Huka Lodge, this leaning towards New Zealand foods and homestyle cooking is what overseas tourists are seeking.

Huka Lodge,
Huka Falls Road, Taupo.
Telephone 85-791. Licensed.

ENTREES

Wild duck pâté
Tua tua patties
Marlin mornay
Venison or wild boar soup
Smoked trout
Whitebait, pan fried in garlic and butter

MAIN COURSES

Roast venison with cranberry sauce
Bush turkey and rabbit pie
Filleted pan fried trout
Roast lamb with river mint sauce
Roast wild boar and apple sauce
Rabbit pie
Roast wild duck

DESSERTS

Plum pie
Blackcurrant tart with Dubonnet and brown sugar
Baked apples with dates in ginger wine
Huka Lodge cherries in rum or brandy
Fruit pudding and rum custard

OYSTER CHOWDER

½KG FRESH BLUFF OYSTERS
2 LITRES WATER
2 SMALL HEADS BROCCOLI, FINELY CHOPPED
2 TABLESPOONS CHICKEN BOUILLON
JUICE OF 3 LEMONS
300ML CREAM
CHOPPED SPRING ONIONS FOR GARNISH

Put the oysters in the water and bring to the boil. Simmer until the oysters are tender. Mince the oysters and return to the stock. Add the finely chopped broccoli, the chicken bouillon and lemon juice. Simmer for 3-4 hours.

Just prior to serving add the cream and sprinkle with chopped spring onions. **Serves 12.**

WILD BOAR CHOPS

1 CUP BREADCRUMBS
1 CUP WHITE FLOUR
1 TABLESPOON GARLIC POWDER
½ CUP SESAME SEEDS
1 TEASPOON SALT
½ TEASPOON CRACKED PEPPER
6 WILD BOAR LOIN CHOPS
2 EGGS, BEATEN
OIL FOR FRYING

Mix the breadcrumbs, white flour, garlic powder, sesame seeds, salt and pepper.

Dip the chops in the beaten eggs and then coat the chops in the dry crumb mixture. Fry the chops in a frypan with hot oil until golden brown on both sides. Then place the chops in a lightly oiled baking pan and bake for 1 hour at 150°C. Serve with apple sauce and fresh vegetables. **Serves 6.**

MARTINI MELON

1 WATERMELON
100G ALMONDS
MARTINI
FRESH MINT LEAVES FOR GARNISH
FRESH LIQUID CREAM

Peel, slice and cube the watermelon and remove the pips. Place the cubes in a large bowl. Halve the almonds, blanche them, and add them to the bowl with the melon. Depending on how many guests you have, make up the equivalent of one martini per person. The original martini recipe is 2 parts gin and 1 part dry vermouth, but if you want an extra dry martini you can use up to 12 parts gin to 1 part vermouth. Shake the martini with ice, and then pour the drink, minus the ice, over the melon and almond mix. Let stand for 2-3 hours. In summer place the dish in the refrigerator; in winter it can stand at room temperature.

To serve, place 4-5 mint leaves over the ingredients to add an aroma, and offer liquid cream in a separate jug. **Serves 10-12.**

Il Casino is Remiro and Fay Breselin's testament to a belief that restaurants, food and dining out should have style and tradition in the manner of Remiro's native city, Venice. Remiro came to New Zealand in 1972 to find a total absence of the Italian eating tradition in which he had been raised – his family had owned restaurants in Venice for more than 100 years. Shortly after arriving in the country, Remiro worked in an Auckland pizza restaurant, before moving to Wellington to open his La Casa Italian BYO on Cambridge Terrace. Meanwhile Fay had been travelling and working in Europe, returning to London to work at the famous Richoux restaurant. On her return to Wellington she opened her very successful Taj pâtisserie and art gallery a few hundred yards away from La Casa. In a move many predicted would end in failure, Remiro found an old two-storey warehouse and converted it into an Italian BYO seating 65 diners. Remiro's partner moved on, Remiro and Fay married in 1979, and Il Casino proceeded to develop into one of this country's finest, most stylish and sophisticated licensed restaurants in the grand Italian manner. The walls are kauri, filled with prints and paintings, many by the famous Italian artist Batelli; there is a baby grand piano in the bar, along with two magnificent leadlight coat of arms in the ceiling, soft leather couches, antiques, and assorted Italian sculptures. Il Casino has been such a success that adjoining properties have been bought, and there are plans to turn one into an Italian bakery. It seems Remiro and Fay leave no stones unturned in the quest to maintain the restaurant's success. In 1982 Remiro returned to Italy, to the city of Padova, to tempt Franco Zanotto, one of that country's top chefs to work at Il Casino's. With Franco now in Il Casino's kitchen, and Remiro and Fay keeping a tight rein over the running of the restaurant, Il Casino is possibly as close as it will ever be to their vision of bringing the Italian traditional to New Zealand.

Il Casino,
108 Tory Street, Wellington.
Telephone 857-496. Licensed.

PRIMI

Gnocchi con Pollo – dumplings with chicken strips and tomato sauce
Bigoli in Salsa di Vitello – wholemeal spaghetti with white veal ragoût
Minestrone del Giorno – Italian soup
Gamberoni ai Ferri – king prawns grilled over charcoal with herbs and olive oil
Cape Sante – scallops in a white wine, orange and fresh herb sauce with puff pastry case

SECONDI

Griglia ta Mistra – seafoods grilled over charcoal
Fagiano Arrosto – braised pheasant
Scallopine al Marsala – white veal sautéed with marsala
Agnello Scottadito – lamb sautéed in olive oil, garlic, Pomodora and sweet basil
Coniglio della Mamma – fresh casseroled rabbit
Bistecchine di Cervo – venison steak
Filetto ai Ferri – prime fillet grilled over charcoal with a herb or green peppercorn sauce.

DESSERTS

Gelati
Various flambéed dishes
From the trolley

BIGOLI E COSTINE
(Large wholemeal spaghetti)

Spaghetti:
200G WHOLEMEAL FLOUR
150G SEMOLINA
OLIVE OIL
4 EGGS
SALT AND PEPPER

PARMESAN CHEESE FOR GARNISH

Sauce:
300G WHITE VEAL RIBS
OLIVE OIL
JUICE OF 2 LEMONS

3 SHALLOTS, SLICED
WHITE WINE
ROSEMARY
3 TOMATOES, PEELED
BUTTER
5 MUSHROOMS, SLICED

To make the sauce: Seal the veal in a pan with olive oil. When the veal juices have vaporized squeeze the lemon juice over the veal, add the shallots, some wine, rosemary, tomatoes and butter. Three-quarters of the way through cooking add the mushrooms and leave to simmer. The sauce will be ready when the meat begins to fall off the ribs.

To prepare the spaghetti: Mix the spaghetti ingredients and extrude through the spaghetti-making attachment of an electric mixer. Otherwise use ready-made spaghetti. Cook the spaghetti and drain well. Place in a heated serving dish, pour the sauce over the spaghetti, and sprinkle liberally with parmesan cheese. Serve immediately. **Serves 6.**

CONIGLIO RIPIENO
(stuffed rabbit)

1½KG BONED RABBIT
1 LITRE WHITE WINE
OLIVE OIL
JUNIPER BERRIES

ROSEMARY
2 PORK FILLETS
SALT AND PEPPER
200G MINCED RABBIT
1 EGG, BEATEN

CENTRE OF LOAF OF FRESH BREAD SOAKED IN MILK
200G SALAMI OR HAM
GRILLED POLENTA FOR GARNISH

Marinate the boned rabbit for 6 hours in the wine and a little olive oil, juniper berries and rosemary.

Quickly seal the pork fillets in a pan, season and remove from heat. Season the minced rabbit and mix with the egg and soaked bread. Lay the boned rabbit on a surface, pat dry, and spread the salami and the mixture over the rabbit. Place the pork fillet in the centre with the rosemary. Roll the rabbit up tightly and secure by sewing. Slowly bake in a heavy dish in the oven for 2-2¼ hours. When cooked, slice the rabbit, place on a heated serving dish, and pour the juices over the rabbit before garnishing with grilled polenta. **Serves 6.**

PASTA FOLLE

Pastry:
300G FLOUR
3 WHOLE EGGS AND 2 YOLKS
VANILLA
ZEST OF 1 ORANGE
100G BUTTER

Topping:
3 EGG WHITES
100G ICING SUGAR
100G ALMONDS, CHOPPED
JUICE OF ½ LEMON

Filling:
100G SPINACH, FINELY CHOPPED
150G RICOTTA CHEESE
4 EGGS
150G SUGAR
JUICE OF 1 ORANGE
30ML RUM

To make the pastry: Mix the pastry ingredients together, and knead. Roll out the pastry and line a 20cm cake tin.
To make the filling: Cook the spinach and drain thoroughly. Mix the spinach with the ricotta cheese. In a separate bowl, beat the eggs with the sugar, add the orange juice and rum, and combine with the spinach and ricotta mixture. Fill the pastry-lined dish with the mixture.

To make the topping: Beat the egg whites, slowly adding the icing sugar. Add the chopped nuts and lemon juice. Spread the topping over the mixture.

Bake at 170-180°C for approximately 40 minutes. This traditional Venetian dessert should be served hot. **Serves 6.**

The idea of a Korean restaurant came to American-born Robert Clark while he was working in Melbourne. He was a regular patron of a Korean restaurant near his home and after a while the owners finally let him into the secrets of Korean cuisine. Restaurants were already in his blood, for his grandmother and his parents had been involved in Chinese restaurants in California. So it was a natural progression that he should search out premises in central Auckland which he then turned into a Korean restaurant. It took a year to strip down the walls, sand the floors, put in a kitchen, and fully renovate the premises. Framed prints of Korean scenes now hang on the bare wood walls, along with huge Korean fans, while bamboo and ritz palms grow out of brass and cane planters. In the reception area there is a cane lounge suite with a cane dividing screen, hanging lamps and peacock chairs. When you are ready to eat, you sit in chairs around specially made tiled tables with a gas cooker in the middle for the bulgogi-style Korean cooking. Plates of marinated beef and pork or various seafooods are brought to the table along with beautifully presented vegetables. Using chopsticks you barbecue the meat or seafoods on the top of the cooker and boil the vegetables in the cooker's moat which contains a broth. Then, at the end of the meal you drink the contents of the moat as your soup.

Because Korea is geographically bound between China and Japan, its cuisine reflects the food of both countries, emphasising the meat dishes and spicier preparation of Northern China and the sauces, marinades and presentation of Japan. Korean cuisine is also famous for its pickled cabbage called Kim Chi, which is ferociously hot due to the chilli content.

Korean Barbecue,
27 High Street, Auckland.
Telephone 33-382. BYO.

MAIN COURSES

Bulgogi-style beef, chicken and pork
Bulgogi-style squid, scallops and oysters
Served with vegetables, rice and soup
Side dishes of toasted sesame seeds and Kim Chi

DESSERTS

Lychees and ice cream
Mandarins and ice cream

Jasmin tea
Green tea
Korean Ginseng tea

BULGOGI DINNER FOR SIX PEOPLE

1 KG CORNER CUT TOPSIDE BEEF

Marinade:
3 TABLESPOONS JAPANESE SOY SAUCE
2 TABLESPOONS WATER
1 TABLESPOON TOASTED, GROUND SESAME SEEDS
2 SPRING ONIONS, WITH TOPS, FINELY CHOPPED
¼ TEASPOON CHILLI SAUCE (OPTIONAL)
3 CLOVES GARLIC, CRUSHED
2 TEASPOONS SUGAR
2 TEASPOONS SESAME SEED OIL

Bulgogi vegetables:
4 CUPS OXTAIL SOUP
1 CAULIFLOWER, BITE-SIZE PIECES
½KG BROCCOLI, BITE-SIZE PIECES
3 COURGETTES, SLICED DIAGONALLY
6 SPRING ONIONS, WITH TOPS, 3CM LENGTHS
¼KG MUSHROOMS, SLICED
PARSLEY FOR GARNISH

Spring Kim Chi (Pickled Chinese cabbage):
1 CHINESE CABBAGE (CELERY CABBAGE)
6 TABLESPOONS SALT
3 SPRING ONIONS, WITH TOPS
3 CLOVES GARLIC, FINELY CHOPPED
2 FRESH CHILLIES, FINELY CHOPPED
3 TEASPOONS FRESH GINGER, FINELY CHOPPED

Roasted sesame seeds:
1 CUP WHITE SESAME SEEDS
2 TABLESPOONS SALT

Bulgogi means 'barbecued.' Traditionally, a bulgogi dome is used, but an electric frypan is sufficient. In summer, an outside barbecue hot plate can also be used, minus the soup stock. Much of the preparation can be done the day before.

To prepare the barbecued beef: Cut all gristle and fat off the meat, cut into long fillets, and then cut each fillet into thin crossways slices. Add the meat to the marinade and let stand overnight or for at least 3 hours.

To prepare the marinade: Add all the ingredients except, the sesame seed oil, together in a bowl, and mix thoroughly. After the meat has marinated add the sesame seed oil.

To prepare the sesame seeds: These can be prepared, stored in an airtight container, and used as needed. Place the sesame seeds in a frypan on medium heat, stirring constantly until they turn golden brown. Remove from the heat, place in a crockery dish and stir in the salt. Leave to cool.

To prepare the Kim Chi: Cut the cabbage into long 2cm wide slices and then chop crossways at 2cm intervals. Place in a container, mix in 3 tablespoons of salt. Let stand for half a day, stirring occasionally to allow penetration. Rinse three times with fresh water. Add the other ingredients, including the remaining salt, and mix thoroughly. Add enough water to cover the Kim Chi and place in an airtight container in the refrigerator.

To serve: Place the sesame seeds and the Kim Chi in individual dishes for the guests. Two hours before the guests arrive, place the meat, vegetables and Kim Chi on dishes, using lettuce and parsley for decoration. Leave the prepared ingredients in the refrigerator until the guests arrive. Prepare the oxtail soup. Place the electric frypan on the table centre on medium heat and supply each guest with chopsticks and a soup spoon. Add half the meat to the frypan, lightly fry, and push to the side of the pan. Lightly fry some of the vegetables and then pour a little oxtail soup in the pan and let simmer for a few minutes. Using chopsticks, eat the meat and vegetables, dipping them in the sesame seeds or the Kim Chi. As the food is eaten, add more ingredients and continue eating at your own pace. Add water to avoid burning. At the end of the meal you have an enjoyable soup to be spooned from the frypan or served separately. Other sauces such as Hoysin and plum sauce can also be used for dipping. **Serves 6-10.**

Kurashiki is undoubtedly the finest Japanese restaurant in New Zealand and comparable to the best overseas, including Japan. The grey slate floor and white pine of the foyer area is reminiscent of the entrance to a Japanese home, complete with a Japanese-style garden. The restaurant itself is a mixture of Shoji paper, dividing screens, hanging ricepaper lights, fine vases, simple but stylish furniture complete with kimonoed waitresses.

Kurashiki, named after Christchurch's sister city, was a natural consequence for Russell Black and his Japanese wife Kumiko after running Sumner's Beachcomber where they had featured a few Japanese dishes. They always had it in mind to open something like Kurashiki, but the plans took a sudden leap when a friend and Japanese chef, Joe Toyama, wanted to become a permanent resident. The only way he would be allowed to stay, according to Immigration officials, was if he worked in a totally ethnic restaurant. Russell and Kumiko decided to bring forward their plans, building Kurashiki on the first storey of a central Christchurch office building, where it was easily accessible to the growing number of Japanese tourists passing through the city. But Kurashiki came into its own when Joe's cousin, Shin Toyama, agreed to come to New Zealand to become the main chef. Shin had been working in one of Japan's most exclusive business clubs but it was not until he began cooking at Kurashiki that Russell and Kumiko realized how brilliant he was. He transformed Kurashiki's dishes into works of art, using bamboo plates, sticks of bamboo, and remarkable presentation. Kurashiki cuts no corners by offering anything other than Japanese dishes; this explains why about 60 percent of its diners are Japanese, the majority of them tourists on their way through to Queenstown.

Kurashiki,
Gloucester and Colombo Streets,
Christchurch.
Telephone 67-092. Licensed.

COURSES

Sashimi — raw fish with green mustard and soy sauce
Sushi — vinaigrette rice ball with fish and soy sauce
Chawan-Mushi — delicate hot soup with egg
Yakitori — marinated chicken grilled on skewer
Sakana-no-Shioyaki — grilled fresh fish
Beef Sashimi — rare fillet with soy sauce
Tempura — seafood and vegetables in crisp batter with sauce
Tonkatsu — pork fillet bread deep fried, sliced and served with a sauce
Teriyaki steak — prime beef fillet marinated, baked and sliced
Sukiyaki — sliced beef and vegetables cooked at the table
Yakiniku — Genghis Khan barbecue of sliced meats and vegetables, barbecued with sauces
Yosenabe — seafoods cooked at the table

DESSERTS

Hatsuyuki — spring snow dessert
Season's fresh fruit

AWABI NO SHIO MUSHI

6 FRESH PAUA

¼ CUP SAKI OR WHITE WINE
1 TEASPOON SALT

⅓ CUP SOY SAUCE

Remove the paua from its shell, remove innards, and wash with salt and water. Use a pot scrubber to remove the black. Boil a pot of water and drop the paua in for 2-3 seconds. Drain off the hot water and run under cold water. When the paua has cooled fill the pot with water. Add the saki or wine and bring to the boil. Turn to a low heat and simmer for 4-6 hours with the lid on. Take off the heat, add the salt and soy sauce and then leave to cool. When cold cut the paua into slices. Serve it with soy sauce, dipping each piece as you eat it. **Serves 6.**

GINGER CHICKEN WINGS

8 CHICKEN WINGS
2 TABLESPOONS WHITE WINE
¼ CUP SUGAR

⅓ TEASPOON CHILLI POWDER
⅓ TEASPOON FRESHLY GRATED GARLIC

1 TABLESPOON FRESHLY GRATED GINGER
2 TABLESPOONS SOY SAUCE

Place the wings in a flat dish and then add the remaining ingredients. Mix together thoroughly. Place the dish underneath a hot oven grill. Cook until golden brown on both sides. Once cooked, place the chicken pieces on a bed of rice. This dish can be served hot or cold. **Serves 4.**

TERIYAKI STEAK

ROLL PRIME FILLET
SALT AND PEPPER
BUTTER

Sauce:
½ CUP SOY SAUCE
1¼ CUPS SUGAR
¼ CUP WATER

GROUND PEPPER AND SALT
¼ TEASPOON CHILLI POWDER
1 CLOVE GARLIC
½ TEASPOON GRATED GINGER

Cut the fillet into 2cm thick rounds, with approximately 2 pieces per person. Sprinkle both sides with salt and pepper. Cook the steak in a hot pan with a little butter for 2-3 minutes each side. Cut each piece into about 4 pieces.
To make the sauce: In a small pot, add the soy sauce, sugar, water, a little ground pepper and salt and the chilli powder. Cook at a low heat for 1 hour but do not boil. When it thickens add the garlic and ginger. The sauce can be made 1-2 days ahead and kept in the refrigerator. Pour the sauce over the steak pieces and serve with steamed short grain rice and salad. **Serves 6.**

Frenchman Jean Claude Rapon has combined the best of both worlds in his seaside French restaurant: cooking and painting. La Bonne Auberge is situated on the first floor of a building in the Orewa shopping centre, looking out over the superb vista of the Pacific Ocean. In summer thousands of holidaymakers flock into Orewa, near Whangaparaoa and Hatfields Beach, where Prime Minister Robert Muldoon has a holiday house. At these times cooking to Jean Claude is an all-consuming affair: picking his herbs grown fresh in his garden, travelling to Auckland to get the best ingredients, choosing fresh fish, crayfish and shellfish from the local fishermen at Leigh, and cooking seven nights a week. After the holiday season, the tempo slows and Orewa resorts to a steady, more refined pace. That is when painting takes its turn. Jean Claude's oils cover the walls of the restaurant, with canvasses of people, ducks on a pond, and still lifes. The paintings, the open terrace where people can eat in summer, and the casual atmosphere give La Bonne Auberge a touch of France similar to the restaurants Jean Claude worked in when he lived in Nice. After leaving France he travelled to South Africa, Germany, Switzerland and England, working in a variety of hotels and restaurants before arriving in Auckland, and then moving to Orewa when he heard he could open La Bonne Auberge in a new complex. Now, with his own restaurant, a myriad of paintings, and a view with few parallels, the travelling days are probably over.

La Bonne Auberge,
Moana Court, Orewa.
Telephone 65-379. BYO.

ENTREES

Soup du Jour
Escargots à la Bourguignonne
Pâté à la façon du chef
Oysters Natural
Scallops Provençal
Parma ham with paw paw

MAIN COURSES

Poisson de Jour Almondines
Coquille St Jacques
Poulet au Citron
Steak au Poivre
Escalope de Veau à l'Orange
Porc Maison
Crayfish in whisky, wine, tomato, herbs

DESSERTS

Chocolate Mousse
Tarte du Jour
Coupe de la Patronne

SOUP AU PISTOU

100G FRESH WHITE HARICOT BEANS
2½ LITRES WATER
500G FRENCH BEANS
3 LARGE POTATOES
1 TABLESPOON SALT
1 TABLESPOON GROUND PEPPER
3 TOMATOES, SKINNED, SEEDED, PULPED
4 SMALL COURGETTES, DICED
3 TABLESPOONS VERMICELLI

Pistou:
LEAVES OF 8 SPRIGS BASIL
3 CLOVES GARLIC
3 TABLESPOONS OLIVE OIL

To make the soup: Put the haricot beans into a large saucepan with the water and boil. Add the green beans and potatoes, and season. Cook for 20 minutes, add the tomatoes, and cook for a further 20 minutes. Add the courgettes, simmer for 5 minutes. Add the vermicelli and cook for a further 5 minutes.
To make the pistou: Pound the basil in a mortar with the finely chopped garlic until it is a smooth paste. Add the oil drop by drop, continuing to pound with the pestle. Work the mixture vigorously with a wooden spatula or spoon to obtain a thickish cream.
To serve: Put the pistou in each of eight soup tureens, and beat in the soup little by little. The soup might need seasoning with freshly ground pepper. **Serves 8.**

LANGOUSTE MAISON

4 LIVE CRAYFISH
WATER
6 TABLESPOONS OLIVE OIL
2 ONIONS
2 CAPSICUMS
4 TOMATOES, PEELED, SEEDED AND CHOPPED
1 CLOVE GARLIC
30ML DRY WHITE WINE
20ML WHISKY
40ML CREAM
3 TABLESPOONS PEPPER AND SALT
2 PINCHES CAYENNE PEPPER

Place the crayfish on a board and stun with a sharp blow to the head with a heavy instrument. Place in boiling water for 15-20 minutes before draining. Cut the crayfish in half from head to tail and remove the viscera.
To make the sauce: Heat the olive oil in a heavy sauté pan and seal the crayfish pieces over a high heat. Remove and reserve. Add the chopped onions and green peppers, and stir thoroughly with a wooden spoon. Add the tomatoes, crushed garlic, white wine, whisky, cream, pepper, salt and cayenne pepper. Arrange the crayfish pieces in their shells and pour the sauce over the crayfish. Heat in the oven for 15 minutes and serve hot, accompanied with Creole rice. **Serves 4.**

COUPE MONT BLANC

1 HEAPED TABLESPOON CHESTNUT PUREE
1 TABLESPOON CREAM
1 SCOOP VANILLA ICE CREAM
3 TABLESPOONS HOT MELTED CHOCOLATE
CHANTILLY CREAM
1 TABLESPOON ALMONDS, FLAKED AND GRILLED
1 GLACE CHESTNUT

Mix the chestnut purée with the cream, without blending completely. Put this mixture into a champagne glass and place a scoop of ice cream on top. Cover with the hot chocolate and decorate the sides with Chantilly cream using a bag with a fluted nozzle. Sprinkle with the grilled almonds and top with the glacé chestnut, or if unavailable, a slice of fruit. **Per portion.**

Landmark, one of the few stately old homes built in Rotorua, has both the distinction of being an excellent restaurant and one of this country's finest buildings. Until 1979 it was a rundown residence, although Auckland *restaurateur* Tony White had plans to restore it and open a restaurant. But he ultimately dropped the idea and Bob and Noeline Sharplin heard on the grapevine that it was up for sale. They had been attracted to the old building for years, partly because Bob worked in real estate and because they were both avid antique collectors. Landmark had been built at the beginning of the century by Charles Kusabs who owned a timber mill at Mamaku. He chose the finest heart rimu and built the two-storey Landmark with its magnificent turret overlooking the geysers of Whakarewarewa. It took nearly six months for the Sharplin's to renovate the building to a 60-seat licensed restaurant, filled with the finest antiques and an Edwardian décor. Because Rotorua is one of the country's major tourist haunts Landmark hosts a lot of American and Australian tourists. Their Yugoslavian chef, George Le Maic, spent a number of years working as a chef on the passenger liner *Queen Elizabeth* before coming to New Zealand, where he spent some time at Bellamy's in Parliament House. His preparation and style of cooking is classical and his dishes international in their approach. However, there is much emphasis on seafoods because of their availability and because so many overseas visitors insist on trying New Zealand whitebait, oysters and carfish. Venison, much of which comes from the Rotorua area, and roasted leg of lamb served with mint sauce and brown gravy, also catch the tourists' eyes.

Landmark,
1 Meade Street, Rotorua.
Telephone 89-376. Licensed.

ENTREES

Poisson Cru
Snails in walnut and garlic butter
Whitebait fritters
Oysters natural
Seafood chowder
Champignons au gratin

MAIN COURSES

Venison steak with orange and green ginger wine sauce
Crayfish Mornay
Chicken Portuguese with orange Drambuie sauce
Orange roughy with a tamarillo sauce
Roast lamb with mint sauce
Filet Mignon

DESSERTS

From the trolley
A selection of New Zealand and imported cheeses

AVOCADO LANDMARK

2 RIPE AVOCADOS
100G BLANCHED MUSHROOMS, FINELY CHOPPED
50G ONIONS, FINELY CHOPPED
50G GHERKINS, FINELY CHOPPED
1 TEASPOON LEMON JUICE
1 TEASPOON MAYONNAISE
PEPPER AND SALT FOR SEASONING
¼ TEASPOON PAPRIKA
LETTUCE LEAF AND PARSLEY FOR GARNISH

Cut the avocados lengthwise, remove their stones and score the flesh. Squeeze some lemon juice on the flesh to prevent discolouration. Fill the halves with the mixed ingredients. Serve on a lettuce leaf, surrounded with crushed ice. Sprinkle with paprika and add a sprig of parsley. **Serves 8.**

CHICKEN PORTUGUESE
with orange and Drambuie sauce

8 CHICKEN BREASTS
8 SLICES SIDE BACON
16 KING PRAWNS
CLARIFIED BUTTER AND COOKING OIL
CHOPPED PARSLEY AND NUTS FOR GARNISH

Sauce:
300ML CREAM
½ CUP ORANGE CONCENTRATE
3 ORANGES, PEELED AND DICED
1 MEASURE DRAMBUIE LIQUEUR
1½ TABLESPOONS CORNFLOUR

Pound the chicken breasts flat and cut the bacon into 8cm lengths. Place one slice of bacon on each breast and wrap these around 2 king prawns. Fold in the chicken breast at the ends and secure with toothpicks. Pan fry the chicken in equal parts of clarified butter and oil till golden brown.

To make the sauce: Heat the cream, concentrate, oranges and Drambuie, and thicken with cornflour. Bring to the boil and stir until the cornflour is cooked.
To serve: Pour the sauce over the chicken rolls and garnish with chopped parsley and nuts. **Serves 4.**

GRAND MARNIER AND CHOCOLATE MOUSSE

1 LARGE BLOCK CHOCOLATE
4 EGG YOLKS
1 MEASURE GRAND MARNIER LIQUEUR
4 EGG WHITES
PINCH OF SALT
WHIPPED CREAM AND GRATED CHOCOLATE FOR GARNISH

Melt the chocolate in a *bain-marie*. Add the egg yolks and liqueur. Stir briskly until smooth.

In a separate bowl, add a pinch of salt to the egg whites and beat the egg whites until they form soft peaks. Pour the egg whites into the chocolate mixture and mix.

Pour the mousse into champagne saucers and refrigerate. Decorate with whipped cream and grated chocolate. **Serves 4.**

Charley Gray is one of Auckland's better known personalities — musical entrepreneur, modern jazz enthusiast, and along with Peter Campbell, the shining light behind the Last and First Café. The title of Café is slightly misleading, because the Last and First is a lot more than simply a café. It is a mixture of restaurant, art gallery and meeting place, attracting a wide variety of people to its café style environment. The idea behind the café grew as a result of Charley Gray's lifestyle, working and living, as he was, on the third storey of a centre city building. The problem was his office-apartment had no kitchen. Each night he ate at restaurants — an expensive way of life. He decided if he was to continue his lifestyle he would have to own his own restaurant. The Last and First opened in what had been a large interior design store, with 2500 square feet downstairs, and enough space upstairs to ultimately open a venue for jazz, theatre and experimental music. From the beginning the Last and First flourished, in what was a new direction for restaurants in this country. A large empty wall was offered to artists to hang, construct or paint works on the spot. Artists such as Gretchen Albrecht, Frank Womble, Pat Hanley, Denys Watkins, Emily Pace and Dick Frizzell have all exhibited there, while a downstairs lounge has become a photography gallery. Seven nights a week till midnight, the Last and First is regularly filled. The kitchen with David Paske and two other cooks rarely has a rest, and Charley and Peter continue their plans to make the Café even more unique. After a trip to Buenos Aires where he ate at a café four times the size of the Last and First, Charley sees room for many more ideas to be implemented.

Last and First Café,
192 Symonds Street, Auckland.
Telephone 792-877. BYO.

ENTREES

Pork, veal, liver and brandy terrine
Fettucini with chicken livers and mushrooms
Smoked fish vol-au-vent
Crêpe Italiano
Spinach and fetta phyllo pie
Red bean and bacon soup

MAIN COURSES

Marinated scotch fillet with mustard butter
Fresh fish of the day
Chicken with soy sauce, ginger and garlic
Lamb kebab
Vegetarian lasagna
Prime beef stuffed with vegetables and chillies

DESSERTS

Dutch apple cake
Chocolate mousse
Poached pears with fruit sauce
Brazilian bananas
Chocolate gâteau

RED BEAN AND BACON SOUP

250G RED KIDNEY BEANS	2 TABLESPOONS COOKING OIL	1 BAY LEAF
2 CARROTS	2 CLOVES GARLIC, CHOPPED	½ TEASPOON CHILLI POWDER
1 STALK CELERY	450G TOMATOES, SKINNED AND PULPED	½ TEASPOON COARSE GROUND PEPPERCORNS
3 SPRING ONIONS		
150G BACON	1200ML CHICKEN STOCK	SOUR CREAM, CHOPPED CHIVES AND PARSLEY FOR GARNISH
1 LARGE ONION	PINCH MIXED HERBS	

Soak the kidney beans overnight. Dice the carrots, celery, spring onions, bacon and onion, and fry in the oil until softened and slightly coloured. Add the garlic, tomatoes, chicken stock, beans, mixed herbs, bay leaf, chilli powder and pepper. Bring to the boil and then simmer for 1 hour. Check seasonings to taste. Other ingredients such as chicken pieces, veal, spinach and peas can be added if desired. To garnish add a generous serving of sour cream and sprinkle with chopped chives or parsley. **Serves 6.**

SOUTH AMERICAN BEEF ROLL

6 PIECES SIRLOIN STEAK	1 CUP MUSHROOMS	2 CLOVES GARLIC, CHOPPED
1 TEASPOON CHILLI POWDER	¼ SMALL CAULIFLOWER	500G FRESH TOMATOES, SKINNED AND CHOPPED
SALT AND PEPPER	1 TOMATO	
1 CARROT	200G BROCCOLI	½ TEASPOON THYME
1 ONION		1 BAYLEAF
1 STALK CELERY	Tomato sauce:	½ GLASS RED WINE
150G BACON	1 ONION, DICED	SALT AND PEPPER
2 LEAVES SPINACH	1 DESSERTSPOON BUTTER	

To make the beef roll: Slice each piece of steak with a 'butterfly' cut nearly all the way through. Open out and flatten with a meat tenderizer. Sprinkle with the chilli powder, salt and pepper.

Finely dice and blanch the vegetables, dice and fry the bacon and thoroughly mix together. Place the mixture on the meat, leaving a quarter of each steak free to allow for overlapping. Roll the meat and secure with toothpicks. Fry the steak turning the roll occasionally.

To make the tomato sauce: Gently cook the onion in the butter with the garlic, until transparent. Add the tomatoes, herbs and wine and cook until the required consistency is reached. Season to taste.

The roll, covered with the sauce, can be served with buttered rice, noodles or potatoes. **Serves 6.**

BRAZILIAN BANANAS

1½-2 BANANAS	2 TEASPOONS COCONUT	1 TABLESPOON GRATED CHOCOLATE
JUICE OF 1 ORANGE	50ML RUM	
1 TEASPOON CINNAMON	¼ CUP RAISINS	FRESH WHIPPED CREAM

Slice the bananas and moisten with freshly squeezed orange juice. Add the cinnamon, coconut, rum and raisins and mix well. Leave to marinate overnight, or for at least 4 hours. Served with grated chocolate and fresh whipped cream. **Per portion.**

Opposite: Blintzes (p. 111). Crêpe making, or at least making the perfect crêpe, is an art in itself, although crêpe makers are now available for those who would rather not use traditional methods. These blintzes from the renowned Orsini's restaurant in Auckland are filled with a delicious mixture including cream cheese, egg yolks, lemon, orange, and nutmeg. *(Photograph by Max Thomson.)*

---

20. Charley Gray, his partner Peter Cameron, and chef David Paske are pictured with other staff from the Last and First Café in Auckland. *(Photograph by Stephen Ballantyne).*

---

21. The building which now houses Landmark restaurant in Rotorua was built at the turn of the century by a timber mill proprietor. The restaurant has retained the Edwardian décor so that patrons can dine in antique filled surroundings.

---

22. Louis and Annabelle Doczi of Louis' in Christchurch, which they designed as a lunchtime BYO but expanded instead into an innovative night-time restaurant. *(Photograph by Stephen Ballantyne).*

20

21

22

23

24

25

26

Opposite: Oxtail with black olives (p. 173). This dish, prepared by Digby Law, takes a little time to prepare and it has to be refrigerated overnight, but the flavour of oxtail with black olives is superb. Served as a casserole with buttered new potatoes and a tossed green salad it makes an excellent winter or summer meal. *(Photograph by Max Thomson.)*

---

23. Rex and Lois Smith of Martini's in Christchurch. The restaurant serves some excellent dishes featuring rabbit, duck, venison and other New Zealand game. *(Photograph by Stephen Ballantyne).*

---

24. Roger Mail of Maggie's Farm, which serves some of the best game foods in New Zealand. *(Photograph by Stephen Ballantyne).*

---

25. Larry Charman's Meridian restaurant at Bucklands Beach has the dual advantage of good French cooking plus one of the best water views in Auckland. *(Photograph by Stephen Ballantyne).*

---

26. Prue and Mark Tatton run Le Petit Café in Masterton, serving a French provincial type fare.

Opening a restaurant in a country town, and daring to be different in the face of conservative tastes, can be a risky enterprise. Changing long-established tastes in food is definitely not an easy task, but this is what Prue Tatton and Mark Barton have achieved with Le Petit Café.

Prue began working in restaurants with Jeff Kennedy in the late 1970s when he ran MacAvity's in Wellington, which went on to become Toad Hall. In those days she was a salad hand and waitress, but the wanderlust set in and she moved to London and the United States, came back to New Zealand, and then moved to Queensland to work there as a chef. Slowly she was picking up a variety of culinary skills. The move to Masterton came with the death of her father. She and Mark were not planning to remain in Masterton but they slowly became enmeshed in the running of Le Petit Café. Initially, it was little more than a coffee bar, but they experimented with opening for dinner on Friday nights. Later, they expanded to other nights and within a short time it had become an excellent French provincial style BYO, with Prue in the kitchen and Mark as waiter. The style of the restaurant was totally new to Masterton, used as it was to a bland country cuisine. But there were people interested in good food and the restaurant filled that void. Along with the introduction of Prue's style of cooking have come changes in the restaurant itself. From its former cottage style, a light café feel has evolved. Working away from the mainstream of New Zealand restaurants, Prue keeps pace with change by regular visits to Wellington restaurants, combined with cookery courses, such as Auckland's Cordon Bleu school. She is determined that Le Petit Café and her cooking will continue to be innovative.

Le Petit Cafe,
8 Bannister Street, Masterton.
Telephone 85-776. BYO.

ENTREES

Scallop mousse with tomato coulis
Vegetable terrine with spinach
Avocado with watercress and cream
Curried crab crêpes
Escargots à la bourguignonne
Hot chicken livers and spinach salad

MAIN COURSES

Pheasant Normandy
Duckling with cherries, oranges and apricots
Pork on spinach with mushrooms and gruyère
Tournedos Rossini
Chicken with camembert and grapes
Fresh fish
White veal with marsala

DESSERTS

Raspberry Mille Feuille Glacé
Fresh fruit flambéed with Cointreau
Crêpes with home-made ice cream
Chocolate gâteau

SCALLOP MOUSSE WITH TOMATO COULIS

1KG SCALLOPS
100ML VERMOUTH
300ML CREAM, WHIPPED
75ML LIQUID CREAM
4 EGG WHITES

SALT, WHITE PEPPER, GARLIC POWDER
1½ TABLESPOONS GELATINE, DISSOLVED IN 225ML BOILING WATER
JUICE OF 1 LEMON

Coulis
8 LARGE TOMATOES
CHOPPED PARSLEY
SALT AND PEPPER
1 CLOVE OF GARLIC, CRUSHED
BUTTER

Poach the scallops in the vermouth over a low heat. Drain and reserve the vermouth, and keep 8 scallops for garnishing. Cut off the red corals from the scallops, and then blend the scallop whites with half the vermouth and half the lemon juice. Season.

Separate the white mixture into two bowls. In each of two separate bowls beat 150ml cream until it forms peaks. Beat 2 egg whites in each of two other bowls.

To each bowl of scallop mixture add a bowl of whipped cream mixture, plus 75ml of gelatine, and then fold in a bowl of the egg whites.

Pour one mixture into a long pâté mould lined with gladwrap and place in the refrigerator for ½ hour until firm. Purée the corals, add seasoning and a dash of vermouth for a smooth consistency, before adding 75ml of liquid cream and 75ml of gelatine. Pour the puréed mixture onto the chilled white mixture. Line 8 whole scallops down the centre of the pâté mould, and then add the second white scallop mixture. Chill again for ½ hour.

To make the tomato coulis: Sweat the tomatoes in a little butter at a moderate heat for 20 minutes. The seasonings should be added at the beginning of the cooking time. Strain, cool and pour the coulis over the demoulded mousse. **Serves 6.**

CRAYFISH AND CHICKEN CREPE GATEAU

1 ROASTED CHICKEN
1 LARGE COOKED CRAYFISH
12 CREPES
SALT AND PEPPER
PARSLEY, CHOPPED
1 CUP GRATED PARMESAN CHEESE

White sauce:
75G BUTTER
75G FLOUR
2 CUPS MILK

1 CUP CREAM
1 TABLESPOON BRANDY
SALT AND PEPPER
1 CUP GRATED PARMESAN CHEESE

To make the sauce: Mix together the butter, flour, milk, cream, brandy and seasonings. Cook over a low heat for 10-15 minutes, then add the parmesan cheese.

Break the chicken into small pieces and remove its skin. Chop the crayfish tail into medallions.

Lay one crêpe on an oiled baking sheet and pour a layer of the white sauce over the crêpe. Sprinkle on some chicken pieces and season with salt, pepper and parsley. Pour over more sauce and top with another crêpe. Pour over more sauce. With a sharp knife, cut the crêpe in half and then into quarters. Garnish each quarter with a medallion of crayfish and pour over a little more sauce. Sprinkle with parmesan.

Assemble the rest of the crêpes in the same way depending on the portions required. Cook at 180°C for 20 minutes or until the crêpes have heated through and the cheese has melted. **Serves 6.**

RASPBERRY MILLE FEUILLE GLACE

Ice cream:
1 PUNNET FRESH RASPBERRIES
2 TABLESPOONS CHERRY BRANDY
60G CASTOR SUGAR
300ML CREAM, WHIPPED

1 PUNNET FRESH RASPBERRIES
ICING SUGAR (OPTIONAL)
FLAKY PASTRY

CREAM, WHIPPED
PIPED CREAM AND RASPBERRIES FOR GARNISH

To make the ice cream: Blend one punnet of raspberries with the cherry brandy and castor sugar for 1 minute, then add the whipped cream. Pour the mixture into a long mould and freeze for 6-8 hours.

Purée the second punnet of raspberries with a little icing sugar to sweeten, and sieve to remove the pips.

Cut some flaky pastry into 15cm by 5cm shapes and bake in the oven until puffed up and lightly browned. Cut the pastry lengthwise to form a thin sheet. On one sheet layer alternate slices of ice cream and cream. Top with the other pastry sheet and pour raspberry sauce over the dessert. Garnish with piped cream and raspberries. **Serves 6.**

Louis Doczi and his wife Annabelle are two of the new young breed of *restaurateur*, bringing to a city starved of good restaurants a modern French style and panache. Christchurch is a conservative city and its restaurants lag behind their North Island counterparts. The restaurants have tended towards a classical approach, virtually ignoring the need for change. This conservatism initially meant a long hard battle before Louis and Annabelle established themselves.

Louis originally did his training in Auckland, before moving to Melbourne to work at the Hilton, and then going to Europe. In London he worked at a French restaurant where he met Annabelle who was waitressing, but in 1979 he decided to head back to Auckland, to be followed later by Annabelle. Louis decided to get away from cooking for a time, and took up a position as a trainee manager with a supermarket chain, but cooking and new ideas were in his blood. Success of the Auckland lunch-time restaurants prompted them to move to Christchurch to try a similar venture there. They found old first-storey premises and spent eight weeks transforming it into a contemporary and elegant lunch-time restaurant, decorating it with soft pinks and greys, spotlit prints on the walls, mauve dinnerware especially imported from France, an antique sideboard, and fine touches such as fresh flowers and candlelit tables. But the conservative Christchurch diners seemed wary of queuing at lunch-time to choose from a buffet, and the venture nearly failed. They decided to open Friday and Saturday nights, and suddenly Louis' had found its niche. They did away with lunches and opened as a night-time BYO, setting a standard comparable to the country's best restaurants.

Louis',
139 Worcester Street, Christchurch.
Telephone 61-969. BYO.

ENTREES

Summer Dream – Mango and banana blended with rum and orange
Volaille Châtaignes – chilled chicken pieces with water chestnuts, red pepper, celery and French dressing
Cari de Bringelle – beef with Madras curry sauce on rice with chutney and coconut
Pasta de Jambo à la Crème – spiral pasta with cream cheese and ham sauce

MAIN COURSES

Poussin Miel – chicken with a honey and lemon sauce
Flondre Louisiana – flounder fillets panfried with bananas and diced red pepper
Entrecôte Dijon – porterhouse with French mustard sauce
Coquilles Saint-Jacques Louis – scallops panfried with courgettes, garlic, tomato and white wine
Agneau au Porto – lamb steak marinaded and finished with pork and rosemary

DESSERTS

Petit Pot de Crème au Café – coffee flavoured cream custard
Glace au caramel – caramel ice cream with brown sugar sauce and toffee chips
Tarte aux Poires – Pear tart poached in white wine and crème pâtisserie

SUMMER DREAM

1 BANANA
½ MANGO OR PAW PAW, PEELED
30ML DARK RUM

1 PASSIONFRUIT
300ML FRESH ORANGE JUICE
6-8 ICE CUBES

4 THIN SLICES CUCUMBER, 4 SMALL FLOWERS (VIOLETS) FOR GARNISH

Take four cocktail glasses. Around the rim rub ½ lemon then turn the glass rims through castor sugar to give a frosted effect. Blend all the ingredients for 1½ minutes or until the ice is broken down. Pour into the glasses.

To garnish gently fold each cucumber slice in half, and cut halfway through the diameter. Place on the edge of each glass and nestle a flower in each slice. **Serves 4.**

COQUILLES SAINT-JACQUES LOUIS

50G BUTTER
800G SCALLOPS
3 CLOVES GARLIC, FINELY CHOPPED

SALT AND GROUND PEPPER
6 COURGETTES, SLICED
6 TOMATOES CUT INTO WEDGES

400ML DRY WHITE WINE
LEMONS, PARSLEY AND BLACK OLIVES FOR GARNISH

Heat the butter in a pan until it is bubbling and just turning pale brown. Add the scallops, stirring gently and cook until a light brown in colour. Add the garlic and seasoning to taste, and then add the courgette fingers and tomato wedges. Stir until the courgettes are just cooked. Add the white wine and simmer for a few minutes. Transfer to a deeper dish, preferably white for contrast, and sprinkle with chopped parsley. Garnish each serving with a lemon cut into a desired shape, contrasting with an olive. **Serves 4.**

GLACE AU CARAMEL

1 TIN CONDENSED MILK
300ML MILK
600ML WHIPPED CREAM
WHIPPED CREAM, MINT LEAF FOR GARNISH

Brown sugar sauce:
1 EGG
50G BUTTER
2 CUPS SOFT BROWN SUGAR
1 CUP CREAM

Toffee chips:
150G SUGAR

Boil the tin of condensed milk for 1-1½ hours in a pan of water to caramelize the contents. Beat the caramel with the milk until blended. Add the whipped cream and gently beat until all ingredients are well blended. Pour into a mould or bowl, and freeze. Unmould by briefly standing the bowl in hot water and running a hot knife around its interior. Cut into wedges and serve on a bed of brown sugar sauce, sprinkled with toffee chips. You can add flavoured liqueur or nuts to vary the icecream. Garnish with whipped cream, a mint leaf or flower.

To make the brown sugar sauce: Whisk the egg in a *bain-marie* and add the butter, brown sugar and liquid cream over a medium heat to melt and blend. Beat well with a wooden spoon and then allow the sauce to cool and thicken.

To make the toffee chips: Gently melt the sugar in a pan until caramelized, but do not burn. Pour into a greased baking tray and put in the freezer for ¼ hour. When set, shatter the toffee by dropping it on a hard surface, breaking it down further by using a sharp knife.
Serves 4-6.

Roger Mail believes in 'bold food', which is one reason why he loves cooking venison, wild duck, wild boar and the stronger meats. Whereas most cooks only prepare the lighter and more delicate fish like orange roughy and snapper, Roger prefers the stronger taste of trevally — catching it himself, bleeding it and cooking it the same day. He refuses to cook beef until it has been hung properly. He also hangs venison for 21 days and then uses the back steaks for fillets, the legs for longer steaks, other sections as cutlets, while the meat trimmings are ground for pâté and the bones are roasted with vegetables and then boiled to make the stocks and demi-glazes. It is a style of cooking that believes in no short-cuts, adding a lot of work to a cooking day. But the proof is in the eating and Maggie's Farm now has the reputation of being one of the best presenters of game foods and other dishes in the country.

Roger began his cooking career with formal training under Bob Sell in the days of the La Boheme restaurant. Then it was off to Auckland's Intercontinental, then to the South Island for four or five years, on to North America, back to Queenstown and finally to the kitchens of Air New Zealand. But this 'factory' style of food preparation did not appeal to Roger, although it did provide good experience in trying to present different styles of food in a management cafeteria where a meal cost just $1.20. At least it was a lesson in costing, and it gave Roger the impetus to go out and open Maggie's Farm as a casual BYO. These days he works long hours preparing and cooking dishes. He even makes his own guava jellies and chutneys to use in various dishes.

Maggie's Farm,
303 Dominion Road, Auckland.
Telephone 602-714. BYO.

ENTREES

Game terrine
Pork spare ribs
Calamares neopolitan
Baked mussels
Chicken crêpes
Seafood chowder
Chicken livers lazzari

MAIN COURSES

Snapper with shrimps and fennel
Porc Avenoise
Entrecôte à lanchoise
Roast duckling
Rack of lamb
Wild boar casserole
Venison bitok

DESSERTS

Apple crêpes
Banana brulle
Kiwifruit mousse
Chocolate gâteau

CALAMARES NEAPOLITAN

3 LARGE SQUID TUBES
CLARIFIED BUTTER
SALT, WHITE AND BLACK GROUND PEPPER
1 TEASPOON CRUSHED GARLIC
½ CUP DRY WHITE WINE
300ML COOKED TOMATOES, SEEDED AND SKINNED
300ML FISH VELOUTE
1 TABLESPOON CHOPPED FRESH BASIL
2 HANDFULS COOKED FETTUCINE
PARMESAN CHEESE FOR GARNISH

Cut the squid into rings and sauté the rings in a hot pan using the clarified butter. Add salt, pepper and garlic. Toss and seal. Keeping the pan hot add the wine and reduce slightly. Add the tomatoes and velouté. Bring to the boil. Add the basil.

Place the hot fettucini in six serving dishes, place the squid rings on top, and pour the sauce over the squid. Garnish with parmesan cheese and serve immediately. **Serves 6.**

PORK AVENOISE

250G GRUYERE CHEESE, GRATED
1 TABLESPOON PREPARED SEED MUSTARD
1 TABLESPOON CHOPPED PARSLEY
1½ CUPS DRY WHITE WINE
2 EGGS
600ML CREAM
12 PIECES CORN FED PORK, PICCATA CUT
CRUSHED GARLIC
CLARIFIED BUTTER
FRESHLY GROUND BLACK AND WHITE PEPPER
FLOUR

Mix the cheese, mustard, parsley, 1 cup of wine, eggs and a little cream until it is a smooth paste.

Lay the pork fillets out and rub with a little crushed garlic. Season and dip in flour. In a hot pan sauté the pork fillets in the clarified butter. When the meat is cooked place it in a baking dish. Place the dish under a hot grill and when the meat is sizzling pour ½ cup of wine over the pork pieces and reduce. Remove the pork from the grill and spoon the mixture over the pork before placing back under the grill to cook until golden brown. Place the pork on a serving dish and then place the baking dish with its remaining contents on to a medium heat. Add the remaining cream and whisk until the sauce thickens. Pour the sauce over the pork and serve. **Serves 6.**

KIWIFRUIT MOUSSE

4 KIWIFRUIT, SKINNED
½ WINE GLASS BENEDICTINE
2½ TABLESPOONS CASTOR SUGAR
600ML CREAM
2 EGG YOLKS
2½ EGG WHITES
2 KIWIFRUIT, UNSKINNED AND SLICED

Cook the kiwifruit with the Benedictine and 1 tablespoon of castor sugar over a gentle heat. When cooked, place the mixture in a dish and cool.

Beat the cream and set aside. Cream the egg yolks with 1 tablespoon of castor sugar and fold the yolks into the cream. Blend the fruit mixture into the cream.

Beat the egg whites with the rest of the sugar and when peaks form fold the egg whites into the cream and kiwifruit mixture. Place in serving glasses and garnish with slices of kiwifruit and a trickle of Benedictine. Refrigerate until ready to serve. **Serves 6-8.**

Martini's, nestling in Oxford Terrace near the tree-lined River Avon, is housed in an old late Victorian building that once belonged to the Canterbury Jockey Club. A sign in the hallway still testifies to the building being the registered offices of the Amberley Racing Club, the Banks Peninsula Racing Club, the Christchurch Hunt Club and the Motukarara Race Course. These days the Jockey Club has gone, to be replaced by the Christchurch Stock Exchange and this restaurant with its deceptively Italian-sounding name; the legacy of a previous owner. Martini's was originally a restaurant in another part of Christchurch but when its building was demolished the chattels and name were sold to new owners, and Martini's was established on its present site. Then early in 1983 Rex and Lois Smith bought the restaurant. They had come to Christchurch from Southland with the intention of purchasing a restaurant, and it turned out that Martini's was the first place they investigated. They made the decision to buy on the spot. There was no need, they felt, to change the name, the style of the place, or the cooks who had created its diverse menu and its excellent game dishes. The only change Lois made, was in the desserts; these were her speciality. Martini's is a homely restaurant, with warm wooden panelling, and the added attraction that from the front tables one can watch the Avon meander slowly along its course.

Martini's,
128A Oxford Terrace, Christchurch.
Telephone 69-363. BYO.

ENTREES

Deep fried camembert — with sweet apricot sauce
Avocado with marinated crab meat, onion and vinaigrette
Frog legs Provençale — marinated, battered and deep fried with a Provençale sauce
Oriental prawns — prawns, water chestnuts and baby corn marinated in honey, soy sauce and sherry

MAIN COURSES

Roast rabbit in a garlic, herb and red wine stock with a game gravy
Duckling Ellesmere — roast duckling with boysenberry and liqueur sauce
Venison braised in red wine and juniper berries with a game gravy and served on noodles
Cherry pork — pork fillets with a special sauce, served with cherries on a noodle base
Tournedos Mexicaine — prime grilled beef with a chilli sauce
Chicken di Martini — stuffed chicken breast with a peach liqueur sauce

DESSERTS

Kiwifruit parfait
Crêpes with marinated fruit
Apricot cream, chilled and layered with fresh grapes
Bananas with orange and Cointreau sauce

CHILLED AND CURRIED APPLE SOUP

3 APPLES, PEELED AND SLICED
1 ONION SLICED
1 TABLESPOON BUTTER
1 TEASPOON CURRY POWDER
PINCH OF PAPRIKA
1 CUP WHITE WINE
3 CUPS CHICKEN STOCK
FRESH GROUND PEPPER
¼ CUP CREAM
SLICED APPLE, WHIPPED CREAM, PAPRIKA FOR GARNISH

Sauté the apples and onion in the butter. Add the curry powder and paprika and cook for 1 minute. Add the wine and chicken stock, and pepper to taste. Cook until the apples and onions are soft and then allow to cool before putting in a food processor to purée. Chill, add the cream, and serve in chilled bowls. Garnish with sliced apple, whipped cream and paprika. **Serves 4.**

CHERRY PORK

1.5KG PORK FILLET
SALT, PEPPER AND MIXED HERBS TO TASTE

Sauce:
2 RASHERS BACON, CHOPPED
1 CUP CRUSHED PINEAPPLE
3 GHERKINS

1 TEASPOON CAPERS
PAPRIKA
300ML CREAM

Seal and brown the whole pork fillet in a frying pan with a little oil. Place the fillet on some foil and sprinkle with mixed herbs, salt and pepper. Wrap the pork in foil and cook in a moderate oven for about 1 hour.
To make the sauce: Sauté the bacon in a little butter and add the pineapple, finely chopped gherkins, the capers and a pinch of paprika. In another pan reduce the cream until thick and then add the bacon mixture. Slice the pork fillet and serve topped with the sauce. **Serves 6.**

HAZELNUT MERINGUE

4 EGG WHITES
PINCH OF SALT
1 CUP CASTOR SUGAR
¼ CUP FINELY GROUND HAZELNUTS
CHOCOLATE
WHIPPED CREAM AND STRAWBERRIES FOR GARNISH

Beat the egg whites and salt until stiff and add the castor sugar. Beat until very stiff and the sugar has dissolved. Lightly fold in the hazelnuts. Cook for 1 hour at 100°C, and then allow to cool in the oven.

To serve: Coat the bottom of each meringue with melted chocolate. Sandwich together with whipped cream and chopped strawberries. **Serves 4.**

The Mekong Restaurant, the first Vietnamese Restaurant in New Zealand, is run by a former journalist Lac Ly and his wife Muoi. They arrived in this country in 1977 as some of the first refugees accepted by New Zealand. Their struggles in escaping from war-torn South Vietnam included a hazardous boat journey and a year-long stay in a refugee camp in Thailand. Their original intention had been to go to America from the refugee camp but a chance meeting with a New Zealander changed their minds. Upon arrival in this country they settled down to work in an office and a factory, saving towards buying a home. In Saigon Lac had been a businessman, and had also been business editor for the English language *Saigon Post*; so he and Muoi decided they would like to run their own business in Auckland. They felt a restaurant was an enterprise where their own experience in cooking ethnic Vietnamese food could be put to advantage. First they tested on their friends many Vietnamese meat and fish recipes with their characteristic spices and herb flavours. Their acceptance gave them the confidence to go ahead. They set up the Mekong, named after Vietnam's main waterway, on the first floor of an old building a few yards from Auckland's main street. The natural brick walls, straw matting and bamboo, with the plants and green tablecloths were chosen to emphasise the natural way of life in Vietnam, where food is gathered from the surrounding land and rivers and simply barbecued or steamed. The basis of their Vietnamese cooking is lemon grass, which gives the dishes much of their unique flavour, and this Lac and Muoi manage to grow for seven or eight months a year.

Mekong,
12 Victoria Street West, Auckland.
Telephone 797-591. BYO.

ENTREES

Vietnamese finger rolls (Cha Gio)
Satay beef (Thit Bo Xa De)
Fried fish balls (Chien Ca Vien)
Crispy chicken wings (Canh Ga Nuong)
Hot-sour soup (Canh Chua)
Pho – thin beef slices in rich beef soup

MAIN COURSES

Grilled beef slices (Bo Nuong) – thin beef slices marinated in honey and wine
Grilled beef wrappers with capsicum (Ot Bo Nuong)
Grilled pork slices (Thit Nuong) – in a wine and lemon grass marinade
Grilled pork balls (Nem Nuong) – served with thick soy bean sauce
Crispy skinned chicken (Ga Nuong)
Squid delight (Ca Muc Chien) – minced squidmeat balls, deep fried
Cold pork mint rolls (Bi Cuon) – sliced steamed pork, mint and lettuce in a thin wrapping
Mekong prawn delight (Chau Tom) – prawn paste wrapped around sugar cane and barbecued

DESSERTS

Rau Cau jellied squares
Fresh fruit salad

VIETNAMESE FINGER ROLLS (CHA GIO)

1KG LEAN PORK	1 TABLESPOON FISH SAUCE	10G VERMICELLI
50G PORK FAT	1 TABLESPOON SUGAR	EDIBLE RICE PAPER
1 TABLESPOON SALT	200G SHELLED GREEN PRAWNS	COOKING OIL
	100G MUNG BEAN SPROUTS	

Mince the pork and pork fat. Add the salt and the fish sauce — obtainable from a Chinese foodstuffs supplier. Add the sugar, prawns, bean sprouts and vermicelli. Mix together.

Soften the rice paper by placing one sheet at a time between the layers of a wrung-out damp towel. After 1-2 minutes cut the paper into squares and put the desired quantity of filling onto each square before wrapping into finger rolls. Deep fry the rolls for 4 minutes in hot oil until crisp and golden. **Serves 6.**

MEKONG PRAWN DELIGHT (CHAU TOM)

1KG KING PRAWN MEAT	1 TEASPOON SESAME OIL	1 TABLESPOON SUGAR
2 EGG WHITES	1 TEASPOON SALT	6 15CM LENGTHS SUGAR CANE OR BABY CARROTS
2 TABLESPOONS MAIZE CORNFLOUR	1 TEASPOON PEPPER	

Remove the spinal passages from the prawns. If the meat is too moist after thawing, dry with paper towel, removing as much moisture as possible. Finely mince the prawn meat and add the egg whites, cornflour, sesame oil, salt, pepper and sugar. Blend the mixture until it becomes a paste.

Dip the sugar cane *or* carrots in the paste, making sure the ends are also covered. In a lightly oiled dish, grill the Chau Tom for 5-6 minutes, turning often. **Serves 4-6.**

RAU CAU JELLIED SQUARES

1 LITRE WATER	5 TABLESPOONS SUGAR	WHIPPED CREAM, CHERRIES FOR GARNISH
20G AGA AGA	1 EGG	

Bring the water to the boil. Add the aga aga and sugar. Once these have dissolved, pour the mixture on to a flat metal tray. Lightly beat the egg and pour it into the mixture, stirring it with chopsticks or a wooden spoon. This will form patterns. Leave for ½ hour and then refrigerate.

Other ingredients, such as coconut or chocolate can also be added when the mixture is hot.

When ready to serve, pour a small amount of sugar water over the rau cau and garnish with whipped cream and cherries.

Larry Charman set up Meridian restaurant in 1982 after a number of years travelling overseas. These days he limits his restaurant to just four nights a week, all of which are packed out with those who enjoy trying a menu that is the culmination of his travels through England, France, Spain and Asia. Larry still remembers his early childhod in Wellington when his fascination with food began with the Edmonds Cookbook which he would thumb through as a seven-year-old, shouting out to his mother the details of his favourite recipes. With that background he was probably predestined to become a *restaurateur*, beginning as a chef in the kitchen of a small Northland hotel before moving to London to do a Cordon Bleu course, and work in restaurants and hotels in London. Later he worked in France as a grapepicker, but ended up working in the kitchen of a little restaurant in Provence where the woman owner would tell him to uncork a fine '75 vintage Bordeaux if he needed a little wine for a particular recipe. It was this experience of French country food that now forms the basis of his style of cooking at the Meridian. After France he went to Spain, working in various restaurants, but he was thrown into jail for overstaying. It was here he maintains that he learnt the basis of true Spanish cooking. Finally a friend sent him his fare out of the country so he headed off to the Channel Isles and then on to Asia, cooking in Goa, Sri Lanka and Thailand, picking up the finer details of spices and curries. Even now he grinds all his own spices for his curries, just as he grows his own herbs for the French dishes. Back in Auckland he found an old dairy at Bucklands Beach, which he turned into the Meridian as it is today — a low-key provincial style restaurant with a casual atmosphere and excellent food.

Meridian,
The Parade, Bucklands Beach, Auckland.
Telephone 534-4943. BYO.

ENTREES

Leek and ham soup
Sautéed squid à la crème
Smoked eel platter
Scallops Normandy
Minced pork balls

MAIN COURSES

French lamb casserole
Snapper with Bluff oyster cream
Escalopes of Veal Cordon Bleu
Roast loin of pork with wine gravy
Baked chicken Provençale

DESSERTS

Chocolate walnut gâteau
Strudel
Asian fruit salad

ALMOND SOUP

200G BLANCHED SKINNED ALMONDS	2 ONIONS, FINELY CHOPPED	¼ CUP LEMON JUICE
2 LITRES MILK	60G BUTTER	PINCH NUTMEG
2 CELERY STALKS, THINLY SLICED	4 TABLESPOONS FLOUR	SALT AND PEPPER
	2 CUPS CHICKEN STOCK	

Pour boiling water over the almonds. Stand for 10 minutes to drain. Blend the almonds with a little of the milk. Simmer the almonds, celery and onions with the rest of the milk for 30 minutes and stir occasionally.

Make a roux with the flour and butter, cook gently for 1 minute and add the milk and almond mixture. Stir with a wire whisk until the milk is absorbed by the roux and the sauce has a creamy consistency. Cook for 3 minutes, then dilute with the chicken stock and lemon juice. Add the nutmeg, salt and pepper to taste, and heat gently for 10 minutes. **Serves 8.**

OYSTER A LA CREOLE

BUTTER	PINCH CAYENNE PEPPER	24 OYSTERS
2 TOMATOES, SKINNED AND MINCED	½ CUP CHIVES	CREAM
½ CUP CHOPPED PARSLEY	1 CUP BREADCRUMBS	

You will need either large scallop shells or small ramekins for this dish.

Brush the inside of the shells or the ramekins with melted butter. Mix together the tomatoes, parsley, cayenne pepper, chives and breadcrumbs. Place a dessertspoon of the mixture on the bottom of the shells and spread with a spoon. Lay 6 oysters in each shell. Top with a little more of the mixture, and add a dash of cream. Bake in a hot oven for 5-7 minutes, making sure not to overcook. **Serves 4.**

MARINATED CHICKEN WITH GREEN PEPPERCORN SAUCE

1 CHICKEN (NO. 6)	SLICED AVOCADO AND CHERVIL FOR GARNISH	2 TABLESPOONS GREEN PEPPERCORNS
½ CUP OLIVE OIL		
½ CUP LEMON JUICE		½ CUP CREAM
½ CUP PREPARED MILD MUSTARD	Sauce:	CHOPPED CHERVIL
SALT AND PEPPER	2 TABLESPOONS BRANDY	

Cut the chicken into 6-8 pieces. Mix the oil, lemon juice, mustard, and salt and pepper together. Pour the mixture over the chicken, making sure the chicken is well coated and leave to marinate for at least 8 hours. When ready cook the chicken and marinade in a pre-heated moderate oven for 20 minutes. Turn the pieces once, remove from the oven, put the chicken pieces on a separate dish and keep warm.

To make the sauce: Place the baking tray over a gentle heat and loosen the chicken residue with the brandy. Add the peppercorns, cream and chervil, mixing thoroughly. Do not boil, but reduce until the sauce is quite thick but can be poured. Arrange the chicken on plates and garnish. Serve with sautéed sesame courgettes, or fresh steamed asparagus and baked potatoes. **Serves 6-8.**

When Phillip and Valerie Littlejohn moved back to Auckland in 1981 after 22 years of running the illustrious Orsini's restaurant in Wellington, their idea was to take a well earned break. But somewhere along the way, their plans to take it easy went astray.

During those years in Wellington, the Littlejohns had turned Orsini's into one of the capital's most renowned restaurants. They had taken over the old two-storey premises in Cuba Street in 1958, spent £2,800 and a lot of energy renovating, and with Phillip cooking and Valerie as hostess they introduced their own distinctive style of cooking and entertaining. Over the years many of the rich and famous dined there, including Alfred Hitchcock and Danny Kaye. Those early days of Orsini's were when Chicken Maryland and Veal Cordon Bleu were the mainstays of the menu, along with fillet steak, accompanied by the usual peas and carrots, with tomato and lettuce as garnishing. Those were also the days of archaic licensing laws when front doors were locked so diners could drink their own wine without being harassed by the police.

In the late 1970s they decided it was time to take a break, but a visit to Auckland meant the discovery of what must be the most remarkable restaurant building in the city. The two-storey mansion had been built as a farmer's town house in 1891 but when they found it, it was an alcoholics' doss house and hostel. They bought the building, and spent eight months transforming it into a restaurant with all the style of its southern counterpart. Old paintings decorate the wall, along with chandeliers, Valerie's magnificent silver collection and antique furniture. Whether the well earned break will now ever occur is pure conjecture.

Orsini's,
50 Ponsonby Road, Auckland.
Telephone 764-563. Licensed.

ENTREES

Marlin Mousse
Seafood Gumbo
Lamb tongues with mustard and cream sauce
Garlic king prawns
Beef satay with peanut sauce
Chicken livers with Marsala and cream sauce
Crumbed lamb brains with orange juice and spring onions

MAIN COURSES

Braised pheasant with smoked ham and red wine sauce
Rack of lamb with blackcurrant sauce
Chicken breast with fresh herb and cream sauce
Roast duckling with orange and apricot sauce
Pork medallions with orange and honey glaze
Fresh fish of the day with a special sauce
Fillet of beef with bearnaise and onion rings

DESSERTS

Cream caramel
Meringue baskets with fresh fruit
Blintzes with citrus flavoured cream cheese
Jamaican bananas flamed at the table
Profiteroles

MARLIN MOUSSE

2 TABLESPOONS ASPIC JELLY	½ CUP MAYONNAISE	30ML BRANDY
½ CUP WATER	30ML HORSERADISH SAUCE	SALT AND CRUSHED BLACK PEPPER
250G BONELESS SMOKED MARLIN	300ML CREAM	LEMON AND CAVIAR FOR GARNISH

Dissolve the aspic jelly in the water and leave to one side to cool. Place the marlin, mayonnaise and horseradish sauce into a food processor and blend into a smooth paste. Fold in the cream and brandy and season to taste. Fold in the aspic jelly and place in a terrine mould lined with cling film. Chill for about 2 hours. To serve, turn the mousse out of the mould and slice. Garnish with lemon and caviar and serve with wholemeal toast. **Serves 6.**

ROAST PHEASANT WITH SMOKED HAM AND RED WINE SAUCE

2 PHEASANTS (NO 2)	Sauce:	
SALT AND PEPPER	1 ONION, DICED	200ML RED WINE
1 TABLESPOON OIL	BUTTER	25G SLICED SMOKED HAM
	50G HAM OR BACON TRIMMINGS	ARROWROOT
	FRESH CHERVIL AND SWEET BASIL	SLICED SMOKED HAM FOR GARNISH

Season the pheasants with salt, pepper and the oil. Place the birds in a roasting dish with a little water. Roast at 190°C for about 1 hour 15 minutes until the flesh is tender. Remove the pheasants from the oven and split them in half. Remove the body and breast bones and place the pheasants in the warmer.
To make the sauce: Boil the stock the pheasants were cooked in along with the bones. In another pan, heat a knob of butter and sweat the diced onion and bacon trimmings with the fresh herbs. Add the red wine and reduce by half. Add the mixture to the stock, strain and thicken with a little arrowroot. Season to taste. Place the pheasants on a serving dish and garnish with sliced smoked ham and glaze with the sauce. **Serves 4.**

BLINTZES

Filling:	VANILLA	10G CASTOR SUGAR
250G CREAM CHEESE	½ TEASPOON NUTMEG	1 TABLESPOON FLOUR
1 EGG YOLK	PINCH SALT	PINCH SALT
60G CASTOR SUGAR		
1 TEASPOON CORNFLOUR	Crêpes:	ORANGE ROUNDS AND CHANTILLY CREAM FOR GARNISH
ZEST OF ½ LEMON	150ML MILK	
ZEST OF ¼ ORANGE	1 EGG	

To make the filling: Cream the ingredients together until they are a smooth paste. Place in the refrigerator and cool for 2 hours.
To make the crêpes: Blend the ingredients together and stand for 1 hour, before proceeding to cook as for normal crêpes. Fill the crêpes with the blintz filling and fold into envelopes. In a frying pan melt a knob of butter and gently cook the blintzes without colouring for about 2 minutes on each side. Garnish with orange rounds and Chantilly cream. **Serves 6.**

Back in the 1860s one of the gold miners wrote from the Shotover River:

> Jack, I am making my pile fast, £100 a week. This is the richest river in the world. I walk in up to my waist, put down the shovel and sometimes I bring up five or six ounces on a shovel.

The miners poured into the Shotover River area seeking their fortune but the problem was the lack of accommodation. However, an enterprising constable, Patrick Gantley (Constable 481), decided to build a wayside inn out of stacked stone just one mile from the point on the Shotover where Thomas Arthur had discovered gold in November 1862. The gold rush ended and Gantley's inn was ultimately abandoned along with the diggings. Instead of housing miners it was used to store hay, until it was rebuilt in 1967 as a restaurant. It is a magnificent building, only 10 minutes drive from Queenstown itself and well worth the visit. The stacked stone is as solid as the day it was built, the shingle roof echoing the rain on a wet night, while an enormous fireplace inside heats the diners during the cold winter.

The owners of Packers Arms, Sally and Mark Costas, have given the restaurant an international appeal. It is fully licensed with silver service, serving a mixture of New Zealand and Continental dishes. Because the Historic Places Trust have designated it a landmark, American and Japanese tourists tend to flock here, to surround themselves with a slice of this country's history.

Packer's Arms,
Queenstown.
Telephone 929. Licensed.

ENTREES

Steak tartare
Aquatic Platter — crayfish, prawns, mussels, whitebait, smoked eel, crab, anchovies
Pot au Feu — rich oxtail broth with vegetables
Seafood Chowder
Vol-au-vent de Ris d'Agneau — creamed lamb sweetbreads in a pastry case
Southland whitebait
Escargot Bourguignonne — served in their shell with garlic butter
Grenouille au vol-au-vent — frogs legs cooked in white wine, served in a pastry case

MAIN COURSES

Loin of lamb
Scallops à la Maison — Nelson scallops, white wine and cream
Golden Cod — pan fried in butter
Crayfish au natural
Châteaubriant — served with chasseur or bearnaise sauce
Pork Ananas — garnished with sautéed onions and pineapple
Chicken Malaya — roasted and glazed in honey, soy sauce and honey
Venison Ragoût — marinated in wine, vinegar and herbs

DESSERTS

A fresh selection daily
New Zealand and imported cheeses

LAMB KIDNEYS A LA SUISSE

1½ TABLESPOONS CLARIFIED BUTTER	3 SMALL LAMB KIDNEYS	1 TEASPOON FLOUR
1 EGG	¼ CUP DEMI-GLAZE	SALT AND PEPPER TO SEASON

Melt ½ tablespoon of butter in a pan and fry the egg so the yolk sets, and then slice. Wash and thinly slice the lamb kidneys. Add the rest of the butter to the pan, combine all the ingredients and cook at a medium heat for a few minutes until the kidneys are cooked. **Per portion.**

PORC AU FROMAGE FONDUE

1 TABLESPOON BUTTER	HOT ENGLISH MUSTARD	1 LARGE CROUTON
1 PORK FILLET	SALT, PEPPER, PAPRIKA TO SEASON	100G DANBO CHEESE, GRATED

Melt the butter in a pan and add the pork fillet. Season with the mustard, salt, pepper and paprika. Fry the fillet until nearly cooked. Remove the fillet from the pan, place it on top of the croûton and cover with the grated cheese. Cook under the grill until the cheese has melted and coloured slightly. Serve hot. **Per portion.**

GRAND MARNIER AND BRANDY ZABAGLIONE

3 EGG YOLKS	100ML WHITE WINE	30ML BRANDY
75G SUGAR	100ML MARSALA	VANILLA ICE CREAM FOR GARNISH
	30ML GRAND MARNIER	

Combine all the ingredients in a *bain-marie*, and over a low heat whisk to combine. When the ingredients are smooth and warm serve with vanilla ice cream. **Per portion.**

The proliferation of restaurants in Auckland's Ponsonby and Herne Bay in recent years has meant many restaurants in the area now face formidable competition. Some restaurants just do not come up with quite the right formula to be successful, while a place only a short distance away seems to have that certain magic that attracts diners. Papillon, run by Michael Ewens, has that magic; a blend of its owner's personality, a relaxing and interesting décor, and excellent food.

Michael originally became involved in the restaurant world more by accident than design. He took a part-time evening position as a wine steward at Auckland's Sorrento, and during the day worked as a kitchen hand at a friend's harbour-side restaurant. He was then elevated to being a chef at the Sorrento, where he stayed for a number of years until he was playing host to 400 patrons on some nights. From there it was such a short step to looking for his own restaurant. The television chefs, Hudson and Halls, had originally occupied the Papillon premises with their Oyster and Fish restaurant before returning to the television world. Michael took it over from the next owner and redesigned the kitchen, redecorated the dining area, added his own menu, and Papillon was flying. Its popularity was immediate, due both to the food and its interesting setting. Framed butterflies decorate the walls, man-made butterflies decorate the candleholders and napkin rings, the music of Ella Fitzgerald and Johnny Mathis wafts through the place, and outside in summer the sun shines through the trellising to warm the garden dining area. Upstairs, one can dine in private, with one's own waiter and a bell to summon service.

Papillon,
286 Jervois Road, Herne Bay, Auckland.
Telephone 765-367. BYO.

ENTREES

Avocado and oranges, celery and walnuts with vinaigrette
Chicken liver pâté with cognac, port, basil and tarragon
Shrimps and pawpaw with lemon and ginger mayonnaise
Calamari marinated in garlic vinaigrette
Chicken yakitori with a spicy sauce
Scallops poached in Noilly Prat

MAIN COURSES

Fresh fish poached in white wine with pepper and sabayon sauce
Aged fillet pan fried with mushrooms and chive sauce
Marinated loin of pork stuffed with prunes and apricots
Chicken boned, stuffed with mango and roasted

DESSERTS

Walnut sponge with apricots and apricot brandy sauce
Fruit Chartreuse – jellied fruit with cream custard
Mille Feuille – layers of pastry, cream, strawberries and fresh fruit
Fresh fruit salad served with champagne

AVOCADO AND HAM MOUSSE WITH TARRAGON DRESSING

4 AVOCADOS
1 TABLESPOON GRATED ONION
2 TABLESPOONS FINELY DICED HAM
SALT AND GROUND WHITE PEPPERCORNS
WORCESTERSHIRE SAUCE

1 TABLESPOON GELATINE
½ CUP COLD WATER
¼ CUP BOILING WATER
¼ CUP WHIPPED CREAM

Tarragon dressing:
1 EGG
2 LEVEL TABLESPOONS CASTOR SUGAR
3 TABLESPOONS TARRAGON VINEGAR
SALT AND PEPPER

Blend the avocado, onion, ham, salt, pepper and a dash of Worcestershire sauce until smooth.

Soften the gelatine in half the cold water and then add the boiling water before stirring in the remaining cold water. Place in the refrigerator until the gelatine is the consistency of egg white. Fold in the whipped cream, ¼ cup tarragon dressing and then the avocado mixture. Put into individual moulds that have been rinsed with cold water. **Serves 4.**

To make the tarragon dressing: Beat the dressing ingredients together and cook in a double boiler until thick.

RACK OF LAMB WITH TAMARILLO AND PORT SAUCE

RACK OF LAMB FOR 4 PEOPLE
GARLIC
SALT AND PEPPER
TAMARILLO FOR GARNISH

Sauce:
500G TAMARILLO, BLANCHED, PEELED, ROUGHLY CUT
250ML PORK

150ML FULL BODIED STOCK
½ TEASPOON TARRAGON
1 TEASPOON RAW SUGAR

Prepare the racks in the usual manner by rubbing lightly with cut garlic, salt and pepper, and roasting for about 25 minutes until the meat is still just pink.
To make the sauce: Simmer the sauce ingredients in a saucepan until the tamarillo is cooked. Rub through a sieve, reheat and adjust seasoning. The amount of sugar used will vary according to the ripeness of the tamarillos used.

Take the racks from the oven, cut up, lay out on the plates, and coat with the hot sauce. Garnish with sliced, blanched tamarillo. **Serves 4.**

ORANGES WITH COGNAC

4 SEEDLESS ORANGES
GRAPES FOR GARNISHING

Sauce:
3 TABLESPOONS SUGAR
1 TABLESPOON CORNFLOUR

125ML ORANGE JUICE
6 TABLESPOONS WATER
½ TEASPOON GRATED ORANGE RIND
4 TABLESPOONS COGNAC

Peel the oranges, taking care to remove all the pith. Slice in circles and lay in a circular pattern in individual shallow dishes.
To make the sauce: Cook the sugar, cornflour, orange juice and water in double boiler over a low heat until thick. Stir in the orange rind, allow to cool, then add the cognac.

Pour the sauce over the oranges and garnish with grapes. **Serves 4.**

Pedro Carazo, from the Basque region of Northern Spain, finds old habits die hard. He arrives at his restaurant around midday each day, works for a few hours preparing the evening meal and from 3.30p.m. he takes his usual two hour siesta, just as he once did in Madrid. These days the resting is much easier. Pedro's — the only Spanish restaurant in New Zealand is an unqualified success. The brilliance of Pedro's is that it is not just another Spanish restaurant swamped with the tourist trivia of bullfight posters and relying on dishes of garlic prawns to keep everyone happy. Pedro would have to be classed as one of the best cooks in Christchurch, interpreting in his own way the Spanish equivalent of recipes used by the top French-style restaurants.

Pedro began his training with the Madrid chefs' school, but over the years he moved to Holland, on to Australia, back to Spain, and finally to Christchurch in 1981 with his wife Fae and son Christiano. With the decision to open a Spanish restaurant here, they brought out from Spain a magnificent old sideboard, blue and white tiles from Pedro's mother's home, framed sets of old banknotes from the days of Franco, mirrors, lamps, and a collection of clay pots in which the Gambas al Ajillo, can go sizzling to the table direct from the heat. The Spanish mats, studded chairs and wrought iron lights give Pedro's the feeling of a Spanish hacienda. As much thought was put into the surroundings as Pedro puts into his cooking. He imports many of the ingredients he needs, rather than relying on inferior local versions. However, the garlic, which he uses at the rate of 1½ kilos per week, is locally grown. Garlic, it seems, varies little from country to country.

Pedro's,
143 Worcester Street, Christchurch.
Telephone 797-668. BYO.

ENTREES

Huevos a la Flamenca — egg dish baked with salami, ham, peas, tomatoes and asparagus
Gambas al Ajillo — garlic prawns
Ostras Buena Hujer — fresh oysters grilled with ham, cheese and Pernod
Boquerones en vinagre — Nelson herring marinated in garlic and parsley
Mejillones a la Andaluza — baked mussels in garlic butter

MAIN COURSES

Brochetta de Pescado — Groper and ham with saffron rice and Remuiard sauce
Zarzuela — fish and scallops with a brandy tomato sauce
Pollo Chilindron — baked chicken with red peppers, bacon, tomatoes and almonds
Ternera Riojana — veal cutlets with ham, red peppers and tomatoes
Chuletas al Ajillo — grilled marinated lamb cutlets in garlic

DESSERTS

Fried bananas flambéed with Cointreau
Caramel custard flan with ice cream
Rock melon stuffed with fresh fruit and port
Fresh fruit marinated in white rum with ice cream

SOPA DE AJO
(Garlic Soup)

100ML OLIVE OIL	100G PROSCIUTTO, RAW HAM OR BACON	1 LITRE BEEF OR CHICKEN STOCK
4 CLOVES GARLIC, CHOPPED	150G STALE FRENCH BREAD	6 EGGS
	25G PAPRIKA	SALT AND PEPPER

Heat the oil in a pan at a medium heat. Add the garlic, the coarsely sliced ham, and the bread which should be sliced into quarters. Fry for 2 minutes, add the paprika, and cook until brown in colour, taking care not to burn. Add the stock and then break in the eggs. Stir until the mixture thickens and season to taste. **Serves 6.**

CORDERO CON BERENGENAS
(Lamb with Aubergines)

1 LARGE LEG OF LAMB	6 CLOVES GARLIC	8 TOMATOES, SLICED
8 EGGPLANT, SLICED	SALT AND PEPPER	COOKING OIL

Roast the lamb and reserve the pan juices. Fry the eggplant with the finely chopped garlic, then place in a food processor and blend until they have become a smooth purée of consistent texture. Season to taste. Sweat the tomatoes in a baking dish in the oven with a little oil. Prepare a mould — a bowl can be used — by greasing it with a little oil. Slice the lamb and make a layer of lamb slices in the mould. Follow with a layer of eggplant purée, a layer of tomato slices, and then pour over some of the reserved pan juices. Repeat these layers until the mould is nearly filled. Gently poach in a *bain-marie* in the oven until heated through. Unmould carefully. **Serves 6.**

TRUCHAS CON JAMON
(Trout with ham)

6 BABY TROUT	Tomato Sauce:	250G TOMATOES, PEELED AND SLICED
SALT	1 ONION, DICED	SALT AND PEPPER
6 SLICES PROSCIUTTO HAM	2 CLOVES GARLIC, SLICED	SUGAR
FLOUR	250ML OLIVE OIL	1 CAPSICUM, DICED

Scale and clean the trout before washing and drying. Rub them lightly with salt and leave for 10 minutes for the salt to be absorbed. Cut the underside of each trout from head to tail. Stuff each stomach cavity with one slice of ham and close with a toothpick. Flour the trout.

To make the tomato sauce: Gently fry the onion and garlic in the oil. Add the tomatoes, salt and pepper to taste and a pinch of sugar. Add the capsicum.

Heat some oil in a pan and fry the trout until golden brown. Serve the trout on a bed of tomato sauce. **Serves 6.**

Experimentation with dishes is extremely important in restaurants. It gives the cook a hint of adventure and discovery, and it is one of those aspects which, in restaurant terms, distinguishes the proverbial 'wheat' from the 'chaff'. It also tells diners that the cook is interested in the new and interesting and is not sitting back resting on laurels or merely getting bored to death cooking and serving the same fare all the time. Margaret Campbell of the North Shore's Penguins' Nest is one such chef who is interested in devising new recipes for her diners. Night after night the blackboard features her interesting creations, from skate — which is like a sting-ray, and which she cooks with capers — to flounder stuffed with prawns and mushrooms and served on a base of fish mousse.

Penguins' Nest is owned by Bryan Crookes, who helps in the front, and his partner, Reinhard Hueber, who also cooks. Since they began working in Auckland restaurants together eight years ago, they have been in a number of ventures, the latest of which began as a result of their wondering what to do with a building they had bought some time before. They turned it into the Penguins' Nest. Seafoods were chosen due to the dire lack of such places on the North Shore, and the name was taken from the fact that penguins actually inhabit the Takapuna shoreline only a few hundred yards away. However, before opening they had to totally renovate the building, and fight the usual battle to get permission to open as a licensed restaurant. Then it was a matter of experimentation with dishes to settle on a menu, and wait to see what would be the response. It has obviously been very successful. The only frustration seems to have been that diners often get very choosy about new dishes, including the skate of which many people have never heard. Nevertheless, Margaret, Reinhard and Bryan are intent on keeping Penguins' Nest as a restaurant trying to present the often unusual and interesting preparation of seafoods.

Penguin's Nest,
174 Hurstmere Road, Takapuna,
Auckland.
Telephone 499-574. Licensed.

ENTREES

Poisson Cru
Mussels with parsley and garlic butter
Tahitian seafood skewer
Blue oysters
Bouillabaisse Aotearoa
Deep fried squid rings with tartare

MAIN COURSES

Flounder stuffed with mushrooms and prawns
Pan fried orange roughy with almonds
Scallops Provençal
Carpetbag steak, stuffed with oysters
Deep fried breast of chicken with ginger and lemon
Rack of lamb

DESSERTS

Hazelnut and kiwifruit meringue
Pineapple kirsch torte
Tamarillos marinated in port
Coffee cream bavarois

MUSSELS WITH PARSLEY AND GARLIC BUTTER

900G LIVE MUSSELS
1 ONION, CHOPPED
1 CUP WATER

GARLIC BUTTER
Topping:
1 TABLESPOON GRATED PARMESAN CHEESE

1 TABLESPOON BROWNED BREADCRUMBS

Scrub the mussels, pulling off the beards, and put them into a large saucepan with the onion and water. Shake occasionally over a medium heat until all the mussels have opened. Allow to cool with the lid half on to prevent the mussels drying out.

Once the mussels have cooled break the shells apart, discard the empty half, and spread garlic butter over the mussels. Place on an oven proof plate or dish.

Mix the cheese and breadcrumbs together, and sprinkle the mixture over the mussels. Brown the mussels in a 200°C oven for about 10 minutes. **Serves 4-6.**

BREAST OF CHICKEN with ginger and lemon

Batter:
55G PLAIN FLOUR, SIEVED
55G CORNFLOUR
1 TEASPOON SALT
30G PARSLEY, CHOPPED
235ML BEER
2 EGG WHITES, WHIPPED

4 CHICKEN BREASTS, SKINNED
30G STEM GINGER IN SYRUP
110G BUTTER
1 LEMON, JUICE AND RIND
1 TEASPOON GINGER POWDER
FLOUR FOR DUSTING
OIL FOR DEEP FRYING

Butter sauce:
15G BUTTER
30G ONION, CHOPPED
30G GREEN OR RED PEPPER, CHOPPED
2 TABLESPOONS SHERRY
2 TABLESPOONS CREAM
PINCH OF CURRY POWDER
1 TEASPOON GROUND GINGER
SALT AND PEPPER TO TASTE

To make the batter: Combine the sieved flour, cornflour, salt and chopped parsley in a mixing bowl. Slowly whisk in the beer until light and smooth. Whisk the egg whites until stiff but not dry, and fold in. Set aside for 2 hours.
To make the sauce: Melt the butter in a frypan. Add the onion and chopped pepper, and cook gently until soft. Add the sherry and simmer for a few minutes. Add the cream, curry powder, ground ginger, salt and pepper, and simmer gently. Check the seasoning and keep warm.

Lay the chicken breasts flat, and slice horizontally not quite through. Open the breasts out and gently beat with a mallet.

Chop the stem ginger and mix it with the softened butter, lemon rind, lemon juice and ginger powder. Spoon the mixture into four sausage shapes, and place one on each breast. Roll tightly to seal. Heat enough oil to deep fry until a crumb will sizzle vigorously. Dust the chicken with plain flour, coat it with batter, and fry for about 10 minutes until golden. Remove, drain, and serve separately with the sauce. **Serves 4.**

WHOLE STUFFED SQUID WITH TOMATO SAUCE

4 SQUID TUBES
2 KIWIFRUIT
2 ROUNDS FRESH PINEAPPLE
½ PAW PAW

Sauce:
2 TABLESPOONS OLIVE OIL
1 ONION, FINELY CHOPPED
900G FRESH OR TINNED TOMATOES

PINCH OF DRIED OREGANO
3-4 SPRIGS FRESH THYME
1 CLOVE GARLIC, CRUSHED
1 TEASPOON SUGAR
150ML CHICKEN STOCK
SALT AND FRESHLY GROUND BLACK PEPPER

Stuffing:
1 ONION, CHOPPED
2 RASHERS BACON, CUT INTO SMALL PIECES
2 CLOVES GARLIC, CRUSHED
2 RED OR GREEN PEPPERS
COOKING OIL
1 CUP LONG GRAIN RICE
SALT AND BLACK PEPPER

Marinate the squid tubes for at least 24 hours in a pulp made from the kiwifruit, pineapple, and paw paw.
To make the sauce: Heat the oil in a medium sized saucepan with a lid. Gently cook the onion until soft and transparent. Add the remaining sauce ingredients and simmer gently for ¾ hour or until the sauce is syrupy. Sieve the mixture.
To make the stuffing: Gently fry the onion, bacon, garlic and peppers in oil until soft. Add the rice and mix well. Season to taste with salt and pepper.

Turn the squid inside out and clean thoroughly. Turn it again and fill with stuffing. Use a skewer at each end to keep the stuffing in. Shallow fry in oil until it turns opaque. Lift out and put in an ovenproof dish, pour the tomato sauce over the squid, and bake in a moderate oven for 20 minutes. **Serves 4.**

Aafke Drake is Dutch, and her husband David, a Yorkshireman; together they run what is one of the country's finest luncheon BYO's. Although only open for dinners on Saturday nights the style and food of Penmarric equates well with long evenings spent on a winter's night in front of a warm fire. But their reasoning is that they are busy enough just presenting luncheons, which include the weekends when people drive from Tauranga, Hamilton and other out-lying districts to while away an afternoon wining and dining. In summer, sitting under the talls trees at wooden benches, eating fresh Bluff oysters, barbecued steaks, washed down with cold white wine, can be a memorable experience. Penmarric was once an old maternity home; now it is divided into various dining areas downstairs, and renovated with the past in mind. Walls are bare brick, covered with chiming clocks, black iron pots and old prints, while David has renovated a number of old sideboards and kauri tables to create more character. Before taking over Penmarric, Aafke was tutoring Continental cookery at the Waikato Technical Institute, while David, who had worked in hotels in Australia and England, had turned his hand to landscape gardening. With their children grown up, they looked to doing something together, and that was the start of their affair with Penmarric. Eventually they will apply for a licence by creating a lounge and bar area in the huge old house. In the meantime Aafke is more than busy in her tiny kitchen, preparing everything herself, leaving David to look after the restaurant and landscape the huge grounds in his spare time.

Penmarric,
50 Hamilton Road, Cambridge.
Telephone 4610. BYO.

ENTREES

Pâté maison
Dutch croquettes
Oysters natural
Vichysoisse
Avocado and prawns
Scallops mornay

MAIN COURSES

Beef Bourguignonne
Pork Lichstenstein
Chicken with walnut sauce
Hot camembert with fruit sauce
Fillet steak aux poivres
Crayfish platter

DESSERTS

Almond torte
Chocolate mousse
Black Forest gâteau

VICHYSOISSE

2 STICKS CELERY
4 LARGE LEEKS, WHITE PARTS ONLY
4 POTATOES
50G BUTTER
1200ML JELLIED CHICKEN STOCK
SALT AND PEPPER
300ML CREAM
CHIVES FOR GARNISH

Finely slice the celery, leeks and potatoes. Sauté, but do not brown the vegetables in butter for 5-10 minutes. Blend in the chicken stock, bring to the boil, season and simmer for 10-15 minutes. Pour into a blender or put through a sieve. Lastly pour in the cream and leave to cool. This can be served hot or cold, but must only be reheated gently. Sprinkle chives on top for garnishing. **Serves 6-8.**

NASI GORENG

250G PRAWNS
100G BUTTER
3 TABLESPOONS OIL
2 ONIONS, FINELY SLICED
2 CLOVES GARLIC, CHOPPED
2 TEASPOONS SAMBAL OELEK
¼ CABBAGE, FINELY SLICED
6 FRENCH BEANS, CHOPPED
2 RED PEPPERS, SLICED
PINCH DRIED SHRIMP PASTE (TRASI)
½ KG RUMP STEAK OF PORK, FINELY SLICED
2 TEASPOONS LETUMBAR
1 TEASPOON DJIENTEN
½ KG LONG GRAIN RICE, COOKED
SALT AND PEPPER TO TASTE
2 TABLESPOONS SOY SAUCE
THIN OMELETTE, SLICED CUCUMBER, SLICED TOMATOES, FRIED SHRIMP SLICES FOR GARNISH

Sauté the prawns in a little butter, then set aside. Sauté the onions and garlic with the sambal oelek in a little of the butter and oil until transparent. Add the onions and garlic to the prawns. Sauté the cabbage, peppers and beans. Then add the trasi and combine with the previously cooked ingredients. Put aside.

Using the remaining oil and butter, fry the meat which should be towel-dried before cooking. Cook for about 10 minutes until tender and add the letumbar and djienten. Combine the ingredients cooked so far in a large casserole or pan, add the cooked rice, and mix well with a fork. Add salt and pepper and the soy sauce. Heat thoroughly, stirring continuously. Serve on a hot platter, garnishing with strips of omelette, sliced cucumber and tomatoes, and fried shrimp slices. **Serves 6.**

ALMOND TORTE

French flan pastry:
145G FLOUR
PINCH SALT
75G BUTTER
70G SUGAR
2 EGG YOLKS
APRICOT JAM

Filling:
150G GROUND ALMONDS
150G CASTOR SUGAR
4 EGGS
2 DROPS VANILLA ESSENCE
2 TABLESPOONS KIRSCH
65G MELTED BUTTER

Decoration:
100G CASTOR SUGAR
100G GROUND ALMONDS
1 EGG WHITE
APRICOT JAM

To make the pastry: Sieve the flour with a pinch of salt and make a well in the centre. Add the butter, sugar, egg yolks and use fingertips to mix together. Make the pastry 1 hour before cooking. Line a quiche dish with the pastry, prick it and brush with a little apricot jam, and chill.
To make the filling: Mix the almonds with the sugar, the egg yolks, vanilla essence and Kirsch. Work well with a wooden spoon till smooth. Stiffly whisk the egg whites and fold into the almond mixture. With a spatula gently fold in the melted butter. Fill the pastry with the mousse and cook in a pre-heated oven at 180°C for 45 minutes.
To decorate: Mix the ground almonds and sugar together. Add the egg white and beat until the paste is moist but not runny. Place in a bag fitted with a 1.5cm pipe and spread the mixture lattice-fashion on top of the slightly cooled torte. Reduce some apricot jam until thick and with a pastry brush glaze the top. **Serves 6-8.**

It took 15 years with a large hotel chain before Swiss-born Pierre Meyer realized he was happiest in the kitchen of his own restaurant. From that came the birth of Pierre's in 1976 — a BYO whose reputation and standard is such, that there is rarely an empty table for lunch or dinner. He never advertizes and many of the diners are out-of-towners who make the pilgrimage there to try the renowned cuisine. Since Pierre's opened there have been few changes. Pierre's original partner, Bruce Hammington, moved overseas, but both Flo Foot and Judy Kelsey have remained as hostesses. There have been the minor changes such as a new coat of bottle-green paint, two extra ovens to increase kitchen flexibility, and even three changes of carpet, but the original wooden cross-patterned tables still remain, along with much of the original decor and many of the wall hangings. It is all very elegant but casual.

There was a time when Pierre worked 14 hours a day but with his new partner Grant Allen, who has been in Pierre's kitchen for the last four years, things run more smoothly. Either Grant or Pierre arrive early each day to check the quality of the meats, fish and vegetables and work out the blackboard menu dishes. Pierre tends to be scathing of the limited choice of vegetables in New Zealand. Whereas in France, there may be a number of different types of lettuce or potatoes to choose from, the choice here is just not available. That accounts for Pierre's continuous experimentation with dishes and new ideas, especially after he has been overseas. On his last trip to France he wanted to see what was happening with nouvelle cuisine. What he found was that only very good restaurants with a kitchen brigade having a sound knowledge of classical cuisine interpreted the new style in the right way. In too many instances, he feels, shortcuts are mistaken for innovation, often to the detriment of taste.

Pierre's,
342 Tinakori Road, Wellington.
Telephone 726-238. BYO.

ENTREES

Terrine maison
Terrine de poisson et langouste
Thon frais fumé sur salad d'oseille
Porc fumé et canteloup
Crème de poireaux et potiron
Ragoût des fruits de mer sur pâtes fraîches

MAIN COURSES

Terakihi à l'amoureuse
Mignonette d'agneau aux herbes fraîches
Poulet sauté au gingembre et citron vert
Filet de boeuf aux échalottes

DESSERTS

Trois tiers au chocolat
L'assiette de sorbets
Tarte au citron
Glace aux kiwifruit
Camembert

FOIES DE VOLAILLE
(Chicken livers and witloaf salad)

4 WITLOAFS, TRIMMED	100ML WALNUT OIL	UNSALTED BUTTER
JUICE OF 6 LIMES OR LEMONS	100ML PEANUT OIL	8 WALNUTS AND CHOPPED
SALT AND FRESHLY GROUND PEPPER	12 CHICKEN LIVERS	CHERVIL FOR GARNISH

Cut the trimmed witloaf on a slant, wash thoroughly and pat dry.

In a food processor, blend the lime or lemon juice with the salt, pepper and the combined oils.

Clean the chicken livers, discarding gristle and fat, and cut into halves. Rapidly sauté the livers in unsalted butter, but do not overcook. Season with salt and pepper and keep warm.

Place the witloaf on individual plates, pour the walnut oil dressing over the witloaf, and place the chicken livers on top.

To garnish: Shell the walnuts, and sprinkle the walnut halves and chopped chervil over the livers. Serve at once. **Serves 4.**

GIGOT D'AGNEAU
(Leg of lamb stuffed with vegetables and basil)

SMALL LEG OF SPRING LAMB	2 STICKS CELERY	100ML WHITE WINE
SALT AND FRESHLY GROUND PEPPER	12 BASIL LEAVES	200ML VEAL DEMIGLAZE
1 LARGE CARROT	1 TABLESPOON OLIVE OIL	50G UNSALTED BUTTER
1 LARGE LEEK, WHITE ONLY	1 TEASPOON TOMATO CONCENTRATE	

Ask your butcher to bone the leg of lamb. Remove all fat from the joint and cavity, and season the cavity with salt and freshly ground pepper. Surround the carrot with the sliced leek then sticks of celery to form a rosette. Insert the vegetables in the leg cavity along with 6 basil leaves. Tie the joint with string. Brush the leg with olive oil. Roast the joint in a pre-heated 200°C oven for about ½ hour, turning after 20 minutes or when nicely brown. Roast for another 30 minutes at 175°C. The meat should be rarish. Remove the joint from the roasting pan and keep it warm. Retain the pan juices.

Put the pan with the retained fat on a medium heat and add tomato concentrate and the white wine, scraping the bottom of the pan and reducing the wine by half. Add the veal demiglaze, or a strong vegetable and bouquet garni stock. Reduce the liquid until it is syrupy. Take the pan off the heat, and stir in the unsalted butter to thicken. Strain the sauce into a sauce boat and keep warm.

Discard the string holding the joint and slice across the grain making 4-5 thick slices. The rest of the joint can be used later. Place each slice on individual serving plates, garnish with the remaining basil leaves or mint leaves and spoon the sauce over the meat. Accompany with French beans. **Serves 4-5.**

TARTE AU CITRON
(Lemon custard tart)

500G SWEET SHORT PASTRY	ZEST OF ½ ORANGE	8 LEMON SEGMENTS WITHOUT SKIN
4 EGGS	125ML FRESH ORANGE JUICE	8 ORANGE SEGMENTS WITHOUT SKIN
250G CASTOR SUGAR	125ML FRESH LEMON JUICE	ICING SUGAR FOR GARNISH
	60ML CREAM	

Line a 22cm French tart mould with removable bottom with a thin layer of pastry and prick the pastry with a fork. Line the pastry with grease proof paper, fill with haricot beans, and bake in a pre-heated 180°C oven on the middle shelf for 12 minutes. Remove the paper and beans and bake for a further 5 minutes.

In a food processor beat the eggs, sugar and orange zest until the mixture is coloured lemon. Then add the juices and the cream with the blender still going. Pour the filling into the pre-baked tart and bake for 15 minutes at 180°C and another 10 minutes at 150°C or until custard is just set. Remove the tart from the oven, decorate the top with the orange and lemon segments, and with a sieve dust the top with icing sugar. Place the tart under a broiler at high temperature to caramelize the sugar, but watch carefully. When cool demould and leave on the rack until cold. **Serves 8.**

Godfrey Meier is a chef with a very classical approach to cooking, yet one tinged with a touch of adventure. Godfrey and his wife Rosa run a superb French style restaurant in the centre of Whangarei. It's a restaurant with such a sense of style, and with such excellent food, that it would do justice to any city in any country. German-born Godfrey did his training in Baden Baden working at the Brenner's Park Hotel, one of the best in Europe. From there he moved to the Richmond in Switzerland, the Grand Hotel in Stockholm, to Montreal, and then to Bermuda's Princes Hotel. He arrived in New Zealand to work at Auckland's Hyatt, formerly the Intercontinental, and there he heard about a little steakhouse that was for sale in Whangarei. That was the start of Plusone. Out went the steaks, in came a blackboard menu, and along with it a totally new decor of dark green walls, striped canvas ceiling, old paintings and prints on the walls, yellow tablecloths, cane backed chairs, and soft classical music. The finishing touch was the arrival of Rosa, his childhood sweetheart who had been working as an air hostess with Iberia airlines for 14 years. They married, and with Godfrey in the kitchen, and Rosa in the restaurant, Plusone developed a very strong following. It was probably as much due to Rosa's personality and efficiency, as to Godfrey's cooking. Her training as an air hostess has been an inestimable asset; she notices when people are left-handed, and will change the cutlery accordingly. When people have a hearing aid she will speak a little louder; she has developed her judgement of people's moods to a fine art. Hers is a talent you see in few restaurants, just as few restaurants possess a cook of Godfrey's experience.

Plusone,
63 Bank Street, Whangarei.
Telephone 89-993. BYO.

ENTREES

Russian chicken cocktail
Consommé with liver dumplings
Glazed fish soup
Brains en bôuchée
Kidneys bordelaise
Spiced pork with red cabbage

MAIN COURSES

Pork loin with apricots
Fillet Ketterer
Saddle of lamb soubise
Pheasant winzerin art
John Dory duglere
Scallops in bird nest

DESSERTS

Crêpe soufflé
Apricot and banana flan
Tortini
Hazelnut parfait
Deep fried ice cream

SNAIL SOUP BADEN BADEN

2 TABLESPOONS BUTTER
1 ONION, FINELY CHOPPED
1 CELERY STALK, FINELY CHOPPED
1 CARROT, FINELY CHOPPED
½ LEEK, FINELY CHOPPED
12 SNAILS, CUT LENGTHWISE
1 TOMATO, PEELED AND SEEDED
2 CLOVES GARLIC, FINELY SLICED
½ LITRE FISH STOCK
1 TEASPOON SALT
½ TEASPOON PEPPER
PINCH OF SAFFRON
100ML DRY WHITE WINE
300ML CREAM
2 TEASPOONS CORNFLOUR
2 EGG YOLKS
CHOPPED CHIVES FOR GARNISH

Sweat the onion, celery, carrot and leek in the butter until soft. Add the snails, tomato, garlic, fish stock, salt, pepper, saffron and white wine. Bring to the boil for 5 minutes. Mix half of the cream with the cornflour and add to the soup and reheat. Add the remaining cream with the egg yolks, and reheat. Do not boil. Serve sprinkled with chopped chives. **Serves 4.**

BUTTERNUT PLUSONE

250G LAMB SWEETBREADS
PINCH OF SALT
4 BUTTERNUTS
4 TEASPOONS BUTTER

Cream sauce:
1 ONION, CHOPPED
50G BUTTER
1 TABLESPOON FLOUR
40G GROUND ALMONDS
200ML CREAM
JUICE OF ½ LEMON
SALT AND PEPPER TO TASTE

Topping:
1 EGG
50G CHEDDAR CHEESE, GRATED
4 TABLESPOONS CREAM

Soak the sweetbreads in running water for 30 minutes. Remove the membrane and place the sweetbreads in a pot. Cover the sweetbreads with cold water. Add a pinch of salt and cook covered for 45 minutes or until tender.

While the sweetbreads are cooking, prepare the butternuts by hollowing out their centres with a spoon. Discard all seeds. Place a teaspoon of butter in each hollowed-out butternut and bake in a 200⅞C oven for 40 minutes or until soft to touch.

To make the cream sauce: In a pot sweat the onion in the butter for 4 minutes. Add the flour and let cook for a further 3 minutes. Add the ground almonds and the stock in which the sweetbreads have been cooking. Whisk briskly until thick. Add the cream, lemon juice, salt and pepper to taste.

Chop the sweetbreads and add to the cream sauce. Fill the butternuts with this mixutre, and top with egg, cheese and cream blended together. Place the butternuts in the oven for 15 minutes at a medium heat and then serve. **Serves 4.**

HONEY PARFAIT

4 EGG YOLKS
125G CLOVER HONEY
500ML CREAM
2 NIPS KIRSCH OR MARASCHINO
WHIPPED CREAM, HONEY, ALMONDS FOR GARNISH

Blend the egg yolks and honey in a bowl and then whisk in a *bain-marie* until thickened. Allow to cool. Whip the cream until firm and then add the Kirsch or Maraschino. Fold this into the egg/honey mixture. Spoon the mixture into individual parfait glasses and freeze for 1½ hours. Decorate with whipped cream, honey and top with roasted sliced almonds. **Serves 6.**

Luigi Paljk is one of the better known characters among New Zealand's restaurateurs; the genial cook and host of Portobello in Hamilton's main street. For many restaurant owners, running a restaurant tends to be just one phase in their life, but for Luigi, cooking is definitely in his blood. For the past 20 years or so he has owned a succession of eating houses in Hamilton and Auckland.

He arrived in Wellington from Yugoslavia when he was just 17 and for a time worked in hotels as he moved around the country. The first venture on his own account was the Red Rooster in Hamilton, before he started the Coachman's Inn in Hamilton, which is still going.

He then spent some time in Europe and on his return bought a small restaurant in Auckland's Parnell called La Trattoria that still has a good name for Mediterranean style food and seafood. Two years later, he moved back to Hamilton and bought the restaurant called Brothers. He renamed it Portobello, re-decorated it in the style of a North Italian country inn and started serving food with a Yugoslav and Northern Italian flavour. Luigi had spent many years in Northern Italy, acquiring such a taste of food which the customers readily accept and come back for more in this cosy, often heavily booked restaurant

Out in the kitchen, Luigi and his co-chef Naomi Levis concentrate on producing some excellent dishes like Ragu Fruit de Mer, Fillet Gigetto, Crayfish Mornay, fresh fish dishes, Veal Valdostana and many others. The herbs they use are from Luigi's garden, although out of season, some dried herbs are used. And while Luigi is in the kitchen, he wife Mayda acts as hostess, tending to the needs of customers.

Portobello,
270 Victoria Street, Hamilton.
Telephone 82-305. BYO.

ENTREES

Oysters natural
Pâté de la maison with brown toast
Chilled pawpaw or rock melon
Avocado with shrimps, seafood or vinaigrette
Shrimp, oyster or seafood cocktail
Soup, freshly prepared each day

MAIN COURSES

Calamari Luciana – pan fried in Neapolitan sauce
Ragu Fruit de Mer – a bouillabaise seafood casserole
Scallops Delmonico
Fisherman's Plate – deep fried fish and shellfish
Fresh fish of the day
Canneloni Casalinga
Lasagna and Ragu
Macaroni Marina

DESSERTS

Cassata
Tortone Ice Cream
Pancakes with various fillings

FETTUCINE AND WHITEBAIT

400G FETTUCINE (PREFERABLY GRANUM DURUM)
GROUND NUTMEG
20G WHITEBAIT
FLOUR
SALT AND PEPPER TO TASTE
1 TABLESPOON CHOPPED PARSLEY
PINCH OF CHOPPED OREGANUM OR MARJORAM
1 DESSERTSPOON OLIVE OIL
SALT TO TASTE
1 TABLESPOON CHOPPED GARLIC
60G BUTTER
2 TABLESPOONS DRY WHITE WINE

Cook the fettucine in boiling salted water until still a little hard (al dente), normally 15-20 minutes. Empty them into a colander and drain. Put the noodles into a saucepan with a little butter and a pinch of ground nutmeg. Mix.

Put the whitebait on a plate and sprinkle with white flour, salt and pepper. Then put the remaining ingredients on top, except the butter and the wine, and mix.

Melt the butter in a non-stick frypan over a low heat and when melted add all the whitebait ingredients and stir gently for about 3 minutes until hot. Pour in the wine, mix again, then pour the lot over the hot, buttered fettucine. Mix it and serve. **Serves 4.**

PORK FILLET RENATO

4 PORK FILLETS
1 DESSERTSPOON SOY SAUCE
1 TEASPOON SESAME SEED
PINCH OF SAGE
2 SOUP SPOONS MARSALA
½ CUP CREAM
½ CUP GRATED GRUYERE

Cut the pork fillets into six slices each. Beat them into medallions, the size of 50¢ coins. Pan fry them in butter and when almost ready add the soy sauce, sesame seed, sage and Marsala. Mix in the frypan until ready. Drain off the liquid, lower the heat and add the cream and gruyère. First cream, then gently simmer until the sauce is smooth and reasonably thick.

Serve with pan fried apple slices and vegetables. **Serves 4.**

FRUIT SALAD IN WINE

4 LARGE PEACHES
6 KIWIFRUIT
1 PAW PAW OR ROCK MELON
4 PEARS
½ CUP CHERRIES OR GRAPES
2 TABLESPOONS SUGAR
JUICE OF HALF A LEMON
1 TABLESPOON VANILLA SUGAR
1 TABLESPOON SAUTERNE
1 LIQUEUR GLASS COINTREAU

Peel and slice the fruit. Sprinkle with the sugar and lemon juice. Add the vanilla sugar and gently mix. Add the sauterne and the Cointreau. Leave in the refrigerator for 1 hour before serving. Serve with ice cream. **Serves 4-6.**

Opposite: Braised pheasant with Madeira Sauce. (p. 175). Another exotic dish is Digby Law's braised pheasant with Madeira sauce. Pheasant is a game bird, and like most game the cooking time varies. But the end result has an excellent flavour. Any leftover pheasant can be used for a crêpe filling, and the carcass for stock. *(Photograph by Max Thomson.)*

---

27. Lac Ly and his wife Muoi were former Vietnamese boat people but they now run their Mekong restaurant a few yards from Auckland's main street. *(Photograph by Stephen Ballantyne).*

---

28. Orsini's began in Wellington but Phillip and Valerie Littlejohn moved north to open their Auckland version in a magnificent old mansion in Ponsonby. *(Photograph by Lianne Ruscoe).*

---

29. Sandra Gordon who runs Palmerston North's Sheraton restaurant, with chef Hugh Cameron. *(Photograph by Stephen Ballantyne).*

27

28

29

30

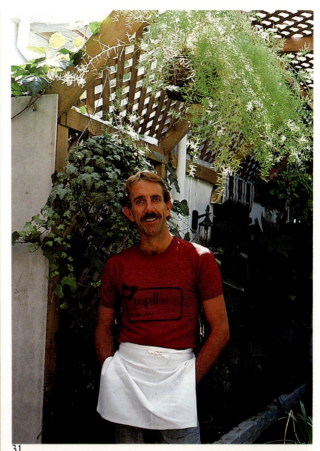

31

32

33

131

34

35

36

37

30. Margaret Campbell and Reinhard Hueber, chefs at Penguin's Nest on Auckland's North Shore, with Bryan Crookes, partner with Reinhard in this mainly seafood restaurant. *(Photograph by Stephen Ballantyne).*

---

31. Michael Ewens in the covered courtyard of his Papillon restaurant in Auckland. *(Photograph by Lianne Ruscoe).*

---

32. Pierre Meyer is another of the country's best-known chefs. His Pierre's restaurant in Wellington attracts gourmets from both the capital and from throughout the country. *(Photograph by Lianne Ruscoe).*

---

33. Although Pedro Carazo was born in Spain's Basque region, his Pedro's restaurant in Christchurch presents a cuisine covering all the regions of Spain. *(Photograph by Stephen Ballantyne).*

---

34. Luigi Paljk of Hamilton's Portobello, a Northern Italian trattoria style restaurant which specializes in seafoods. *(Photograph by Lianne Ruscoe).*

---

35. Shiraz is New Zealand's only Persian restaurant. It also offers Indian cuisine in stylish surroundings. *(Photograph by Stephen Ballantyne).*

---

36. Armando Cozzolino, the effervescent cook-owner of Auckland's Vesuvio's restaurant, was once a chef on an Italian passenger liner. *(Photograph by Stephen Ballantyne).*

---

37. Brian and Raewyn Milicich of Hamilton's Seddon House. Rather than buy an existing restaurant they built Seddon House so it would be exactly what they wanted. *(Photograph by Lianne Ruscoe).*

Roaring Meg's has its roots in London where Peter Bonifant, originally from Feilding, met up with fellow New Zealanders, Rob and Louise Ongley. Peter was working in a restaurant after doing the Cordon Bleu cookery course, while Rob and Louise were catering. The trio had high hopes of owning their own restaurant, but it was not until Rob and Louise returned to New Zealand that it became a reality. The *Woman's Weekly* published an article about the couple, and they were then approached by a Queenstown businessman who wondered if they would like to take over an old building there and convert it into a restaurant. Peter promptly returned from London and the trio moved to Queenstown to take over an ageing miner's cottage more than 100 years old. For many years the cottage had served as a school house in nearby Skipper's Canyon, before being moved into the town. By the time they took it over it was badly rundown but, after months of effort and ingenuity, they converted it into a restaurant full of character and with an excellent reputation. It still has the character of its heritage with wood panelled walls, flower printed wallpaper, a coal range set in stacked schist, oval mirrors and old prints and paintings, brassware, and old style chairs. White Rosenthal china, crystal glasses, green tablecloths and fresh flowers combine to give it a very homely and intimate atmosphere. The background music of this BYO is from the 1920's and 30's, but there is also a piano which is mainly decorative though sometimes it does get played by the occasional diner. Peter changes Roaring Meg's menu four times a year but it always has a good range of dishes with emphasis on New Zealand cuisine, such as the whole Takaka Salmon and Jackson Bay whitebait.

Roaring Meg's,
57 Shotover Street, Queenstown.
Telephone 968. BYO.

ENTREES

French onion soup
Smoked eel pâté
Chicken liver pâté
Mushrooms Marakesh, with bacon, flamed in brandy
Jackson Bay whitebait served in a light omelette
Avocado fruit salad

MAIN COURSES

Sirloin steak with a herb butter
Scallops Gratinée
Southland lamb in apricot and almond sauce topped with flaked pastry
Takaka salmon baked whole
Skipper's Chinese chicken with a honey and soy gravy
Fiordland venison fillets rolled in breadcrumbs and pan fried

DESSERTS

Knickerbocker glory — fruit, icecream, liqueur, cream and nuts
Brandy snaps
Chocolate mousse
Fresh fruit sorbet
Pavlova

SMOKED EEL PATE

300G SMOKED EEL
100G BUTTER
125G CREAM CHEESE
2 TABLESPOONS OIL
2 TABLESPOONS SOUR CREAM
JUICE OF ½ LEMON
SALT AND FRESHLY GROUND BLACK PEPPER
LEMON FOR GARNISH

Bone and skin the eel and purée it in a food processor. Set the eel aside and then purée the butter, cream cheese and oil. When creamy add the smoked eel, sour cream, lemon juice, salt and pepper to taste. Pour into ramekins or a large bowl and allow to set. Serve with French bread and crudités. Garnish with lemon slices.

LAMB AND APRICOT PIE

1KG LAMB, CUBED
1 ONION, DICED
1 TEASPOON CHOPPED ROSEMARY
1 CLOVE GARLIC, CHOPPED
400G APRICOT PUREE
2 TABLESPOONS TOMATO PUREE
300ML BEEF STOCK
½ CUP CHOPPED DRIED APRICOTS
½ CUP CHOPPED ALMONDS
SALT AND PEPPER
FLAKY PASTRY
1 EGG, BEATEN
APRICOT AND ROSEMARY FOR GARNISH

Seal the cubed lamb in a large pan with hot fat. Remove the lamb and to the pan add the onion, rosemary and garlic. Cook slowly until soft. Then add the apricot purée, tomato purée and the beef stock. Cook until thickened and then add the lamb, dried apricots, almonds, salt and pepper. Simmer for 2 hours before placing in a pie dish to cool. Cover with flaky pastry and glaze with the egg before baking at 225°C for 15-25 minutes. Garnish with fresh apricot and rosemary sprigs. **Serves 6.**

ICED ZABAGLIONE

6 EGG YOLKS
30G SUGAR
6-8 TABLESPOONS MARSALA SHERRY
1 TEASPOON GELATINE
1 TABLESPOON WATER
¼ TEASPOON VANILLA
3 TABLESPOONS BRANDY
300ML CREAM, WHIPPED
WHIPPED CREAM AND FRUIT FOR GARNISH

Place the egg yolks, sugar and sherry in a *bain-marie* and heat well. Heat slowly, beating constantly until the mixture has thickened. Remove from the heat and add the gelatine which has been dissolved in the water. Pour the mixture in a bowl, and then place the bowl in ice, stirring the mixture until cold but not set. Stir in the vanilla, brandy and the whipped cream. Pour into a serving dish and place in the freezer for 1 hour until set but not frozen. Garnish with whipped cream and fresh fruit. **Serves 4.**

Roger and Anne Weston are purists as far as their commitment to their restaurant is concerned. Rogann's serves only seafood, and despite the pressures of people coming to the restaurant and asking for steak or chicken, the Weston's have resisted the temptation to stray from only specializing in seafoods. The only concession has been Anne's scallop and chicken pie.

Rogann's — derived from a combination of their christian names — is their third restaurant. Their first venture was a small café in Greytown, serving Devonshire teas at their home on a property which also cultiveated 20,000 glass-house carnations. Along came the Health Inspector; the Riot Act was read, and they had to get official approval for what had turned into an excellent little BYO. In 1982 they decided to move to Whitianga on the Coromandel Peninsula where they opened their Greenhouse restaurant with a strong emphasis on seafoods. However, they did not enjoy Whitianga, so they moved to Auckland where developer Les Harvey showed them the old Observer printing works. Built around 1840, the building still had solid brick walls, kauri floors stained with printer's ink, and even an old press. The first floor shambles was quickly turned into Rogann's within a matter of months, with Ann in the kitchen and Roger out the front. Anne's approach to cooking seafoods is to take care not to mask the natural flavour by using sauces which are too strong. She provides a heady range of seafoods, through crayfish, crab, mussels, cockles, squid, to prawns and whitebait.

Rogann's,
12 Wyndham Street, Auckland.
Telephone 398-689. Licensed.

ENTREES

Seafood chowder
Whitebait mousse
Brandied seafood mornay
Smoked roe on wholemeal crackers
Mussels in the shell with garlic and wine
Poached scallops in sauce Beaujolais

MAIN COURSES

Sautéed seafoods with Marsala sauce
Crayfish grilled with garlic butter
Flounder baked with paprika and lemon
Hapuka steak with garlic butter, camembert and minted apple sauce
Scallop and chicken pie
Fish of the day with seafood caper sauce

DESSERTS

Drambuie fruit and nut ice cream
Fresh fruits in season
Oranges, glazed in liqueur

SCALLOPS POACHED IN BEAUJOLAIS SAUCE

1 LITRE BEAUJOLAIS WINE
1 LITRE WATER
3 BUNCHES SPINACH, CHOPPED
4 CARROTS, PRECOOKED AND CHOPPED
10 LETTUCE LEAVES
2 LARGE ONIONS, CHOPPED
6 CLOVES GARLIC, FINELY CHOPPED
2 CANS TOMATO JUICE
GROUND BLACK PEPPER AND SALT TO SEASON
RAW SUGAR
36 SCALLOPS

Simmer the vegetables in the Beaujolais wine and water. This liquid can be used a number of times if stored in the refrigerator. When the vegetables are tender blend to a smooth paste.

In a heavy saucepan make a roux, breaking it down with a little Beaujolais or water. Add a little roux at a time to the vegetable mixture until a smooth consistency is acquired. This should 'run' freely when hot. Season and sweeten with sugar.

In a separate pot add the required number of scallops for your guests — about 6-8 scallops for every ladle of the Beaujolais sauce. To cook the scallops bring the mixture quickly to a high heat, but do not boil. **Serves 6.**

SMOKED SEAFOOD SOUP

10G BACON
1 TABLESPOON BUTTER
1 LEEK
2 CARROTS
½ BUNCH CELERY
1 ROOT FENNEL
½ TEASPOON TURMERIC
½ TEASPOON SWEET BASIL
½ TEASPOON GARLIC, FINELY CHOPPED
½ TEASPOON MARJORAM
½ TEASPOON THYME
½ LITRE DRY WHITE WINE
3 LARGE POTATOES, QUARTERED
½ LITRE FISH STOCK
200G WET FISH FILLETS
300ML CREAM
SALT AND PEPPER TO TASTE
1 KG SMOKED FISH OF CHOICE

Cut the bacon into squares and sauté in the butter until clear. Julienne the leek, carrots, celery and root fennel and sauté in the pan. Add the herbs and garlic, dry white wine, potatoes, fish stock, fish, and simmer for about 10-15 minutes. Take out the fish, and then blend the potatoes and half the soup in a blender, before mixing with the rest of the soup. Add the cream, season to taste, and add the fish and smoked seafoods of your choice. This can include eel, roe, salmon, any smoked fillets of fish, and even oysters. **Serves 12.**

SCALLOP AND CHICKEN PIE

2 FRESH CHICKENS (NO 5)
WORCESTERSHIRE SAUCE
½ TEASPOON PAPRIKA
½ TEASPOON MARJORAM
½ TEASPOON ANGOSTURA BITTERS
BLACK GROUND PEPPER AND SALT TO SEASON
1 TEASPOON RAW SUGAR
FLAKY PUFF PASTRY
15-20 SCALLOPS
600ML MORNAY SAUCE MADE WITH WHITE WINE
EGG WHITE

Sprinkle a generous amount of Worcestershire sauce inside the chickens, and place them in an oven dish. Sprinkle with the paprika, marjoram, Angostura bitters, pepper, salt and raw sugar. These amounts can be varied slightly to taste. Cover and cook in a 180°C oven for 1½ hours.

When the chickens have cooled, take the meat off the carcasses, reserving the bone and liquid for future soups.

Line a large shallow roasting dish with pastry and spread with the chicken meat. Lay enough scallops over the top to cover the chicken, and then pour the mornay sauce over the scallops. Top with pastry brushed with egg white, and decorate. Bake at 250°C for 15 minutes, and then reduce to 180°C for 15-20 minutes. **Serves 6.**

When Brian and Raewyn Milicich decided they wanted to open their own restaurant they went about it the hard way. Rather than buying an existing restaurant they went site hunting around Hamilton and found an empty block of land next to Seddon Park about half a mile from the city centre. They wanted a restaurant that would have a comfortable and intimate atmosphere. The single-storey building took seven months to build but by the time it was finished it was exactly what they wanted, right down to the cobblestoned courtyard with fountain and old cast iron stove. There was one main dining area, two smaller dining rooms, reception area, and there was the big advantage that they could live on the premises which with a young son made life a lot easier. To give the restaurant warmth and atmosphere they kept a dark colour scheme, and added a myriad of antiques, including an old set of brass scales and brass hatrack, an ancient zither, framed photographs of their great-great grandparents, and an old tiled fireplace. A mirrored wall, cane divider, velvet drapes and greenery gave the modern touch.

Once opened, Seddon House became quickly established as one of the Waikato's better restaurants. For a place that seats 64 it's quite an achievement, as is the fact that the menu offers three appetizers, a soup, 10 entrées, 11 main courses and seven desserts. In those early days of the restaurant when they were ironing out initial problems it was pure bliss to stumble those few yards to bed after a hard night. Now with Seddon House running virtually like clockwork they've moved into a house well away from the restaurant, but the restaurant is definitely still a second home.

Seddon House,
67 Seddon Street, Hamilton.
Telephone 78-294. BYO.

ENTREES

Tropical prawn salad with vinaigrette
Oysters Czarina — raw oysters with caviar
Mushrooms Romanoff — with sour cream and paprika on a croûte
Brandied chicken liver pâté
Calamari — crumbed with Green Goddess dressing
Ham and asparagus mornay

MAIN COURSES

Chicken Valdostana — boned breast with cream cheese, chives and ham, poached in white wine
Fresh Fish — stuffed with Alaskan crab meat and pan fried
Camembert Apricot Chicken — with an apricot and ginger sauce
Fritto Misto — Italian-style deep fried seafoods
Tournedos Rossini — eye fillet with chicken liver pâté and Madeira sauce
Veal Marsala — finished with Marsala and lemon cream sauce

DESSERTS

Pineapple Kirsch with deep-fried ice cream
Peach Melba with toasted slivered almonds
Deep fried walnut cheese with toffee sauce
Apple strudel
Apricot passion parfait with a brandy snap

TROPICAL PRAWN SALAD

1 AVOCADO	1 CUP SMALL PRAWNS	Vinaigrette:
½ PAW PAW	2 KING PRAWNS	4 TABLESPOONS WHITE VINEGAR
4 SPRING ONIONS	4 SLICES RED CAPSICUM	2 TABLESPOONS LIQUID HONEY
½ SMALL LETTUCE	1 STALK DIAGONAL SLICED CELERY	2 TABLESPOONS SUGAR
8 CUCUMBER SLICES	4 LEMON AND TOMATO WEDGES	1 TEASPOON FRENCH MUSTARD
4 RADISH SLICES	PARSLEY FOR GARNISH	PEPPER
		1 TEASPOON SALT
		COOKING OIL

Arrange the salad ingredients imaginatively on individual serving dishes, using the lettuce leaves as a bed.
To make the vinaigrette: Boil the vinegar, honey, sugar, French mustard, ground pepper and salt. Mix this with the same quantity of high quality cooking oil. **Serves 2.**

CHICKEN VALDOSTANA

4 BONED CHICKEN BREASTS	1 TABLESPOON GRATED PARMESAN CHEESE	1 TABLESPOON LEMON JUICE
SALT AND FRESHLY GROUND BLACK PEPPER	¼ TEASPOON PAPRIKA	2 SLICES HAM
75G CREAM CHEESE	1 TABLESPOON FINELY CHOPPED CHIVES	12G BUTTER
1 TABLESPOON FRESH CREAM		1 TABLESPOON OIL
		75ML DRY WHITE WINE

Lightly beat the chicken breasts to soften and then sprinkle with salt. In a bowl combine the cream cheese, cream, parmesan, paprika, chives, lemon juice and pepper to make a thick paste. Spread half the mixture on half of each slice of ham and then fold over and sandwich each slice between two chicken breasts. Press the edges of the breasts together and secure with toothpicks around the edges. Refrigerate for at least 1 hour before dipping the breasts in flour. Mix the butter and oil in a large shallow frypan, and fry the breasts until lightly browned on both sides. Add the white wine and cover and simmer for 5 minutes or until the chicken is tender. **Serves 2.**

PERSIAN DELIGHT

COFFEE ICE CREAM	4 LYCHEES	2 TABLESPOONS SLIVERED TOASTED ALMONDS
1 FRESH MANGO, SLICED	2 TABLESPOONS CREME DE CACAO	
	WHIPPED CREAM	

Place four scoops of coffee ice cream in a sundae dish and arrange the mango slices over the ice cream, with the lychees on the side. Pour over the Crème de Cacao and decorate with the whipped cream, before spiking with toasted almonds slivers. **Per person.**

In 1908 the North Island cattle king, Roderick McKenzie, built his magnificent rambling homestead on 300 acres just outside Palmerston North. For decades it continued as a cattle stud farm but over the years the acreage was gradually whittled down to just 3¼ acres of what is now beautiful gardens and towering trees. To reach the old homestead, now the Sheraton, there is a long driveway framed with flower beds. The Sheraton operated as a restaurant, albeit not a particularly good one, for a number of years, but it was not until 1982 that it really came into its own when Sandra Gordon and Hugh Cameron took over. The first task was to paint and refurbish the Sheraton and to transform it into an elegant affair, complete with velvet regency wallpaper and drapes, new crystal, cutlery and china, white linen tablecloths, cane-backed chairs, chandeliers, ritz palms, silver candelabra on the tables, old oil paintings, silver teapots and three open fireplaces with ornate carved mantelpieces. Hugh, who had finished his basic chef's training in Oamaru a decade before, had worked in Australia, West Germany, England and Scotland, including periods at the Gloucester and Cumberland Hotels in London. He brought back to New Zealand a host of new ideas for what is an extraordinarily comprehensive menu backed by a fine wine cellar. With Sandra's flair for decoration, and Hugh's cooking skills, the Sheraton was quickly transformed into what is now one of the better restaurants in the country, recreating a touch of elegance in a part of New Zealand that has sadly lagged behind in its restaurant standards in the past years.

Sheraton,
Milson Line, Palmerston North.
Telephone 77-686. Licensed.

ENTREES

Huîtres Montuigo Bay – oysters, prawns and coconut cream broiled, with toasted coconut
Bisque D'Huîtres – Bluff oyster chowder
Anguille Fumée Chaude – eel fillets, hot with butter sauce
Escargots à la Pâtisserie – snails and burgundy sauce in pastry and deep fried
Crêpes – with seafoods and kiwifruit with a cream champagne sauce

MAIN COURSES

Fresh fish poached in white wine with a cream sauce and grapes
Petit Diable – baby chicken with mustard, breadcrumbs and a spicy sauce
Filet Shrewsbury – lamb fillet with redcurrant jelly and Worcestershire sauce
Canard Poivre Vert – duckling with green peppercorns and cognac
Tournedos Rossini – with croûtons, pâté, and a burgundy sauce
Homard Thermidor – lobster with wine and mustard, grilled with parmesan

DESSERTS

From the trolley or cheeseboard

FILET DE POISSON SHERATON

4 PAUPIETTES OF FRESH FISH FILLETS	1 KIWIFRUIT	PRAWN, PARSLEY, KIWIFRUIT
FISH STOCK	½ CUP CREAM	FOR GARNISH
PUFF PASTRY	1 CUP CHAMPAGNE	

Poach the fish fillets in the fish stock until nearly cooked and place in a 10cm by 15cm pastry case along with the kiwifruit. Make a cream and champagne sauce from the fish velouté and pour over the pastry case. Replace the lid on the pastry base and garnish with a whole peeled prawn, a sprig of parsley and a wedge of kiwifruit. **Per portion.**

FILET D'AGNEAU SHREWSBURY

1 LARGE LAMB FILLET, TRIMMED	SALT AND PEPPER	½ TABLESPOON WORCESTERSHIRE
BUTTER	1 TABLESPOON REDCURRANT JELLY	SAUCE
		3 TABLESPOONS DEMI GLACE

Season and sauté the fillet in butter until nearly cooked.
Meanwhile, melt the redcurrant jelly and Worcestershire sauce in a pan, and add the demi glace. When simmering add the lamb fillet and coat well with the sauce, turning the fillet often until cooked. Remove and slice the fillet, coat it with the sauce which should be a dark colour and have a syrup consistency. Add finely chopped truffles if available. **Per portion.**

HOMARD NANTUA

1 LOBSTER	60G SMALL SHRIMPS	SALT AND PEPPER
FISH STOCK	BUTTER	2 TABLESPOONS CREAM
60G TOMATO FLESH, LESS SKIN AND PIPS	1 CUP DRY WHITE WINE	LEMON, PARSLEY AND PRAWN
	FISH VELOUTE	FOR GARNISH

Poach the lobster in court boullion or the fish stock and split in half, removing all the meat. Cut the meat into bite-size pieces and fold into a sauce made by sautéeing the tomato and shrimps in a little butter. Add the white wine and reduce by half. Then stir in enough fish velouté to make approximately 1 cup of sauce. Finish with cream. Place the cooked meat and sauce into the lobster shells and garnish with lemon, parsley and a whole peeled prawn. **Per portion.**

Veer Charan, herself a Fijian Indian, opened Shiraz in 1982 as the country's first Persian-Indian restaurant. Over a period of months the interior was torn out of what was previously a basic curry house. The roof was altered, new walls added and the building was transformed into the intimate and elegant restaurant Veer had always wanted to open. The reception lounge is decorated with grey carpet, a sofa and chairs, an Indian brass table, hanging brass lamps, a carved Indian wallpiece and a ceiling of draped silk forming a pyramid. A circular staircase leads to the dining area on the top floor which seats 30 people in two rooms. Upstairs is a continuation of the elegant décor with peach coloured walls, another pyramid ceiling and brasswork Veer imported from Singapore. A lot of the ideas for the restaurant she brought back from overseas.

Shiraz' cuisine mixes the Punjabi mild curries of India with Persia's more exotic dishes which use a lot more dairy products, such as cream and yoghurt, often combined with nuts. The curries also tend to be less meat oriented than the usual Indian meat curries. Shiraz also serves chapatis, puri, papadums, various picklets and chutneys, dhal, a yoghurt Lassi, and a spiced Indian milk tea. But one of the major differences that sets Shiraz apart from the usual curry restaurant, other than its décor, is its garnishing, presentation and sense of style. It is the only one of its type in New Zealand which puts it into a class of its own.

Shiraz,
470 Richmond Road, Grey Lynn,
Auckland.
Telephone 766-276. BYO.

ENTREES

Palak Puri — spinach sautéed in spices wrapped in wholemeal puri
Begam Zohra — lambs kidneys sautéed with herbs and spices and flamed in rich port wine sauce
Sultan's Dream — chicken pieces, tossed in brandy cream sauce, garnished with melon balls

MAIN COURSES

Tandoori Shehnaz — chicken marinated in spices, yoghurt and roasted
Murag Shahzahani — chicken cooked in sour cream, spices and almonds
Boti Amritsari — lamb curried with fruits, spices or traditional lamb curry
Boti Rani — lamb cooked in spices and spinach
Shikari Balochi — pork with mushrooms, herbs and spices in cream sauce
Machli Molee — fresh fish cooked in spicy coconut cream sauce
Persian Pilau — Pilau rice with orange peel and almonds
Navarita — seasonal vegetables cooked with herbs and spices

DESSERTS

Red Delicious Desire — baked apples stuffed with spiced fruit, flamed in brandy, with hazelnut ice cream
Bombay Surprise — assorted Indian sweets
Persian Paradise — Liqueur mousse

SAMOSAS

2 TABLESPOONS BUTTER
1 ONION, CHOPPED
2 CLOVES GARLIC, CRUSHED
2 GREEN CHILLIES, CHOPPED
2.5CM FRESH GINGER, PEELED AND SLICED
½ TEASPOON TURMERIC
½ TEASPOON HOT CHILLI POWDER
350G POTATOES, PEELED AND DICED
1 TEASPOON SALT
2 TEASPOONS GARAM MASALA
JUICE OF ½ LEMON
150G PEAS
COOKING OIL

Pastry:
2 CUPS FLOUR
½ TEASPOON SALT
2 TABLESPOONS BUTTER
⅓ CUP WATER

Melt the butter in a frying pan and add the onion, garlic, chillies and ginger and fry until the onions are golden brown. Stir in the spices, potatoes and salt. Cook until tender and then stir in the garam masala, lemon juice and peas. Cook for 5 minutes, stirring occasionally. Cool.
To make the pastry: Mix the pastry ingredients together. Knead until smooth and elastic.

Divide the dough into 15 portions. Roll each portion into a ball, flatten, then roll out into a 10cm diameter circle and cut each circle in half. Fill the cones with a little of the filling, dampen the top and bottom edges and pinch together. Deep fry the samosas in the cooking oil – a few at a time. Fry for 3-5 minutes, until crisp. Drain on kitchen towels. Serve with tomato sauce or chutney. **Serves 4-6.**

TANDOORI MURGI

1½ KG CHICKEN, SKINNED
1 TEASPOON HOT CHILLI POWDER
1 TEASPOON SALT
½ TEASPOON BLACK PEPPER
2 TABLESPOONS LEMON JUICE
4 TABLESPOONS MELTED BUTTER

Marinade:
3 TABLESPOONS YOGHURT
4 CLOVES GARLIC, PEELED
1 TABLESPOON RAISINS
2 DRIED RED CHILLIES

1 TEASPOON CUMIN SEEDS
½ TEASPOON RED FOOD COLOURING
5CM FRESH GINGER, PEELED

Make gashes in the thighs and breast of the chicken. Mix the chilli powder, salt, pepper, lemon juice and the melted butter. Rub the mixture over the chicken and set aside for 20 minutes.
To make the marinade: Purée all the ingredients except the food colouring in a blender. Transfer to a bowl and add the colouring. Spread most of mixture over the chicken, rubbing it into the gashes. Cover and chill in the refrigerator for 24 hours.

Place the chicken in a roasting pan with just enough water to cover the bottom and prevent the drippings burning. Spoon the remaining marinade over the chicken. Roast in a pre-heated 200°C oven for 1 hour, or until cooked. Serve with side salad. **Serves 4-6.**

TURKISH DELIGHT

½ PINT WATER
2 CUPS GRANULATED SUGAR
25G GELATINE
4 TABLESPOONS LEMON JUICE
½ LEVEL TEASPOON TARTARIC ACID
ICING SUGAR, SIEVED
RED FOOD COLOURING

Put most of the water and sugar into a heavy saucepan and stir until the sugar dissolves. Soften the gelatine in the remaining cold water and add to the sugar mixture, stirring until well blended. Add the lemon juice and acid and boil steadily, stirring once or twice, for 8-10 minutes. Remove from the heat and pour half into a tin dusted with icing sugar. Add a few drops of red colour to the other half and stir before pouring into the tin. Allow the mixture to cool and set then cut with a knife dipped in hot water. Add more icing sugar before serving. **Serves 4-6.**

Graeme Berry's kitchen in the tiny 110-year-old Stanmore Cottage on Whangaparaoa is a tribute to the art of efficient cooking. From a space, barely sufficient to toss a crêpe, he manages to single-handedly prepare at least 32 meals a night. To come across Stanmore Cottage, in its extremely isolated location near a peninsula beach is extraordinary — you would expect it to collapse at any time from insufficient patronage. But it is rarely quiet, with people regularly driving from Auckland to dine there, while in summer when the nearby beach resorts of Orewa and Red Beach are packed with holidaymakers, Graeme and his wife Anne nightly turn away 100 or more people.

Graeme originally did his apprenticeship in Rotorua and Queenstown in the big hotels, before moving to Queensland and then to Mt Hotham in Victoria to run a ski resort restaurant. The incredible business they did there gave them the capital to return to New Zealand and buy the large property on which the cottage stood. It took nearly two years to turn the old building into a small intimate restaurant with such modern touches as soft pink napkins, fine white china and silverware, but still evoking the past are old prints, aged wooden chairs, and lots of bare wood. You can look over beautiful lawns, gardens and trees, and in summer dine outside on the verandah surrounding the building. It's a setting that would be difficult to reproduce except in the country. In winter the Cottage's open fires warm the restaurant. Winter is also the time when Graeme prefers working in the confined kitchen which gets dreadfully hot in summer.

Stanmore Cottage,
201 Brightside Road, Stanmore Bay,
Whangaparaoa.
Telephone HBC-7074. BYO.

ENTREES

Venison Terrine
Cream of pumpkin soup
Lambs' fry with plum sauce
Snapper and ham crêpe
Scallops au gratin
Paw paw and smoked beef

MAIN COURSES

Snapper in phyllo
Salmon kebab
Chicken with camembert
Venison with red wine and mushroom sauce
Veal Jurrusianne
Rabbit Connoisseur
Sautéed king prawns

DESSERTS

Crème caramel
Apricot pavlova
Home-made coffee ice cream
Mexican chocolate cake

SALMON AND ORANGE KEBAB

1KG SALMON	Sauce:	KNOB OF BUTTER
2 ORANGES	ZEST OF 1 ORANGE, FINELY GRATED	LIQUID CREAM
	500ML BECHAMEL	WATERCRESS FOR GARNISH
	25ML GRAND MARNIER	

Fillet the salmon. Skin and cut it into uniform cubes. Alternate a salmon cube with orange segments cut from the two oranges. Set aside.

To make the sauce: Mix the orange zest with the bechamel, Grand Marnier, butter, and enough cream to give a desired consistency.

Lightly poach the salmon. Pour the sauce over the salmon and garnish with watercress. **Serves 6.**

STEAK MADAGASCAR

4 300G EYE FILLETS	1 PUNNET STRAWEBERRIES, HULLED AND HALVED	25ML DRAMBUIE
2 TABLESPOONS CRUSHED BLACK PEPPERCORNS		

Cook the fillet steak with the crushed black peppercorns in a heavy skillet. Remove the fillets from the skillet and keep warm. Place the strawberries in the skillet, add the Drambuie and allow the strawberries to heat but not overcook. Spoon the strawberries and liquid over the steak and serve immediately. **Serves 4.**

KAHLUA SOUFFLE

2 TEASPOONS CASTOR SUGAR	40G SUGAR	4 EGG WHITES
15G BUTTER	3 EGG YOLKS	PINCH OF SALT
30G FLOUR	25ML KAHLUA	WHIPPED CREAM AND KAHLUA FOR GARNISH
230ML MILK	1 TEASPOON VANILLA	

Prepare a 15cm soufflé dish by making a collar of greaseproof paper approximately a third higher than the soufflé dish. Lightly butter the base and sides and dust with 1 teaspoon of castor sugar. Set aside. Heat the 15g of butter and add the flour. Cook for 1 minute over a low heat. Add the milk and sugar and whisk to a smooth sauce. Remove from the heat, add the egg yolks, Kahlua and vanilla.

In a separate bowl, beat the egg whites and salt until they will stand in soft peaks. Gently fold the egg whites into the Kahlua mixture. Transfer to the soufflé dish and bake in a pre-heated 190°C oven for 25-30 minutes. Remove from the oven, dust with the remaining teaspoon of castor sugar and serve garnished with whipped cream and lots of Kahlua. **Serves 4.**

Russell and Judith Foster, with chef John Appelman, run this little Queenstown restaurant, one of the few in this tourist oriented town that actually has character. When Upstairs Downstairs first began a few years ago, it was in premises in Queenstown's Mall, now occupied by Westy's. But the transfer to its current, more spacious site, had already been made when Russell, Judith and John took over in mid-1982. It was the Fosters' first venture into a restaurant, though John had cooked in restaurants in Holland and France, and was a chef at Nelson's Capistrano when the opportunity arose to take over Upstairs Downstairs.

The name of the restaurant evokes memories of the famous television series 'Upstairs Downstairs' and its nostalgic portrayal of Edwardian England. Likewise, Upstairs Downstairs is an interesting restaurant for both the nostalgic feel it evokes and its dishes. It is set on two levels, with old oak tables, paintings of George V, antiques from old Canterbury and Southland homesteads, an ancient brass flame-thrower, a copper 'Wonder' tea kettle salvaged from a closed down railway station, old bottles and stone jars, and a piano that neither Russell, Judith nor John can play, but which the occasional customer tries. In this informal atmosphere John concentrates of preparing both French provincial and more traditional dishes but he has a great belief in the use of garlic in his creations. He buys fresh garlic from Gore and Oamaru by the kilo, using it in all but a few dishes. This explains the interesting but heady aromas that waft through the restaurant at preparation time.

Upstairs Downstairs,
66 Shotover Street, Queenstown.
Telephone 2203. BYO.

ENTREES

Scallop Bonne Femme
Garlic king prawns
Chicken livers in a sweet sherry sauce
Gypsy Kebab
Frog legs with ginger, pineapple and soy sauce
Spaghetti and mushrooms

MAIN COURSES

Chicken glazed with honey and lemon
Lamb noisettes pan fried with thyme and red wine
Fresh fish with tarragon and cream sauce
Seafood pancake
Venison marinated in red wine and herbs
Fillet steak with garlic, tomato and herbs

DESSERTS

Caramel mousse
Half camembert pan fried with an apricot sauce
Chocolate or home-made cheesecake
Almond parfait

FROG LEGS IN GINGER AND PINEAPPLE

SALT
2 PAIR FROG LEGS
1 DESSERTSPOON BUTTER
1 TABLESPOON CHOPPED GREEN GINGER
3 TABLESPOONS CHOPPED PINEAPPLE
2 TABLESPOONS SOY SAUCE
½ CLOVE GARLIC
3 TABLESPOONS WHITE WINE
FRESHLY CHOPPED PARSLEY
TOMATO FOR GARNISH

Salt the frog legs and lightly dip in flour before pan frying in the butter until cooked. This will not take long as the meat is quite tender. Keep the frog legs warm on a plate. To the frying pan add the green ginger, pineapple, soy sauce, garlic and white wine. Return the frog legs to the sauce and simmer until the legs are soft. Add the parsley last and serve on a bed of rice with a tomato as garnish. **Serves 2.**

BEEF MEDALLIONS

500G TENDERLOIN
SALT AND PEPPER
2 DESSERTSPOONS BUTTER
1 CLOVE GARLIC
JUICE OF ¼ LEMON
150ML CREAM
1 DESSERTSPOON CHOPPED PARSLEY

Cut the fillet into thin slices of approximately ½ cm and then tenderize with a wooden mallet. Season the medallions with salt and freshly ground black peppercorns and dip lightly in flour. Heat the butter in a frying pan until golden brown and place the medallions in the pan individually. Add the garlic and lemon juice and pan fry for 1 minute each side. Add the cream and parsley and then remove the meat, reducing the cream until it is the thickness of sauce. Pour this over the medallions which have been kept warm. Serve with sautéed potatoes and a green salad. **Serves 2.**

ALMOND PARFAIT
(home-made almond ice cream)

500ML CREAM
5 EGG YOLKS
1 EGG WHITE
50G SUGAR
1 CUP CHOPPED ALMONDS
1 LIQUEUR GLASS AMARETTO LIQUEUR

The cream should be stored in the fridge for 24 hours. Beat the cream until almost thick and place in the fridge. Put the eggs and sugar in a stainless steel bowl and place in a *bain-marie*, beating until lukewarm. Remove and continue beating until cool, and then add the cream by folding in. Add the chopped almonds and liqueur. Pour the mixture into a 2 litre container, seal and freeze. This can be served in slices, garnished with cream and chopped almonds.

Opposite: Brandy Cake (p. 179). The imagination can run riot with this magnificent brandy cake by Digby Law. If you want a predominantly brandy taste just add more brandy, or you can add as much whipped cream and cherry conserve as you like. Likewise you can use your favourite chocolate cake recipe with as much chocolate as you wish. *(Photograph by Max Thomson.)*

Double page: Chicken with rosemary and tomatoes (p. 171). This dish, prepared by Digby Law, features the use of whole, unpeeled cloves of garlic cooked with the chicken. But its secret is the addition of fresh tomatoes just before serving. It is a superb summer or winter dish, and is surprisingly easy to prepare. *(Photograph by Max Thomson.)*

Opposite: Fruit baskets (p. 63). This fruit basket, prepared by Wendy Lever or Auckland's Flamingos Restaurant, can contain whatever fruits you prefer. Kiwifruit though, because of its taste and effect, is definitely a must. The brandy snap baskets can be prepared well in advance and filled when it is time to serve dessert. *(Photograph by Max Thomson.)*

Six years ago, Vesuvio's was little more than a pizza parlour. During quiet moments Armando Cozzolino would go over the road to the Seamen's Mission to watch the nightly movie. Whenever a customer came in his wife would rush across, Armando would come back and prepare the meal, and then go back to the movie. Eventually Armando decided there was little enjoyment in cooking thousands of pizzas each year. After 12 years of being a cook on the Lloyd Triestino Shipping Line, and working in restaurants in Naples, he wanted to get back into working in an Italian restaurant. Out came a few walls, in came a myriad of decorating ideas, and Vesuvio's was transformed into a busy Italian restaurant with a reputation for fine Italian fare, including outstanding pasta and seafood dishes. To give it a warm and interesting interior, Armando asked an artist friend to run free with some ideas. The artist, Don Jack, has over the years covered the ceiling with clouds, built a little model aeroplane which is in a steep dive, added Leo and Cancer symbols, painted Italian countryside scenes on the walls, and added false windows. Along with the raffia covered Chianti bottles, red tablecloths, and Italian music, Vesuvio's has lots of character and on a busy night plenty of noise. Armando frequently wanders out from the kitchen to see how things are going, and more often than not he will usually know some of the diners. He also goes out of his way to find out how a particular person likes this or that dish to be prepared. He is definitely a cook with a heart who enjoys what he is doing, and it would be hard imagining Armando not in a restaurant environment. He does all the preparation himself, is forever tasting, testing, and pushing the staff to get the dish from the bench to the tables before it cools. It's a restaurant whose character embodies that of its owner — colourful.

Vesuvio's,
16 Swanson Street, Auckland.
Telephone 794-769. BYO.

ENTREES

Minestrone soup
Stuffed peppers
Tortellini stuffed with chicken
Mussels Vesuvio
Whitebait Partenopia
Calamari in a creamy sauce

MAIN COURSES

Scallops with a garlic, cream and brandy sauce
Pan fried snapper with mornay
Flounder Aurora stuffed with crabmeat
Eye fillet with a mushroom and garlic sauce
Spaghetti Marinara, lasagna or ravioli
Pollo D'Oro — chicken with camembert

DESSERTS

Zabaglione Marsala
Profiteroles with chocolate sauce
Cassata

STUFFED PEPPERS

4 GREEN PEPPERS
1 CUP OF RICE
1 TABLESPOON OLIVE OIL
1 SMALL ONION, DICED

50G MINCED MEAT
15G CHICKEN LIVERS
1 CUP OF MUSHROOMS
25G PEAS
3 TABLESPOONS PARMESAN CHEESE

2 EGGS
PEPPER, FRESHLY GROUND
2 CUPS FRESH TOMATO SAUCE, HEATED

Prepare the peppers (capsicums) by cutting the tops off just enough to allow you to scoop out the seeds so the peppers can be stuffed. Cook the rice in boiling water. Gently fry the onion in the olive oil. Add the meat and chicken livers. Cook for 2-3 minutes until the chicken livers have changed colour. Take the mixture off the heat and allow to cool before putting into a mixing bowl with the rice, mushrooms, peas, 1 tablespoon of parmesan cheese, eggs and pepper. Using your hands combine the mixture and then stuff the mixture into the peppers. Place in a medium oven until the peppers are crisp to well done. To serve, pour the heated tomato sauce over the peppers and top with the remaining parmesan cheese. **Serves 4.**

SPAGHETTI MARINARA

2 ONIONS, CHOPPED
3 TABLESPOONS OLIVE OIL
2 CLOVES GARLIC, SLICED
1 TEASPOON OREGANO
500G SNAPPER FILLETS

100G SQUID
2 TEASPOONS CHOPPED PARSLEY
½ CUP WINE
ANCHOVIES (OPTIONAL)
3 TOMATOES, SKINNED AND PULPED

SALT AND PEPPER
6-8 MUSSELS
100G PRAWNS
12 SCALLOPS
SPAGHETTI

In a frypan sauté the onions in the olive oil, adding the garlic and oregano. Chop the snapper and squid into bite-size pieces and add to the frypan, with the parsley and wine, cooking gently for 10 minutes. If you have a taste for anchovies these can now be added. Add the tomato pulp. Season with salt and pepper, and lastly add the mussels, prawns and scallops. Cook for 1 minute.

The amount of spaghetti needed depends on appetites, but it should be cooked in salted water for only about 7 minutes or until *al dente*. Drain the spaghetti, put on plates, and pour the seafood mixture over the top. **Serves 4-6.**

CASSATA

2 LITRES VANILLA ICE CREAM
500G MIXED GLAZED FRUIT

100G CHOCOLATE, BROKEN OR GRATED
½ CUP MANDARIN OR ORANGE LIQUEUR

1 TABLESPOON VODKA OR TIA MARIA

Melt the ice cream in a pot, and when soft add the rest of the ingredients, stirring thoroughly. You can experiment freely with the ingredients, altering to suit your taste. Pour the mixture into a container and put in the deep freeze. It will be ready to slice in 2 hours. You can also put a sponge in the bottom of the container and pour the soft mixture on top of this before freezing. **Serves 8.**

Westy's is without doubt one of the most unusual restaurants in Queenstown. The majority of restaurants in this tourist area opt for the French or international approach to food to cater for the holidaymakers. But Kevin Templeton and Ansley Evans have adopted a different stance with a menu incorporating both vegetarian and more conventional dishes. Kevin, a New Zealander, met Ansley, a Canadian, in Cairns during a working holiday. Ansley was washing dishes at the Travelodge while Kevin was working for an Italian family cooking in their pâtisserie. Eventually they travelled to Europe, England, back through Asia and on to Adelaide, before moving to Queenstown. Both were working at Queenstown's Travelodge, when Upstairs Downstairs shifted premises, where upon they took over the lease of the then derelict restaurant. They gave it a pole-house look to try to disguise the fact the restaurant was part of an arcade, with the kitchen on one side, and tables on the other. The addition of a pot belly stove, pine tables and chairs and various antiques gave it warmth and character.

The original idea was for a vegetarian restaurant but that only lasted as long as it took to realize that people were walking in, seeing that there was no meat dishes on the menu, and rushing off somewhere else. Their decision was to blend vegetarian dishes with more acceptable fare. Kevin still cooks his home-made kibbled rye loaf and creates interesting menus that change with the seasons. Fresh vegetables are brought in twice a week, whereas the majority of the town's restaurants order only once every two weeks. Because they both love cooking, they refuse to compromise by taking shortcuts with preparation and ingredients.

Westy's,
The Mall, Queenstown.
Telephone 609. BYO.

ENTREES

Tamblin Triangles – paper thin pastry filled with asparagus cream with home-made chutney
Jingha Molee – prawns in coconut milk served on rice
Whitebait Roulade – crumbed cold whitebait omelette on toast with applemint and cucumber sauce
Rumaki Chicken – skewered grilled chicken balls with sweet chilli sauce on rice

MAIN COURSES

Stilton Fillet – eye fillet with mushrooms in Stilton butter
Oriental Lamb – lamb hot pot with Asian spices and garlic bread sticks
Beef and Spinach Blintzes – with a rich tomato sauce
Pan Fried Cod – with sautéed potatoes and English lemon cheese
Avocado Marinara – prawns, mussels, scallops and sole on buttered pasta
Crêpes Marengo – crêpes with sautéed vegetables in a spicy sour cream sauce

DESSERTS

Carob honey velvet mousse with biscuit sticks
Raw apple pie with yoghurt, cream or cheese
Blueberry cake with sauce
Blackberry apple shortcake
Fresh ginger cheesecake

GRUYERE AND MUSHROOM PÂTÉ

Mushroom mixture:
450G MUSHROOMS, CHOPPED
⅓ CUP CHOPPED CELERY
⅓ CUP CHOPPED SHALLOTS
4 TABLESPOONS MELTED BUTTER
¼ CUP CHOPPED PARSLEY
2 EGGS, BEATEN
125G COTTAGE CHEESE, SIEVED
¾ CUP BREADCRUMBS
¼ TEASPOON CRUSHED BASIL
¼ TEASPOON CRUSHED OREGANO
¼ TEASPOON CRUSHED ROSEMARY
1 TEASPOON SALT
¼ TEASPOON CAYENNE PEPPER
½ TEASPOON GROUND BLACK PEPPER

Cheese sauce:
3 EGGS
1 CUP CREAM
1 TABLESPOON FLOUR
1 TABLESPOON BUTTER
2 CUPS GRATED GRUYERE

To make the mushroom mixture: Sauté the mushrooms, celery and shallots in butter until the juices run. Remove from heat. Add the remaining ingredients and blend to form a thick paste.
To make the cheese sauce: Blend the eggs, cream, flour and butter in a double boiler until thickened. Stir in the gruyere.

Line a loaf tin with foil. Put in a layer of mushroom mixture and pour a layer of cheese sauce over the mixture. Place in a roasting tin of water and bake at 170°C for 20 minutes or until set. Cool. **Serves 6-8.**

PORK AND PINEAPPLE LOG WITH TRIPOLI SAUCE

Pork mixture:
1KG PORK, MINCED
2 EGGS
1 CUP CHOPPED STEWED APPLES
1 ONION, MINCED
150ML CREAM
1 CUP CHOPPED PARSLEY
½ TEASPOON BASIL
½ TEASPOON MARJORAM
½ TEASPOON CRUSHED GARLIC
1 TEASPOON SALT
3 TEASPOONS PEPPER
WHOLEMEAL BREADCRUMBS

Filling:
2 CUPS CRUSHED PINEAPPLE
4 TOMATOES, PEELED AND DICED
1 TABLESPOON TOMATO PASTE
1 TABLESPOON CHOPPED SPRING ONIONS
CORNFLOUR

Pastry:
400G WHITE FLOUR
12 TABLESPOONS ICE-COLD WATER
1 TEASPOON SALT
BUTTER, CHOPPED

Tripoli Sauce:
3 TABLESPOONS OLIVE OIL
1 ONION, DICED
1 CUP SUGAR
¼ CUP CIDER VINEGAR
1 TEASPOON BLACK PEPPER
1½ TEASPOONS SALT
1 TEASPOON CRUSHED GARLIC
6 TOMATOES, PEELED AND DICED
2 TABLESPOONS TOMATO PASTE
1 CHILLI, CRUSHED
150ML CREAM

To make the pork mixture: Blend the ingredients together and work in enough breadcrumbs to make a rollable texture.
To make the filling: Bring the pineapple, tomatoes, tomato paste and spring onions together and thicken with cornflour and cold water. Cool.
To make the pastry: Blend together the flour, water and salt. Knead. Weigh to find out how much butter to add — butter should be ½ total weight. Roll out the dough, place the chopped butter in the middle and fold ⅓ towards you, ⅓ away from you, roll, refold and turn 90° to the right after each fold. Repeat six times.

On greaseproof paper or foil, roll the dough out into an oblong shape. Using ½ pork mixture make a flat sausage down the length of the pastry. Make a slight hollow down the centre. Fill the hollow with the pineapple filling. Flatten the remaining pork mixture and cover the filling. Lift the pastry up over the sides to meet at the top — to form an enclosed log. Glaze with egg white or water. Pinch the pastry. Prick the top, brush with egg and seal the ends. Sprinkle liberally with sesame seeds. Bake in a pre-heated 150°C oven for ¾ hour.
To make the Tripoli Sauce: Sauté the onions in the olive oil. Add the remaining ingredients except the cream. Sweat with the pan lid on until tender. Put through a blender. Stir in the cream. Pour the sauce over the log. **Serves 6-8.**

WHOLEMEAL HAZELNUT CRACKERS

½ CUP WARM WATER
1 TABLESPOON DRY YEAST
1½ CUPS WHOLEMEAL FLOUR
2 TEASPOONS NON-IODISED SALT
¼ CUP OIL
2 CUPS CHOPPED HAZELNUTS

Dissolve the yeast in the warm water and leave for 15 minutes. Mix the flour, salt, and oil. Add the yeast. Knead the dough in a bowl and leave to double in size.

Flour a baking tray. Turn out the dough onto the tray. Using a rolling pin, roll out to an even thickness (about 2mm thick). Sprinkle with chopped nuts and roll lightly to partially submerge the nuts. Leave to rise. Put into a pre-heated 150°C oven for 20 minutes. Keep a close eye on them, as they burn easily. Cool on racks.

FRESH GINGER CHEESECAKE

1 CUP MELTED BUTTER
1 PACKET DIGESTIVE BISCUITS, CRUSHED
¼ CUP COCONUT
¼ CUP WHOLEMEAL FLOUR
400G CREAM CHEESE
110G SUGAR
2 EGGS
1 TABLESPOON LEMON JUICE
300G SOUR CREAM
3 TABLESPOONS CREAM
5 TABLESPOONS RAW SUGAR
1 TABLESPOON FRESHLY GRATED GINGER
3 TABLESPOONS CRYSTALLIZED GINGER
WHIPPED CREAM AND TOASTED COCONUT FOR GARNISH

Line a springform pan with paper, allowing a 4cm collar for the cheesecake to rise. Make the crust by mixing the butter, crushed biscuits, coconut and flour. Press the crust into the base of the tin, coming up 5cm around the sides.

Beat together the cream cheese, sugar, eggs and lemon juice. When the mixture is thick and creamy pour it into the tin and cook in a pre-heated 150°C oven for 25 minutes.

Beat together the sour cream, cream, raw sugar and grated ginger, until smooth. Remove the cake from the oven and gently pour the sour cream mixture over the cake — starting at the rim to prevent the middle sinking. Sprinkle the crystallized ginger over the top. Return to the oven for 20 minutes. Leave the cake to cool — be careful when removing the paper collar.

Garnish with whipped cream and toasted coconut. **Serves 6-8.**

Digby Law

The abundance, variety and quality of fresh meat and produce in New Zealand is amongst the best in the world. Indeed our market gardens are probably only equalled by those in California. We are told we eat too much meat and not enough fibre; we are told we eat too much altogether. Whether such allegations are correct or not, we do eat extremely well with a proliferation of imaginative restaurants and a multitude of excellent home cooks.

Over the past 10 years the standard of our cuisine has gone from a monotonous roast meat and boiled vegetables, followed by stodgy puddings, to the gastronomic delights evolved by following the cuisines of other countries. In the past few years this has gone a step further as we increasingly adapt and create dishes using foods so readily available here: delightful seasonal produce, varieties of fish and shellfish, new and different types of meat cuts, imported Pacific Island tropical fruit, and foods that are more or less unique and abundant in New Zealand. Silver beet, which we almost take for granted, is considered a luxury in some countries; as are asparagus, avocados and globe artichokes. Our kumara is the most succulent and waxiest of the world's sweet potatoes. Pumpkin, which we use so well, is virtually shunned elsewhere. New Zealand kiwifruit, apples, tamarillos, boysenberries, strawberries and pears are among the fruits shipped all over the world. New fruits are constantly appearing – pepinos, babacos and prince melons to name a few. Our lamb is perfection, as is our beef. Fish is abundant and of superb quality. So too are our shellfish; crayfish, paua, tua tua and toheroa are all unique to our shores. Game is plentiful and venison, duck and pheasant are now readily available.

It is this abundance of such exciting food which provides a firm basis for imaginative cooking in this country.

Digby Law.

Entrées and Soups

The three course dinner is very much the standard style of New Zealanders' eating habits. Once it would have been a seafood cocktail, a roast and vegetables, followed by a heavy pudding. Today, everything goes and the entrée or first course is more often than not particularly imaginative. In America, the entrée refers to the main course while the first course is usually known as the appetizer. Although we have appropriated the word from the French — meaning 'entry' or 'coming in' — in France, the term usually refers to the third course, and it precedes the roast but follows the fish course. In France it is usually a made-up dish served with a sauce. Therefore, although our use of the term entrée is more or less correct, we variously label it: starter, appetizer, hors d'oeuvres, or first course.

Any entrée should be fairly light so that white meats (chicken or fish), shellfish, vegetables, salads, offal, pâtés, terrines and mousses are all ideal. Slightly larger portions of an entrée can be served as a main course and entrée dishes make excellent lunch fare.

Soups make admirable entrées. They can usually be prepared well ahead and so save the cook at least some last minute fuss. Hot soups are ideal in the winter as are chilled soups in summer, though, of course, this is not necessarily the rule. An entrée soup should be light, though small quantities of a heavy soup can be served. It is a good idea to serve soup at the table from a tureen, ladling hot soups into hot bowls and chilled soups into chilled bowls.

CREAMY ROE PATE

125G SMOKED ROE

125G CREAM CHEESE

1 SMALL ONION, FINELY GRATED
JUICE OF ½ LEMON

So simple yet so delicious when served with croûtons or crusty French bread and black olives as a dinner party starter.

Remove the skin from the roe and put the roe in a basin, adding the cream cheese and onion. Mix to a creamy consistency, gradually adding the lemon juice. Alternatively, it can all be mixed in a food processor.

Pile the pâté into a small bowl and refrigerate until ready to serve. **Serves 4.**

TERRINE OF HAM, VEAL AND PORK

500G COOKED HAM
500G RAW PORK
500G RAW VEAL
1 CLOVE GARLIC, FINELY CHOPPED
6 JUNIPER BERRIES, CRUSHED
THYME AND MARJORAM
SALT AND FRESHLY GROUND BLACK PEPPER
½ TEASPOON MACE
½ CUP DRY WHITE WINE
2 TABLESPOONS BRANDY
150G BACON
BAY LEAVES

A terrine is a coarse type of pâté, highly revered for its flavour. Its name is derived from the dish in which it is cooked. This is a superb version of the 'country' terrine.

In a mincer or food processor, mince the ham, pork and veal. Mix the meats well, adding the garlic, juniper berries, a little fresh thyme, a little marjoram, mace, plenty of pepper and very little salt — the ham is probably very salty. Transfer the mixture to a bowl, pour the wine and brandy over the mixture. Stand for several hours.

Cover the bottom of a large, fairly shallow terrine with little strips of bacon. Add the meat mixture, cover with more strips of bacon and put several bay leaves in the centre.

Cover the terrine and put in a baking dish half-filled with hot water. Bake in a slow oven for 2½-3 hours. Leave to cool before serving with toast.

CHICKEN LIVER AND BACON PATE

50G BUTTER
4-6 RINDLESS RASHERS BACON, COARSELY CHOPPED
1 LARGE ONION, CHOPPED
2 CLOVES GARLIC, CHOPPED
500G CHICKEN LIVERS
¼ CUP DARK RUM
½ CUP SHERRY
1 CUP CREAM
½ CUP FINELY CHOPPED PARSLEY
SALT AND FRESHLY GROUND PEPPER

A smooth pâté with a delicious bacon taste. Make sure that the bacon is a good smokey one, and to ensure that the pâté is really smooth purée it in a blender rather than the food processor.

In a frying pan, lightly fry the bacon in butter. Add the onion, the garlic and chicken livers. Cook for 10 minutes, stirring often, until the chicken livers are cooked through. Add the rum and sherry. Purée in batches in the blender. Pour the purée into a bowl, adding the cream and parsley. Add salt and pepper to taste. Mix well. Pour into pâté pots, cover and refrigerate a few days before using. This pâté also freezes well.

BLUE CHEESE MOUSSE

6 EGG YOLKS
2 CUPS CREAM
1½ TABLESPOONS GELATINE
300G BLUE VEIN CHEESE
GREEN FOOD COLOURING
3 EGG WHITES
SALAD VEGETABLES FOR GARNISH

Light, creamy and tangy — this dish is ideal when served with plain crackers and bread either with drinks or as a first course.

Beat the egg yolks with ½ cup cream in a saucepan over a low heat until the mixture is creamy. Soften the gelatine in 4 tablespoons of cold water, dissolve over hot water and add to egg yolks.

Force the blue vein cheese — at room temperature — through a sieve and add to the gelatine mixture along with 3 drops of green food colouring. (Blue food colouring looks distasteful). Cool.

Fold in 1½ cups cream, whipped, then fold in the egg whites, stiffly beaten. Pour into an oiled mould and chill until well set.

When ready to serve, turn the mousse out onto a bed of lettuce and garnish with salad vegetables.

GARLIC SCALLOPS

500G FRESH SCALLOPS	4 TABLESPOONS BUTTER	⅓ CUP FINELY CHOPPED PARSLEY
FLOUR	2-3 CLOVES GARLIC	1 LEMON
2 TABLESPOONS OIL	SALT AND PEPPER	

Some say garlic is far too strong for such a delicately flavoured seafood. In fact, the addition of garlic actually enhances the flavour of the scallops. Steamed mussels are equally delectable when treated like this.

Dry the scallops and roll them in flour. Heat the oil and butter in a frying pan; add the scallops. Fry the scallops quickly, a few minutes each side, until they are white throughout. Add the finely chopped garlic and mix in well. Add salt and pepper to taste.

Just before serving add the parsley, tossing the scallops until they are well coated in parsley. Serve with the juices poured over the scallops and with lemon wedge. **Serves 4 as an entrée or 2 as a main course.**

SWEET AND SOUR FISH

	Sweet and sour sauce:	
COOKING OIL		⅔ CUP VINEGAR
1 KG FISH FILLET OR PIECES	3 TABLESPOONS OIL	1⅓ CUP WATER
3 TABLESPOONS CORNFLOUR	1 CUP SUGAR	2 CUPS FINELY CHOPPED ONION
3 TABLESPOONS WATER	4 TABLESPOONS CORNFLOUR	1 TABLESPOON FINELY CHOPPED FRESH GINGER
	4 TABLESPOONS SOY SAUCE	

The sweet and sour sauce can also be used for meats or poultry. Ideal as an entrée or as a main course.

Heat until very hot, enough cooking oil for deep frying. Dredge the fish in a mixture of the cornflour and water. Fry the fish until just cooked on both sides. Drain well.

To make the sauce: In a saucepan mix together the oil, sugar, cornflour, soy sauce, vinegar and water. Bring to the boil. Add the onion and ginger. Boil for 1 minute; pour over the fish and serve hot. The sauce may be made in advance and re-heated. **Serves 6 as a main course or 8-10 as an entrée.**

BRAINS TERRAPIN

2 SHEEP'S BRAINS	SALT AND CAYENNE PEPPER	1 EGG
1 TABLESPOON BUTTER	1 CUP CREAM	1 TABLESPOON DRY SHERRY
1 TABLESPOON FLOUR	75G MUSHROOMS	CHOPPED PARSLEY FOR GARNISH

This dish is so good that it should cause those opposed to this delicious food to re-consider their aversion.

Parboil brains in salted water for about 20 minutes, or until firm and tender. Remove membranes and blanch in cold water. Cut into desired cubes or slices.

In a saucepan melt the and stir in the flour, ½ teaspoon salt and a dash of cayenne pepper. Slowly stir in the cream, and still stirring heat until the sauce thickens.

Slice the mushrooms and gently fry in a little butter until they are just limp. Keep warm.

Into the cream sauce stir a well-beaten egg and remove from heat after about a minute. Add the sherry, mushrooms and the prepared brains and reheat for a few seconds. Serve with toast points and garnish with chopped parsley. **Serves 4-6.**

EGGS WITH HAM AND MUSHROOMS

4 SLICES COOKED HAM
100G MUSHROOMS
4 EGGS
8 TABLESPOONS CREAM
GRATED PARMESAN CHEESE
SALT AND FRESHLY GROUND PEPPER
CHOPPED PARSLEY FOR GARNISH

Grease four individual ovenproof dishes. Line each with a slice of ham. Fry the mushrooms in a little butter until soft. Spread the mushrooms over the ham and break an egg into each dish. Top each with 2 tablespoons cream and liberally sprinkle with grated parmesan cheese and season with salt and pepper.

Bake in a moderate oven for 10 minutes, or until the eggs are just firm. Sprinkle each dish with chopped parsley and serve immediately. **Serves 4.**

KIDNEYS WITH MUSHROOMS AND FENNEL

4 TABLESPOONS BUTTER
1 CLOVE GARLIC, FINELY SLICED
1 ONION, FINELY CHOPPED
6 SHEEP'S KIDNEYS
1 TABLESPOON FLOUR
1 TEASPOON PAPRIKA
1 CUP BEEF STOCK
200G MUSHROOMS, SLICED
2 TEASPOONS FENNEL SEEDS
SALT AND PEPPER

The exciting flavour of fennel makes this dish something quite different. Serve it on toast or rice; as a light dinner, first course or lunch dish.

Melt the butter in a frying pan, add the garlic and onion and cook until soft. Skin the kidneys, slice them into quarters lengthwise and remove their cores. Add the kidneys to the pan and cook them, turning often.

Stir in the flour, then add the paprika, beef stock, mushrooms and fennel seeds. Stir until the sauce is thickened and then season with salt and pepper. Cover and gently simmer for a few minutes. **Serves 4.**

MARINATED RAW FISH WITH COCONUT CREAM

500G SKINNED AND BONED SNAPPER
  OR TERAKIHI PER PERSON
LEMON JUICE
Cream:
1 CUP DESSICATED COCONUT
1 CUP MILK
2-3 SPRING ONIONS, FINELY CHOPPED
SALT AND FRESHLY GROUND PEPPER
TOMATO, CUCUMBER OR PARSLEY
  FOR GARNISH

Raw fish recipes abound around the world. Here is a New Zealand recipe. Any white fish can be used but snapper and terakihi are particularly good.

Cut the fish into small pieces; place it in a bowl and cover with freshly squeezed lemon juice. Refrigerate for at least 3 hours — or all day if you wish. By this time the fish will have turned white.
To make coconut cream: Heat to almost boiling the coconut and milk. Let stand for about 10 minutes then strain through muslin.

Add the spring onion — including the green part — to the coconut cream, and add some salt and pepper to taste. Drain off most of the unabsorbed lemon juice and mix the fish with the coconut cream. Chill well and serve either in lettuce cups or squat glasses. Serve as an entrée with thinly sliced tomato and cucumber or parsley. **Serves 6-8.**

WHITEBAIT FRITTERS

2 CUPS WHITEBAIT	1 TEASPOON BAKING POWDER	2 EGGS, SEPARATED
1 CUP FLOUR	SALT AND WHITE PEPPER	½ CUP MILK
		COOKING OIL

If you have a plentiful supply of whitebait an excellent way to present them is to lightly flour them and quickly fry in butter. Another way is to combine masses of whitebait with a French omelette mixture and make into fritters. The following recipe is both economical and tasty.

Wash and drain the whitebait. In a bowl mix the flour with the baking powder and add some salt and pepper. Stir in the whitebait. Beat the egg yolks with the milk and stir into the whitebait mixture. Beat the egg whites until stiff and fold them in.

Drop the mixture by the spoonful into hot oil and fry until golden brown on both sides. Serve hot with lemon wedges or tartare sauce. **Serves 6.**

CHUNKY MUSTARD

125G YELLOW MUSTARD SEED	¼ CUP OLIVE OIL	4 TEASPOONS SALT
125G BLACK MUSTARD SEED	1 CUP RED WINE	1 TEASPOON DRIED BASIL
4 TABLESPOONS WHOLE BLACK PEPPERCORNS	1 CUP WINE VINEGAR	½ TEASPOON DRIED OREGANUM

This mustard goes well with beef, ham or cheese and mellows lightly with age. Instead of red wine, white wine or vermouth can be used. Curry powder can also be added, or the herbs varied.

In the blender combine both mustard seeds and blend for ½ minute or until the seeds are well chopped. Pour into a bowl.

In the blender blend the peppercorns until they resemble cracked pepper. Add to the mustard.

Add the remaining ingredients. Stir well — it should be quite sloppy. Let stand over night to thicken. If it is too thick add more olive oil. Pack into small jars or crocks with lids. Store in a cool cupboard.

BREAD AND BUTTER PICKLES

8 LARGE CUCUMBERS, UNPEELED	9 CUPS COLD WATER	1 TEASPOON YELLOW MUSTARD SEED
3 LARGE ONIONS	1.8 LITRES MALT VINEGAR	
4 LARGE GREEN PEPPERS	1.5 KG WHITE SUGAR	1 TEASPOON CELERY SEED
1 CUP SALT	1 TABLESPOON TUMERIC	

Wash and slice the cucumbers, onions and green peppers; combine in a bowl. Sprinkle the salt over the vegetables and add the cold water. Let stand for 3 hours, then drain thoroughly without rinsing.

In a large saucepan combine the remaining ingredients. Heat to boiling then add the vegetables. Bring to the boiling point again but do not boil.

Pack the vegetables in sterilized jars and seal by the overflow method. Chill before serving. Serve on thin slices of buttered brown bread with pre-dinner drinks. **Yields about 6 litres.**

LEMON AND RAISIN CHUTNEY

4 MEDIUM ONIONS
5 LARGE LEMONS
25G SALT
600ML CIDER VINEGAR
1 TEASPOON GROUND ALLSPICE
25G MUSTARD SEED
500G SUGAR
125G SEEDLESS RAISINS

Peel and slice the onions. Cut the lemons into small pieces – discarding the pips. Combine the onions and lemons in a bowl, sprinkle with salt and let stand for 12 hours.

Combine all the ingredients in a saucepan and bring to the boil. Simmer until tender – about 45 minutes. Spoon the chutney into sterilized jars and seal when cool.

CHILLED CREAM OF HERB SOUP

3 CUPS CHICKEN STOCK
¼ CUP FINELY CHOPPED FRESH PARSLEY
⅓ CUP FINELY CHOPPED FRESH BASIL
⅓ CUP SNIPPED FRESH CHIVES OR SPRING ONION TOPS
2 TABLESPOONS FINELY CHOPPED FRESH MINT
2 EGG YOLKS
300ML CREAM
SALT AND WHITE PEPPER
FINELY CHOPPED FRESH HERBS FOR GARNISH

An elegant creamy soup perfect in the summer when fresh herbs are available. It is best made with home-made chicken stock rather than the commercial variety.

In a saucepan bring the chicken stock to the boil, and add the parsley, basil, chives and mint. Cover and simmer for 20 minutes.

In a bowl beat the egg yolks with the cream. Add 1 cup of the hot stock in a stream, whisking, and return the mixture to the saucepan, whisking, then slowly heat the soup for about 5 minutes, until it has thickened slightly but not boiled. Add salt and white pepper to taste. Allow the soup to cool, then chill well.

Check the seasoning, ladle the soup into chilled dishes, and sprinkle with finely chopped fresh herbs. **Serves 4-6.**

HAMBURGER SOUP

500G MINCED BEEF
1 ONION, FINELY CHOPPED
1 CLOVE GARLIC, CRUSHED
COOKING OIL
1 MEDIUM CARROT, FINELY CHOPPED
1 LARGE STALK CELERY, FINELY CHOPPED
3 TOMATOES, PEELED AND CHOPPED
CHILLI PASTE
OREGANUM AND MAJORAM
2 CUPS BEEF STOCK
SALT AND FRESHLY GROUND PEPPER
SOUR CREAM, HOME-MADE TOMATO SAUCE AND CHOPPED PARSLEY FOR GARNISH

A robust winter soup using the ingredients of a hamburger – hence the name. Good minced beef is essential; minced gristle and fat just won't do.

In a saucepan gently fry the beef, onion and garlic in some oil, until the mince is separated and browned. Add the carrot, celery and tomatoes to the saucepan. Add a little chilli paste, some oreganum, majoram and the beef stock. Cover and simmer for about 1 hour. Add salt and pepper to taste and some more beef stock if the soup is too thick.

Serve with sour cream or a swirl of home-made tomato sauce and garnish with chopped parsley. Accompany by toasted split hamburger buns. **Serves 6.**

SHELLFISH CHOWDER

100G GREEN STREAKY BACON
1 LARGE ONION, CHOPPED
1 STALK CELERY, CHOPPED
1 GREEN PEPPER, CORED, SEEDED AND CUBED
2 MEDIUM POTATOES, PEELED AND CUBED
1 BAY LEAF
2 CUPS WATER
SALT AND WHITE PEPPER
5 TABLESPOONS FLOUR
2½ CUPS MILK
400G SELECTED CHOPPED SHELLFISH
CHOPPED PARSLEY FOR GARNISH

A richly flavoured soup in which either tuatua, cultivated mussels, pipis, oysters or toheroa can be used.

Remove the rind from the bacon and dice. Gently fry the bacon in a dry saucepan until it starts to brown. Add the onion and the celery and cook until golden. Add the green pepper, potatoes, bay leaf, water and salt and pepper to taste. Bring to the boil and simmer until the potatoes are just tender.

Mix the flour with ½ cup of milk and stir into the chowder. Stir until boiling. Add the remaining milk and the shellfish. Simmer for 4-5 minutes. Serve garnished with chopped parsley. **Serves 4-6.**

COLD KIWIFRUIT AND WINE SOUP

2½ CUPS PEELED AND DICED KIWIFRUIT
2 CUPS SAUTERNE
1 CUP WATER
¼ CUP SUGAR
SALT
1 TABLESPOON CORNFLOUR
WHIPPED CREAM FOR GARNISH

As the first course of a meal Kiwifruit Soup makes a welcome change from the usual kiwifruit, melon and ginger cocktail.

In a saucepan combine the kiwifruit, 1 cup sauterne, water, sugar and a dash of salt. Bring to the boil and cook over a medium heat for 5 minutes.

Dissolve the cornflour in ¼ cup sauterne. Stir the mixture into the soup and boil for 1 minute, stirring constantly. Remove from heat and stir in the remaining sauterne.

Purée half the soup in a blender. Stir the purée into the remaining soup. Chill well and serve garnished with whipped cream. **Serves 4-6.**

Vegetables and Salads

Timing is the important thing about cooked vegetables. To get them to the table in perfectly cooked condition is no mean feat. Gone are the days when we presented soggy cauliflower or beans boiled to an unrecognizable greyness. Today, vegetables are offered 'crisp-tender' or 'barely cooked'. Select your vegetables carefully — there are over 40 varieties to choose from — and whenever possible use vegetables that are in season, for economy as well as flavour. If you are offering a selection of vegetables make sure they are of differing colours. A selection of white, green and orange or yellow vegetables looks far better than merely three white or green vegetables. Nor is it always necessary to offer potatoes. If you require a starchy food, kumara, pumpkin, rice or noodles are all suitable alternatives.

When entertaining it is often easier to offer a salad. They can be prepared well in advance and dressed when necessary, thus eliminating last minute cooking fuss. In America, the salad is served before the main course; in France, sometimes before but usually afterwards. A salad served after the main course is refreshing to the palate and can be an extra course of the dinner. If the salad is served with the main course, offer individual salad bowls or plates. Putting a chilled salad on a hot dinner plate will only ruin the salad. Vegetables and salads also make excellent entrées.

There are a number of recipes for French dressing, but the one I prefer uses 3 parts olive oil to 1 part wine vinegar, cider vinegar or lemon juice. Place the dressing in a screw-top jar and season well with salt and freshly ground black pepper. Shake well and use as desired. The dressing will keep almost indefinitely in the refrigerator. To this can be added one or two of the following flavours: crushed garlic, a little mustard powder or prepared mustard, dried herbs (fresh herbs should be added directly to the the salad), tomato paste or concentrate, chopped anchovies, horse radish, to name a few.

RAW VEGETABLE PLATTER WITH AVOCADO CREAM

RADISHES, CAULIFLOWER, CELERY CUCUMBER, TOMATOES, BUTTON MUSHROOMS, CARROTS, GREEN BEANS, GREEN OR RED PEPPERS, ETC.

Avocado Cream:
1 LARGE AVOCADO, PEELED, PITTED AND CUBED
⅓ CUP SOUR CREAM
1 TABLESPOON MAYONNAISE
1 TABLESPOON LEMON JUICE
1 TEASPOON GRATED ONION
1 CLOVE GARLIC, CHOPPED
SALT AND FRESHLY GROUND PEPPER

Raw vegetables not only look good but also taste good, especially if accompanied with this delightfully smooth avocado cream and served at a party or as a first course.

On a large platter arrange an array of raw salad vegetables cut into bite-size pieces. In the centre, place a bowl of Avocado Cream and allow everyone to dip each vegetable into the cream.

To make the cream: In a blender purée the avocado, sour cream, mayonnaise, lemon juice, onion, garlic and salt and pepper to taste. Transfer the cream to a serving bowl. If the Avocado Cream is not to be eaten immediately keep it in a refrigerator with the avocado seed placed in the cream to prevent discolouring.

RAW PUMPKIN SALAD

| IRON-BARK PUMPKIN | SALT | FRENCH DRESSING |

The secret of this salad is to grate the pumpkin in long coarse shreds. The food processor won't do this so you'll have to grate the pumpkin by hand.

Peel and seed the pumpkin and grate on a coarse grater to get longish shreds. Sprinkle some salt over it, cover with cold water and leave overnight. This removes the sliminess and softens the pumpkin.

Drain it well. Make up some french dressing, using lemon juice instead of vinegar. Toss it well and serve. An interesting variation is to add some mung bean sprouts.

APPLE, CELERY AND WALNUT SALAD

2 EATING APPLES
2 SWEET ORANGES
2 CUPS DICED CELERY
50G WALNUT HALVES
PAPRIKA FOR GARNISH

Whipped cream dressing:
1 CUP CREAM
1 TABLESPOON SUGAR
1 TABLESPOON LEMON JUICE

1 TEASPOON DRY MUSTARD
SALT AND FRESHLY GROUND BLACK PEPPER

A crisp and refreshing combination of fruit, vegetables and nuts, with a delightfully different dressing. Ideal as an entrée salad or when accompanying all meats.

Chop the apples with the skin on. Peel and chop the oranges and mix together with the celery and walnut halves. Pour over the whipped cream dressing and chill until ready to serve. Either serve in a pottery or glass salad bowl or in individual lettuce cups. Garnish with paprika. **Serves 6-8.**
To make dressing: Mix together the ingredients for whipped cream dressing and beat until thick.

MUSHROOM AND BEANSPROUT SALAD

FRESH MUSHROOMS
LEMON JUICE

BEANSPROUTS
FRESHLY GRATED ROOT GINGER

FRENCH DRESSING

A good example of the importance of textures in food, especially in salads. The smoothness of the mushrooms combines admirably with the crunchy beansprouts.

Slice mushrooms and marinade them in lemon or lime juice for several hours.

Toss gently with plenty of beansprouts and some freshly grated root ginger, and dress with a peppery French dressing.

SILVER BEET SALAD
with bacon, almonds and cream cheese

1 BUNCH FRESH SILVER BEET
3 RASHERS BACON
50G UNBLANCHED ALMONDS
125G CREAM CHEESE

Salad dressing:
⅔ CUP OLIVE OIL
¼ CUP WHITE VINEGAR
1 TEASPOON FINELY CHOPPED TARRAGON

2 CLOVES GARLIC, CRUSHED
1 TEASPOON SALT
¼ TEASPOON BLACK PEPPER
1 TABLESPOON BACON FAT

This salad can be used either as an entrée or as an accompaniment to any rich main course. Make sure the silver beet is very fresh.

Wash the silver beet. Remove the white stalks and break the green leaves into salad-sized pieces. Drain well and place in a large salad bowl.

Fry the bacon until crisp. Remove from the fat and crumble it. Reserve 1 tablespoon bacon fat for salad dressing. In the remaining fat, fry the almonds taking care not to burn them. Set the almonds aside with the bacon.
To make the dressing: In a screwtop jar combine the dressing ingredients and shake well.

Just before serving, toss the silver beet carefully in the dressing. Strew with the bacon, almonds and the cream cheese, cut into small pieces. **Serves 8.**

GREEN AND WHITE SALAD

| SALAD VEGETABLES | BASIL | FRENCH DRESSING |
| | OREGANUM | |

The idea of this salad is that all the vegetables are cut into bite-sized pieces. Everything is chunky and the salad colours are green and white.

In a salad bowl combine chunks of cucumber, green pepper, slices of celery, courgette, some coarsely chopped bulb fennel, cauliflower and cabbage.

Add plenty of basil and some oreganum. Dress with a garlic flavoured french dressing.

PICKLED RED PEPPERS

1 CUP WHITE VINEGAR	2 TEASPOONS SALT	14 RIPE, RED SWEET PEPPERS
2 CUPS WATER	1 TEASPOON PICKLING SPICE,	CINNAMON STICK
1 CUP WHITE SUGAR	LESS CLOVES AND ONLY 1 CHILLI	

These can be served as an hors-d'oeuvre, or added to salads, sandwiches and filled rolls, or used as a garnish. By themselves they make an excellent salad.

In a large saucepan combine the white vinegar, water, sugar, salt and pickling spice. Bring to the boil and boil for 5 minutes.

Wash, core and remove the seeds from the peppers. Slice into 4 lengthways. Add the peppers to the syrup and simmer for ½ minute. Pack into sterilized jars. Add a piece of cinnamon stick to each jar and cover to overflowing with syrup. Seal. They are ready for use in about 3 weeks.

WHIPPED KUMARA, APPLE AND RAISINS

2KG KUMARA	½ CUP MELTED BUTTER	½ TEASPOON FRESHLY GRATED NUTMEG
2½ CUPS APPLE PULP	¼ CUP MOLASSES	½ TEASPOON FINELY GRATED ORANGE RIND
1 CUP MILK	3 EGGS, BEATEN	
⅓ CUP BROWN SUGAR	½ TEASPOON GROUND CINNAMON	⅔ CUP SEEDLESS RAISINS

A wonderful dinner party vegetable dish to accompany any meat — especially lamb, chicken or turkey.

Peel the kumara and cook in boiling water until tender. Drain and mash well. Add the apple pulp and mix well. Gradually add the milk, beating until smooth. Stir in the brown sugar, butter, molasses, eggs, cinnamon, nutmeg and orange rind. Beat until thoroughly mixed. Stir in the raisins.

Pour the mixture into a greased, large casserole and bake uncovered for 1 hour in a 160°C oven. **Serves 10-12.**

VEGETABLE CASSEROLE

500G BROCCOLI	2 EGGPLANT	1 LARGE CAN TOMATO PUREE
2 LARGE ONIONS	750G COURGETTES	3 CUPS GRATED TASTY CHEESE
750G KUMARA	4 TABLESPOONS BUTTER	SALT AND PEPPER

Delicious as a vegetarian dish or as a meat accompaniment. Whichever way you use it, the vegetables can be varied, depending on what is in season or what is available.

Cut the broccoli into flowerets. Peel and slice the onions and kumara. Cube the unpeeled eggplant and slice the courgettes.

Put 1 tablespoon butter in the bottom of a casserole and layer a third of the vegetables on top. Pour over a third of the tomato purée, then sprinkle with 1 cup cheese and some salt and pepper. Repeat twice, finishing with cheese. Dot with 3 tablespoons butter.

Cover and cook in 210°C oven for 2 hours or until the vegetables are tender. If the casserole dries out add a few tablespoons water. Serve hot or cold.

Another excellent vegetable combination includes cauliflower, onion, tomatoes, mushrooms and potatoes. **Serves 6.**

Main Courses

The main course should be the main feature of the meal. However, more often than not the first course or dessert will attract the most attention. It's all a matter of luck but there is also a certain amount of good planning involved. Like the other dishes the main dish should be in the style of the rest of the meal. Never repeat the main ingredients in any of the courses and if the main course is rich, make sure that the accompanying vegetables or salad are simple and not doused in heavy sauces.

Although a dinner is usually planned around the main course there are always exceptions. For instance, you may have acquired some avocados you wish to present as the entrée. Having determined the method of presentation, you select a main course that you feel will be compatible with the first course.

Keep your menu interesting, don't feel it has to be overly elaborate to impress — simple food can be most impressive. And forget about out-doing dinners thrown previously by your guests. That sort of thing went out ages ago. Remember that as well as taste, colour and texture in food is also important. Present the food with style, whether it's silver service and fine china or merely pottery and stainless steel around the fire or at the picnic table. Always serve a hot main course on heated plates.

PEANUT CHICKEN

50G BUTTER
6 LARGE PORTIONS CHICKEN
5 TABLESPOONS CREAM
2 TABLESPOONS MILK
2 TABLESPOONS PEANUT BUTTER
3 TABLESPOONS FLOUR
SALT AND PEPPER

Chicken has so little flavour these days that it needs something like the tang of peanuts to bring it out of itself. This dish is excellent served with baked kumara or baked potatoes and a green vegetable or salad.

Melt the butter in a baking dish. Wash and dry the chicken portions. Slowly mix the cream and milk with the peanut butter to make a smooth paste. Roll each chicken portion in the peanut butter mixture, spreading it on where necessary. Mix the flour with salt and pepper and coat the chicken with it.

Place the chicken in the baking dish, skin side up, and cook in 200°C oven for 40-50 minutes or until the chicken is tender and the coating crisp. **Serves 6.**

CHICKEN WINGS WITH THIN SOY SAUCE

10 CHICKEN WINGS
CHOPPED SPRING ONIONS
  FOR GARNISH

Thin soy sauce:
½ TABLESPOON PEANUT OR
  MAIZE OIL
½ CUP SOY SAUCE
1½ TABLESPOONS SUGAR
2 TABLESPOONS SHERRY
2 CLOVES GARLIC,
  PEELED AND WHOLE
3 THIN SLICES FRESH GINGER
2 CUPS WATER
6 ANISE SEEDS

Boiling chicken wings is preferable to baking them which only shrivels them. These delicious morsels can be partly prepared beforehand and the stock used again. All kinds of meat can be cooked using this sauce, even pre-cooked dishes for trips.
To make sauce: In a saucepan combine the ingredients of the thin soy sauce and bring to the boil. Simmer for half an hour.

Chop the chicken wings into three at the two joints. Cook the big pieces in the sauce for 15 minutes, the middle pieces for 10 minutes and the tips for 5 minutes. Do not overcook otherwise they go sticky. Remove from the sauce and serve with plain rice, garnished with chopped spring onion. **Serves 4.**

CHICKEN BAKED IN SHERRY

6 LARGE PIECES CHICKEN
50G BUTTER
1 CLOVE GARLIC, FINELY SLICED
1 SMALL ONION, HALVED
¼ TEASPOON FRESHLY GROUND
  PEPPER
1 TEASPOON SALT
1 TABLESPOON CHOPPED PARSLEY
½ CUP DRY SHERRY

Served hot or cold, the sherry ensures that the chicken is moist and succulent. When served hot, it is the ideal buffet fare; when cold, it's great to take on picnics.

In a roasting dish lightly brown the chicken in the butter, along with the garlic and onion. Add pepper, salt, parsley and sherry. Cover and bake in a moderate oven for 1 hour or until the chicken is tender.

While cooking, occasionally baste the chicken. If serving cold, allow the chicken to cool in the pan. **Serves 6.**

CHICKEN WITH ROSEMARY AND TOMATOES

6 LARGE PORTIONS CHICKEN
SALT AND FRESHLY GROUND PEPPER
OLIVE OIL
2-3 TEASPOONS CHOPPED, FRESH
  ROSEMARY
6 SMALL WHOLE CLOVES GARLIC,
  UNPEELED
½ CUP DRY WHITE WINE
6 TOMATOES

The secret of this delicious chicken recipe is the addition of fresh tomatoes just before serving. The rest can be made well in advance and reheated. An unusual feature is the use of whole, unpeeled cloves of garlic. This gives a hint of garlic to the dish and to garlic lovers, the taste of the garlic so-cooked is exquisite.

Rub the chicken portions with salt and freshly ground pepper. Fry until golden brown in some olive oil. Add the rosemary, garlic and white wine — and cook quickly until the wine has almost disappeared. Cover and simmer gently until the chicken is just cooked.

Peel the tomatoes, remove the seeds, chop them into small pieces, add them to the chicken, heat them through and serve immediately. Serve with brown rice and a green salad. **Serves 6.**

DUCK WITH PORT

1 COMMERCIAL DUCK OR 2 WILD DUCKS	1 ORANGE, UNPEELED 1 ONION, PEELED	THYME 2-3 RASHERS BACON
1 APPLE, UNPEELED AND CORED	SALT AND PEPPER	½ BOTTLE PORT

Use either wild or commercial duck. A wild duck is about half the size of a commercial duck and takes twice as long to cook.

Wipe the inside and out of the duck with a damp cloth. If it has been frozen reserve the juices.

Coarsely chop the apple, orange and onion. Mix them together and fill the duck's cavity.

Rub the outside with salt, pepper and plenty of thyme. Place the duck in a covered roasting dish, cover with bacon rashers, add any duck juice to the pan. Pour in the port. Cover the pan and cook in a 200°C oven for 20 minutes. Then turn the heat down to 160°C and bake, basting occasionally until the duck is tender (1½ hours for a commercial duck or up to 3 hours for a wild duck).

Before serving remove any fat from the pan juices and thicken slightly, adding more port if you wish. Serve the sauce with the duck and accompany with baked kumara and a watercress salad. **Serves 4.**

LAMB WAIATARUA

1 LEG OF LAMB OR HOGGET	GARLIC	FRESH ROSEMARY
		1-2 LEMONS

Garlic and rosemary give a wonderful flavour to lamb or hogget while the lemon juice helps cut down the fattiness and makes a pleasantly tangy sauce.

Make 12 deep incisions with a sharp pointed knife into the lamb. Into each incision stuff a sliver of garlic, several rosemary leaves and a little grated lemon rind.

Place the joint in a baking dish — no fat is needed — and bake in a hot (210°C) oven for 10 minutes. Turn the oven down to a moderate heat (180°C) and continue cooking until the meat is tender — 1-2 hours — depending on the size of the joint. Baste the joint from time to time with the juice of 1 lemon. When cooked there should be plenty of juice in the pan. After carefully removing most of the fat, thicken the remaining lemon-flavoured sauce. Add salt, dry sherry and extra lemon juice to taste. Serve with roast vegetables.

LAMB FONDUE

200G PRIME LEG OF LAMB PER PERSON	Condiments: MINT SAUCE OR JELLY,	CHILLI SAUCE, MUSHROOM SAUCE, FRUIT CHUTNEY
PEANUT OIL	GUAVA JELLY, PLUM SAUCE	SOY SAUCE WITH CRUSHED GARLIC

Similar to Fondue Bourguignonne — this is an exciting way to serve lamb as a main course.

Remove all the skin and fat from the lamb and cut into 2.5cm cubes.

Fill the fondue pot ⅓-½ full with peanut oil. Heat the oil until a dice of bread browns in less than a minute, then regulate the heat to maintain an even temperature.

Each person selects a piece of meat, spears it with a fondue fork and cooks it in the hot oil. It should cook in a few minutes. Transfer the cooked meat to another fork and dip it in a condiment. To be accompanied by salads, crisp French bread or hot baby potatoes.

FILLET OF BEEF WITH SOUR CREAM FILLING

1 LARGE CARROT, FINELY CHOPPED
1 STALK CELERY, FINELY CHOPPED
1 MEDIUM ONION, FINELY CHOPPED
4 TABLESPOONS BUTTER
1 KG FILLET OF BEEF
SALT AND FRESHLY GROUND PEPPER
WATERCRESS, LETTUCE AND TOMATOES FOR GARNISH

Sour cream filling:
250G BACON, CUBED
1 TABLESPOON COOKING OIL
1 CRUSHED CLOVE GARLIC
1 CUP SOUR CREAM
1½ TABLESPOONS PAN JUICES
1 TABLESPOON GRATED ONION
1 TABLESPOON CHOPPED CHIVES
SALT AND WHITE PEPPER

In a large roasting pan, gently fry the carrot, celery and onion in 2 tablespoons butter for 10 minutes — or until the vegetables are soft. Place the fillet on top of the vegetables, sprinkle with salt and pepper and dot with the remaining butter. Roast in a pre-heated 260°C oven for 20-25 minutes — depending on the thickness of the fillet. Let it cool in the pan for at least 1 hour, then transfer the fillet to a serving platter, reserving the juices.

To make the filling: In a frying pan cook the bacon in the oil with the crushed garlic, until the bacon is crisp. Remove the bacon and drain on paper towels. Discard the fat or reserve it for future use.

In a bowl combine 1½ tablespoons of the reserved pan juices, sour cream, onion and chopped chives. Add the bacon, season with salt and pepper, and combine the mixture well. Cut a wedge along the length of the fillet 4cm wide and 2.5cm deep. Transfer to a serving platter. Fill the cavity with the filling, spooning the remainder into a separate serving dish. Cut the fillet wedge into slices crosswise and reassemble it on top of the filling. Garnish the platter with watercress or lettuce and tomatoes. Serve cold, not chilled. **Serves 6.**

CAPER SCHNITZELS

SCHNITZELS
SALT AND PEPPER
COOKING OIL

Caper Sauce:
1 TEASPOON DRY MUSTARD
1 TABLESPOON DRAINED CAPERS

CREAM
½ LEMON
WINE OR SHERRY
SALT AND PEPPER

A quick and easy dish for the busy person. Serve with crisp potatoes and a green vegetable or salad.

Rub trimmed schnitzels with salt and pepper and pound them well to tenderize. In a frying pan quickly cook the schnitzels in the cooking oil. Remove from the pan and keep them hot.

To make the sauce: To the juices remaining in the pan stir in the mustard, capers, some cream, the lemon juice and enough wine or sherry to make a thickish sauce. Stir until bubbling, season with salt and pepper and serve the schnitzels with the sauce poured over.

OXTAIL WITH BLACK OLIVES

1 LARGE OXTAIL, CUT INTO SECTIONS
FLOUR
COOKING OIL
1 LARGE ONION, SLICED
1 LARGE CARROT, SLICED
1 CLOVE GARLIC, FINELY SLICED
3 SPRIGS PARSLEY
1 SPRIG THYME
1 BAY LEAF
1 TEASPOON DRIED BASIL
SALT AND PEPPER
1 CUP RED WINE
1 CUP WATER
150G MUSHROOMS, SLICED
½ CUP WHOLE BLACK OLIVES
CHOPPED PARSLEY FOR GARNISH

Because of its fattiness, oxtail takes some time to prepare but the effort is well worthwhile to produce this succulent stew/casserole.

Rub the oxtail pieces with flour, shake off any excess flour and brown them in a little oil in a saucepan. Add the onion, carrot, garlic, parsley, thyme, bay leaf, basil and salt and pepper. Stir in the red wine and the water. Cover and simmer until the meat is tender — about 2-2½ hours.

Allow the oxtail to cool and refrigerate it overnight. Remove as much fat as possible, add the mushrooms and the black olives. Simmer for ½ hour. If you wish, it can be thickened but this is not really necesssary. Serve sprinkled with chopped parsley and accompanied by buttered new potatoes and a tossed green salad. **Serves 3-4.**

SPINACH AND COTTAGE CHEESE TART

PIE PASTRY	¼ CUP MILK	250G COTTAGE CHEESE
⅓ CUP FINELY CHOPPED ONION	FRESHLY GRATED NUTMEG	½ CUP GRATED PARMESAN CHEESE
2 TABLESPOONS BUTTER	SALT AND PEPPER	2 TOMATOES
½ CUP COOKED SPINACH OR SILVER BEET	4 EGGS	

Roll out the pie pastry and fit into a 23cm flan tin with a removable fluted rim. Prick the bottom of the shell with a fork and chill for 30 minutes. Line the shell with greaseproof paper, fill the paper with raw rice and bake the shell in a pre-heated 210°C for 15 minutes. Remove the paper and rice, bake the shell for a further 10 minutes or until golden. Allow to cool.

In a frying pan sauté the onion in the butter for a few minutes until soft but not browned. Add the cooked, well-squeezed and chopped spinach or silver beet, stirring the mixture for several minutes. Remove the frying pan from the heat, stir in the milk and nutmeg, salt and pepper to taste.

In a bowl beat together the eggs, cottage cheese, Parmesan cheese and stir into the spinach mixture. Pour the mixture into the shell and decoratively arrange thin slices of tomato on top and sprinkle them with salt and pepper. Bake the tart in a pre-heated 180°C oven for 35-40 minutes, or until a knife inserted in the centre comes out clean. Allow the tart to cool for about 10 minutes before serving. **Serves 6.**

OYSTER SOUFFLE

3 TABLESPOONS BUTTER	⅔ CUP MILK	18 CHOPPED OYSTERS
6 TABLESPOONS FLOUR	1 TABLESPOON LEMON JUICE	6 EGGS
1 TEASPOON SALT	GRATED ONION	½ TEASPOON CREAM OF TARTAR
⅓ CUP OYSTER LIQUOR	CAYENNE PEPPER	

In a large saucepan melt the butter, add the flour and salt and mix thoroughly. Add the oyster liquor and milk, stirring constantly, until very thick and smooth.

Remove from the heat. Add the lemon juice, a little grated onion, a dash of cayenne pepper and the chopped oysters. Beat the egg yolks in, one at a time.

In a bowl, beat the egg whites until foamy. Add the cream of tartar and beat until the egg whites are stiff but not dry. Fold into the oyster mixture and pour into a souffle dish, greased only on the bottom.

Place in a pan of hot water and bake in a 160°C oven until brown and firm (about 1 hour). Serve at once, accompanied with thin slices of buttered brown bread and lemon wedges. **Serves 6-8.**

TROUT BAKED WITH HERBS

1 MEDIUM-SIZED TROUT	1 LEMON	WATERCRESS AND TOMATOES FOR GARNISH
SPRIGS OF THYME AND PARSLEY	BUTTER	
	SALT	

This trout recipe makes it taste like salmon. It can be served hot but is preferable served cold.

Place the trout in the middle of a large strip of aluminium foil. In the trout's cavity, place sprigs of parsley and thyme. Cut half a lemon into thin slices and arrange on top; along with further sprigs of parsley and thyme. Dot with butter, season with salt and wrap foil around the fish.

Bake in a moderate oven, allowing 20 minutes per 500g.
To serve hot: Heat the juices in a saucepan and serve over the skinned trout.
To serve cold: Allow the trout to cool in the foil before skinning and transferring to a platter. Garnish with extra lemon slices and surround with watercress and tomatoes. Serve with a herb mayonnaise. **Serves 8-10.**

MARINATED FILLET OF VENISON
with sour cream and calvados sauce

1.5 KG PIECE EYE FILLET OF VENISON	**Marinade:**	1 TEASPOON FRESHLY GROUND BLACK PEPPER
2 CLOVES OF GARLIC, SLIVERED	1½ CUPS DRY RED WINE	**Sour cream and calvados sauce:**
125G STREAKY BACON	1 CUP WATER	1 CUP STRAINED MARINADE
	4 PEPPERCORNS	½ CUP CALVADOS
	2 BAY LEAVES	250G SOUR CREAM
	2 TABLESPOONS TARRAGON	

Venison is slowly becoming available commercially in New Zealand. It is a gamey meat but tends to be dry so needs marinating and larding and serving with a creamy sauce.

With a sharp knife remove as much skin as possible from the venison. Insert slivers of garlic in the fillet.

To prepare the marinade: Add the ingredients of the marinade to a container just large enough to hold the venison. Stir thoroughly.

Place the fillet in the marinade and refrigerate for 24 hours, turning 3 or 4 times and making sure it is covered by the marinade. Remove from the marinade, place in a shallow roasting pan and cover with the bacon rashers.

Place in a pre-heated 200°C oven for 1 hour 15 minutes or until a skewer inserted in the meat renders pink juices. Baste frequently with the drippings. Remove from oven, remove bacon and place the fillet on a serving platter in the warming oven.

To make the sauce: Place the roasting pan over a medium heat and stir in 1 cup of strained marinade and the calvados. Stir briskly and slowly add the sour cream. Check seasoning and pour the sauce over the fillet. Carve in slices across the grain, about 1cm thick. **Serves 6-8.**

BRAISED PHEASANT WITH MADEIRA SAUCE

2 MEDIUM (NO. 3) PHEASANTS	1 RASHER BACON, CHOPPED	⅓ CUP MADEIRA OR MARSALA
2 SMALL TANGERINES OR 1 ORANGE, PEELED	50G BUTTER	½ TEASPOON SALT
¼ CUP LARD OR OIL	4 SHALLOTS OR 1 SMALL ONION, FINELY CHOPPED	FRESHLY GROUND BLACK PEPPER
6 MEDIUM MUSHROOMS, SLICED	2 TABLESPOONS FLOUR	SPRIG OF FRESH FENNEL
		2 CRUSHED JUNIPER BERRIES

Like most game, the cooking time for pheasant depends on its age and whether it was wild or cultivated. This recipe can take from 1½ to 3 hours cooking time so plan on the maximum time and if the pheasants are cooked much earlier, keep them sealed and hot in a low oven – they don't spoil. Any leftover pheasant will make a delicious crêpe filling – mix the shredded meat with leftover sauce. The carcass can be boiled up to make a superb stock.

Wash and dry the pheasants and insert a tangerine or half an orange in each cavity. In a large heavy frying pan, heat the lard or oil and brown the birds one at a time, turning and basting until golden.

Place in a casserole.

Add the mushrooms and bacon to the frying pan and cook, stirring for a few minutes. Add to the casserole.

Melt the butter in the frying pan and add the shallots or onion, then stir in the flour and cook for a few minutes but do not brown. Slowly stir in the Madeira or Marsala and add the salt and some pepper. If it is too thick, add a little water. Pour this into the casserole and add the fennel and juniper berries.

Cover the casserole and bake in a 200°C oven for 1½ hours then test for tenderness every quarter hour. The birds could take up to 3 hours to cook but should be done in about 2 hours. While cooking baste and turn the pheasants occasionally. Add water if the sauce becomes too thick. Serve the pheasants with the sauce and accompany with brown rice, currant jelly and a green salad. **Serves 4-6.**

PORK LOIN WITH APRICOT STUFFING

Apricot stuffing:
175G DRIED APRICOTS
2 ONIONS, FINELY CHOPPED
1 TABLESPOON BUTTER

100G FRESH BREADCRUMBS
1 TEASPOON DRIED ROSEMARY
1 TEASPOON DRY MUSTARD
1 LEMON

SALT AND PEPPER
MILK

2.5KG BONED LOIN OF PORK
2 TEASPOONS DRY MUSTARD

To make the stuffing: Barely cover the apricots with cold water, bring to the boil and simmer for 5 minutes. Drain the apricots and cut into strips. In a frying pan, cook the onions in the butter until soft but not browned. Mix the onion, apricots and breadcrumbs together. Add the rosemary, mustard and the grated rind and juice of 1 lemon. Season well with salt and pepper, mix, and if necessary moisten with a little milk.

Spread the inside of the pork with the stuffing, roll up, and secure it firmly with string. Alternatively, make pockets in the flesh from each end and stuff the loin. Rub the scored loin all over with the mustard – this gives a crisp, well-flavoured crackling.

Roast for ½ hour in a pre-heated 200°C oven before turning the oven down to 180°C and cooking a further 1½ hours or until the pork is very tender, basting occasionally with the juices. **Serves 6-8.**

HARE WITH WHITE WINE AND FRUIT

100G BACON
25G BUTTER
4 HARE JOINTS
8 SMALL ONIONS

1 TABLESPOON FLOUR
2½ CUPS DRY WHITE WINE
SALT, PEPPER, THYME
1 CUP RAISINS OR SULTANAS

8 PITTED PRUNES
3 TABLESPOONS SUGAR
1 TABLESPOON WHITE VINEGAR

Either hare or rabbit can be used for this casserole. It is very rich so serve with plain boiled potatoes and several simple vegetables or a salad.

Cut the bacon into thin strips and lightly brown in the butter in a frying pan. Transfer to a heavy saucepan or casserole. Brown the hare joints in the frying pan, then transfer to the saucepan. Brown the onions in the pan, then transfer to the saucepan.

Sprinkle the flour in the saucepan and mix in well. Add the wine to the frying pan and bring to the boil, removing the brown bits sticking to the pan. Pour into the saucepan. Add salt, pepper and thyme in moderation, and simmer, covered, for 1 hour. Add the raisins and prunes, and simmer for 1 further hour.

Just before serving, melt the sugar in the vinegar over a low heat. When it starts to colour or caramelize, add it to the hare sauce and stir in well. Check the seasonings before serving. **Serves 4.**

Desserts

Desserts, puddings, sweets, call them what you may, they all add up to the sweet course at the end of the meal. The dessert is something at which most New Zealanders excel. For years, while other courses were stodgy and monotonous, it was the dessert that had all possible attention lavished upon it. Interestingly, dessert making, particularly dessert cakes, can be termed 'constructive' cooking — the ingredients are completely transformed in the process. Savoury cooking, on the other hand, can be likened to 'destructive' cooking. Ingredients like onion and tomatoes often reduce and almost disappear into the dish.

It is generally accepted that the dessert is the last course of the meal. However, if a cheese platter is offered, and if we follow the English, then it is the cheese that is served last. In France cheeses are served before the dessert.

Desserts are particularly delicious if made from fruit and alcohol. However, possibly the easiest dessert to make is a dessert cake. It is usually rich and sticky and can be made well in advance. Meringues, brandy snaps and other small sweetmeats also make excellent desserts.

PAVLOVA

3 EGG WHITES
PINCH OF SALT
2 CUPS WHITE SUGAR
2 DROPS VANILLA ESSENCE
1 TEASPOON VINEGAR
3 TABLESPOONS BOILING WATER
200ML CREAM, WHIPPED
KIWIFRUIT, PASSIONFRUIT OR STRAWBERRIES FOR GARNISH

In a bowl, combine the egg whites, a pinch of salt and cover with the sugar. Add the vanilla essence and the vinegar. Add the boiling water and place the bowl in a pan of hot water on the stove. Beat the mixture for 15 minutes.

Grease an oven tray with butter, cover with greaseproof paper and grease again. Put under the cold tap and shake off the excess water from the tray before pouring the mixture on.

Place in a pre-heated 150°C oven then turn down to 100°C and cook for ¾ hour.

When cool, remove to serving platter, smother with whipped cream and garnish with kiwifruit, passionfruit, strawberries or other fruit. **Serves 4-6.**

FRUIT AND RUM FONDUE

| APPLES, PINEAPPLES, ORANGES, KIWIFRUIT, PEARS, BANANA (WITH LEMON JUICE), STRAWBERRIES | DARK RUM
BROWN SUGAR | WHIPPED CREAM |

First prepare the fruit. Acidic fruits are best but any fruit can be acidified by coating with lemon juice. Cut, slice, cube the fruit into small portions.

Half fill a small stainless steel bowl with methylated spirits and place the small bowl in a large container — in case it is knocked.

Fill three other bowls — one with dark rum, one with brown sugar and one with whipped cream.

With a fork, spear a piece of fruit, dip it in the rum, then the sugar, then hold it over the methylated spirit flame to caramelize. Dip it in the whipped cream and eat it carefully — it's hot.

Refill the methylated spirit bowl when empty and the flames have died. On no account add meths until you are positive the flame is out. The meths bowl will be a mess when you have finished so soak it immediately.

CHERRY LIQUEUR CHOCOLATES

| 250G RIPE, FRESH CHERRIES
BRANDY | 500G MARZIPAN OR ALMOND PASTE
300G MILK CHOCOLATE | BUTTER |

Home-made chocolates are always fascinating and these sweetmeats are ideal as an after-dinner offering.

Pit the cherries and place them in a screw-top jar. Cover them with brandy, put the lid on, and leave in the refrigerator for 2 weeks.

Drain the cherries — and perhaps drink the brandy while you are making the chocolates.

Roll out the marzipan thinly and wrap completely around each cherry.

In a double boiler melt the chocolate, adding a little butter if necessary.

Roll each marzipan-covered cherry in the chocolate, covering them completely. Put them on a plate and refrigerate until set. Makes about 36 chocolates. Best kept in a cool place.

PRALINE SOUFFLE

| Praline:
50G UNBLANCHED ALMONDS
4 TABLESPOONS CASTOR SUGAR | Soufflé:
4 EGGS, SEPARATED
8 TABLESPOONS CASTOR SUGAR
2 TABLESPOONS LIQUID HONEY | 300ML CREAM, WHIPPED
1 TABLESPOON GELATINE
5 TABLESPOONS COLD WATER |

Praline is a term for caramelized nuts, almonds in particular.

To prepare the praline: Gently heat the almonds and the castor sugar in a saucepan. Stir continuously until the sugar dissolves and coats the almonds. Take care not to burn the almonds when toasting them. Turn the almonds onto an oiled tin and when cold crush them finely.

To make the soufflé: Prepare a 15cm soufflé dish with a paper collar. In a basin, beat the egg yolks, the castor sugar and honey until thick. Lightly whip the cream and fold into the egg mixture, reserving some for decoration. Soften the gelatine in 5 tablespoons cold water, dissolve over heat, allow to cool then add to the mixture.

Beat the egg whites until stiff then fold them into the soufflé with half the praline. Turn into the soufflé dish and refrigerate until set.

To serve, remove the paper collar and decorate the top with the remaining cream and praline. **Serves 6-8.**

LEMON CREAM PIE

125G BUTTER	¼ CAN SWEETENED CONDENSED MILK	600ML CREAM
250G PLAIN BISCUITS	¼ CUP LEMON JUICE	FINELY GRATED LEMON RIND

The secret of this recipe is to use lots of finely grated lemon rind. It cuts down the sweetness and makes the dessert rich and refreshing.

Melt the butter and crush the biscuits. Combine the butter with the biscuits and press into a medium-sized springform pan to make a pie shell.

Mix together the condensed milk, lemon juice and 300ml cream, whipped. Pour into the biscuit shell and set for 8-12 hours in the refrigerator.

Whip the remaining 300ml cream and spread over the pie. Smother with masses of finely grated lemon rind. Serve chilled. **Serves 10-12.**

BRANDY CAKE

1 RICH DARK CHOCOLATE CAKE	CHERRY CONSERVE	GRATED CHOCOLATE AND CHERRIES FOR GARNISH
BRANDY	WHIPPED CREAM	

Cut the cake into three crosswise. Put the bottom layer on a serving platter and generously dowse in brandy. Then spread it with cherry conserve and then whipped cream. Put the middle layer on top and repeat the process.

Dowse the top layer with brandy and place on top of the cake. Cover the entire cake with whipped cream and garnish with grated chocolate and cherries. Either refrigerate for 2-3 hours or deep freeze for 1 hour. Serve chilled.

STRAWBERRY SHORTCAKE

150G BUTTER	1 TEASPOON BAKING POWDER	2 CHIPS STRAWBERRIES
2 CUPS SIFTED FLOUR	PINCH OF SALT	ICING SUGAR
½ CUP CORNFLOUR	1 EGG, BEATEN	300ML CREAM, WHIPPED
½ CUP SUGAR	CREAM	

To make the shortcake: Rub the butter into the flour. Add the cornflour, sugar, baking powder and a pinch of salt. Mix in the beaten egg and enough cream to make a scone consistency. Divide the mixture into three and roll into three rounds, about 20cm in diameter, on greaseproof paper. Bake in a 150°C oven for 20 minutes or until light brown. Allow to cool then store in an air-tight container until ready to use.

Hull the strawberries. Reserve some to garnish the top and mash the remaining berries with icing sugar to taste.

Spread half of the mixture on one shortcake, place the second shortcake on top and spread with the remaining mixture. Place the third shortcake on top of these. Store in the refrigerator for at least 3 hours — the longer the better. This will allow the mashed strawberries time to soak into the shortcakes.

Just before serving, whip the cream until stiff — sweeten with icing sugar if you wish. Spread the cream on top of the shortcake. Decorate with reserved strawberries. **Serves 6-8.**

Index

APPETIZERS AND ENTREES

Asparagus and Brie parcels, 71
Avocado,
    Avocado and ham mousse with tarragon dressing, 115
    Chilled avocado with orange soup, 71
    Avocado Landmark, 89
Awabi No Shio Mushi, 85
Bacon and Chicken Liver pâté, 161
Bigoli e costine, 81
Blue cheese mousse,
    Blue cheese and ham mousse, 33
Brains Terrapin, 162
Bread and butter pickles, 164
Calamares Neapolitan, 103
Cheese soufflé, 61
Chicken,
    Chicken Biriani, 49
    Ginger chicken wings, 85
    Chicken liver and bacon pâté, 161
    Chicken livers and witloaf salad, 123
Chunky mustard, 164
Chutney, Lemon and raisin, 165
Creamy roe pâté, 160
Eggs with ham and mushrooms, 163
Fettucine and whitebait, 127
Foies de volaille, 123
Frog legs in ginger and pineapple, 147
Gruyère and mushroom pâté, 157
Ham,
    Ham and blue cheese mousse, 33
    Ham and avocado mousse with tarragon dressing, 115
Jelly fruit salad, 45
Kidneys with mushrooms and fennel, 163
Kiwifruit cocktail, 31
Lambs kidneys à la Suisse, 113
Lemon and raisin chutney, 165
Marinated raw fish and coconut cream, 163
Marlin mousse, 111
Mousse,
    Avocado and ham mousse with tarragon dressing, 115
    Blue cheese mousse, 161
    Ham and blue cheese mousse, 33
    Marlin mousse, 111
    Scallop mousse with tomato coulis, 99
Mushrooms,
    Mushroom and gruyère pâté, 157
    Mushrooms Alton, 29
Mussels,
    Mussels Fraser, 65
    Mussels with parsley and garlic butter, 119
Mustard, Chunky, 164
Pâtés,
    Chicken liver and bacon pâté, 161
    Creamy roe pâté, 160
    Gruyère and mushroom pâté, 157
    Smoked eel pâté, 135
Pel'meni (Siberian meat-filled dumplings), 59
Peppers, Stuffed, 155
Pickles, Bread and butter, 164
Prawns,
    Gong Ho prawns, 35
    Tropical prawn salad, 139
Raw vegetable platter with avocado cream, 167
Raisin and lemon chutney, 165
Salmon,
    Salmon and orange kebab, 145
    Salmon crème, 67
Samosas, 143
Scallops,
    Gainsborough scallops, 69
    Garlic scallops, 162
    Honey and ginger scallops, 55
    Scallop mousse with tomato coulis, 99
    Scallops poached in Beaujolais sauce, 137
Seafood feuillete, 61
Soufflé, Cheese, 61
Smoked eel pâté, 135
Squid,
    Calamares Neapolitan, 103
    Deep fried squid, 47
Summer dream, 101
Terrine of ham, veal and pork, 161
Veal in pastry, 43
Venison feuillette, 63
Vietnamese finger rolls (Cha Gio), 107
Whitebait,
    Fettucine and whitebait, 127
    Whitebait fritters, 51, 164
Wholemeal hazelnut crackers, 158

SOUPS

Ajo, Sopa de (Garlic soup), 117
Almond soup, 109
Apple soup, chilled and curried, 105
Avocado and tomato soup, 53
Bacon and red bean soup, 91
Garlic soup, (Sopa de Ajo), 117
Hamburger soup, 165
Herb soup, Chilled cream of, 165
Kiwifruit and wine soup, Cold, 166
Mulligatawny soup, 67
Orange soup with chilled avocado, 71
Oyster chowder, 79
Pistou, Soup au, 87
Pumpkin soup, 55
Red bean and bacon soup, 91
Shellfish chowder, 165
Smoked seafood soup, 137
Snail soup Baden Baden, 125
Tomato and avocado soup, 53
Tua Tua, Cream of, 51
Vichysoisse, 121
Wine and cold kiwifruit soup, 166

BEEF AND VEAL

Beef,
    Beef medallions, 147
    Fillet of beef with sour cream filling, 173
    South American beef roll, 91
Bulgogi, 83
Oxtail with black olives, 173
Pel'meni (Siberian meat-filled dumplings), 59
Schnitzels, Caper, 173
Steak,
    Steak Madagascar, 145
    Teriyaki steak, 85
Veal
    Veal in pastry, 43
    Veal Saltimbocca, 57
    Veal Venezian, 57

LAMB

Kidneys
    Lambs Kidneys à la Suisse, 113
    Kidneys with mushrooms and fennel, 163
Brains Terrapin, 162
Lamb,
    Lamb and apricot pie, 135
    Filet d'agneau Shrewsbury, 141
    Lamb fondue, 172
    Lamb stuffed with vegetables and basil, 123
    Lamb Waiatarua, 172
    Lamb with aubergines (Cordero con berengenas), 117
    Lamb with tamarillo and port sauce, 115

HAM AND PORK

Bacon and chicken liver pâté, 161
Ham and blue cheese mousse, 33
Ham and avocado mousse with tarragon dressing, 115
Ham with eggs and mushrooms, 163
Pork,
    Pork and pineapple log with Tripoli sauce, 157
    Pork Avenoise, 103
    Porc au fromage fondue, 113
    Cherry pork, 105
    Pork fillet Renato, 127
    Paupiettes of pork, 61
    Pork with apricot stuffing, 176
    Pork with mushrooms and parsley stuffing, 65

POULTRY AND GAME

Boar chops, 79
Chicken,
    Chicken and crayfish crêpe gâteau, 99
    Chicken and scallop pie, 137
    Chicken baked in sherry, 171
    Chicken Biriani, 49
    Braised soy sauce chicken, 35
    Chicken breasts with Maraschino sauce, 45
    Curry Chicken Malaysian style, 35
    Deep fried breast, with ginger and lemon, 119
    Foies de volaille (chicken livers and witloaf salad), 123
    Ginger wings, 85
    Hazelnut chicken, 69
    Chicken legs stuffed with camembert, 33
    Chicken livers and witloaf salad (Foies de volaille), 123

Chicken liver and bacon pâté, 161
Chicken marinated with Greenpepper sauce, 109
Old fashioned chicken and rice pie, 59
Peanut Chicken, 170
Chicken Portuguese (with orange and Drambuie sauce), 89
Supreme of Chicken, with sherry, cream and pineapple, 65
Tandoori Chicken, 49
Tandoori Murgi, 143
Chicken Valostana, 139
Chicken wings with thin soy sauce, 171
Chicken with rosemary and tomatoes, 171
Chicken Yakitori, 47
Duck with pork, 172
Duckling with orange sauce, 53
Goat, Braised saddle, 55
Hare with white wine and fruit, 176
Pheasant,
    Pheasant, with madeira sauce, 175
    Pheasant with smoked ham and red wine sauce, 111
    Pheasant with wine and cherry sauce, 31
Rabbit, stuffed (Coniglio Ripieno), 81
Turkey and fruit platter, 67
Venison,
    Venison feuillette, 63
    Marinated fillet, with sour cream and calvados sauce, 175

PASTA AND RICE

Bigoli e costine, 81
Fettucine and whitebait, 127
Nasi Goreng, 121
Old fashioned rice and chicken pie, 59
Spaghetti Marinara, 155

VEGETABLES AND SALADS

Asparagus and Brie parcels, 71
Avocado,
    Avocado and ham mousse with tarragon dressing, 115
    Chilled Avocado with orange soup, 71
    Avocado Landmark, 89
Butternut Plusone, 125
Casserole, vegetable, 169
Kiwifruit cocktail, 31
Kumera, Whipped, with apple and raisins, 169
Mushrooms Alton, 29
Peppers,
    Pickled red peppers, 169
    Stuffed peppers, 155
Salads,
    Apple, celery and walnut salad, 168
    Green and white salad, 169
    Jelly fruit salad, 45
    Mushroom and beansprout salad, 168
    Raw pumpkin salad, 168
    Silver beet salad (with bacon, almonds and cream cheese), 168
    Whitloaf salad and chicken livers, 123
Spinach and cottage cheese tart, 174
Vegetable platter with avocado cream, 167

FISH AND SHELLFISH

Crayfish,
    Crayfish and chicken crêpe gâteau, 99
    Crayfish Captain style, 51
    Crayfish in champagne, 43
    Langouste Maison, 87
Creamy roe pâté, 160
Fish,
    Fish fillets with tamarillo sauce, 29
    Filet de poisson Sheraton, 141
    Marinated raw fish with coconut cream, 163
    Melanesian fish salad, 63
    Sweet and sour fish, 162
Homard Nantua, 141
Marlin mousse, 111
Mussels,
    Mussels Fraser, 65
    Mussels with parsley and garlic butter, 119
Neptune's Treasure Chest, 47
Oysters,
    Oyster à la Creole, 109
    Oyster chowder, 79
    Oyster Soufflé, 174
Paua, Awabi No Shio Mushi, 85
Prawns,
    Gong Ho prawns, 35
    Mekong prawn delight, 107
    Tropical prawn salad, 139
Salmon,
    Salmon and orange kebab, 145
    Salmon crème, 67
Scallops,
    Coquilles Saint-Jacques Louis, 101
    Scallop and chicken pie, 137
    Gainsborough scallops, 69
    Garlic scallops, 162
    Honey and ginger scallops, 55
    Scallop mousse with tomato coulis, 99
    Scallops poached in Beaujolais sauce, 137
Seafood Feuillete, 61
Seafood Soup, 137
Shellfish chowder, 165
Smoked eel pâté, 135
Squid,
    Calamares Neapolitan, 103
    Deep fried squid, 47
    Whole stuffed squid with tomato sauce, 119
Trout,
    Trout baked with herbs, 174
    Trout with ham (Truchas con Jamon), 117
Tua Tua Soup, Cream of, 51
Whitebait,
    Whitebait and fettucine, 127
    Whitebait fritters, 51, 164

DESSERTS

Almond,
    Almond parfait, 147
    Almond torte, 121
Bananas, Brazilian, 91
Blintzes, 111
Brandy,
    Brandy cake, 179
    Brandy and Grand Marnier zabaglione, 113
Cassata, 155
Caramel glacé, 101
Cheesecake, Fresh ginger, 158
Chocolate,
    Chocolate and Grand Marnier mousse, 89
    Cherry liqueur chocolates, 178
    Chocolate cream, 53
    Chocolate hazelnut torte, 61
    Marquise au chocolat, 33
Coupe Mont Blanc, 87
Fruit,
    Fruit and rum fondue, 178
    Fruit baskets, 63,
    Fruit salad in wine, 127
Gâteau, Tia Maria ice cream, 69
Glacé,
    Glacé au caramel, 101
    Raspberry mille feuille glacé, 99
Ginger cheesecake, 158
Gulab Jambu (sweetmeats), 49
Grand Marnier,
    Grand Marnier and chocolate mousse, 89
    Grand Marnier and brandy zabaglione, 113
    Soufflé Grand Marnier, 43
Grand panache, 31
Hazelnut meringue, 105
Honey parfait, 125
Ice cream and parfaits,
    Almond parfait, 147
    Cassata, 155
    Honey parfait, 125
    Tia Maria ice cream gâteau, 69
Kahlua soufflé, 145
Kiwifruit mousse, 103
Lemon,
    Lemon cream pie, 179
    Lemon custard tart (Tarte au citron), 123
Martini melon, 79
Meringue, Hazelnut, 105
Middle Eastern salad, 29
Mousse,
    Grand Marnier and chocolate mousse, 89
    Kiwifruit mousse, 103
Oranges with cognac, 115
Pasta Folle, 81
Pavlova, 177
Persian delight, 139
Praline soufflé, 178
Profiteroles with hot walnut sauce, 45
Raspberry mille feuille glacé, 99
Rau Cau jellied squares, 107
Rock melon with ginger, 59
Shortcake, Strawberry, 179
Soufflé,
    Kahlua soufflé, 145
    Praline soufflé, 178
    Soufflé Grand Marnier, 43
Strawberry shortcake, 179
Tarte au citron (Lemon custard tart), 123
Tia Maria ice cream gâteau, 69
Toot sweet, 71
Torte,
    Almond torte, 121
    Chocolate hazelnut torte, 61
Turkish delight, 143
Zabaglione,
    Grand Marnier and brandy zabaglione, 113
    Iced Zabaglione, 135
    Zabaglioni, 57

Restaurant Index

Altons   28
316 Cameron Road, Tauranga.
Telephone 87-360. BYO.

Anderson's   30
104 London Street, Hamilton.
Telephone 395-957. Licensed.

Antoine's   32
333 Parnell Road, Parnell, Auckland.
Telephone 798-756. Licensed.

August Moon   34
Cnr Albert and Victoria Streets, Auckland.
Telephone 34-141. Licensed.

Bacchus   42
8 Courtenay Place, Wellington.
Telephone 846-592. Licensed.

Bartups   44
222 Ponsonby Road, Auckland.
Telephone 767-888. BYO.

Beachcomber   46
The Esplanade, Sumner, Christchurch.
Telephone 266-592. BYO.

Bengal Tiger   48
83 Willis Street, Wellington.
Telephone 728-706. Licensed.

Captain Crab   50
1 Teed Street, Newmarket, Auckland.
Telephone 504-273. Licensed.

Coachman   52
46 Courtenay Place, Wellington.
Telephone 848-200. Licensed.

Coach Trail Lodge   54
Waiwera.
Telephone 0942-64792. Licensed.

Colosseo   56
368 Karangahape Road, Auckland.
Telephone 771-694. BYO.

Country Life   58
Highway 1, Waikanae.
Telephone (0583) 6353. Licensed.

95 Filleul   60
95 Filleul Street, Dunedin.
Telephone 777-233. BYO.

Flamingos   62
242 Jervois Road, Herne Bay, Auckland.
Telephone 765-899. BYO.

Fraser's   64
Tinakori Road, Wellington.
Telephone 730-342. BYO.

Fraser's Place   66
116 Parnell Road, Parnell, Auckland.
Telephone 774-080. BYO.

Gainsborough House   68
61 Ulster Street, Hamilton.
Telephone 394-172. Licensed.

Harley's   70
25 Anzac Avenue, Auckland.
Telephone 735-801. BYO.

Huka Lodge   78
Huka Falls Road, Taupo.
Telephone 85-791. Licensed.

Il Casino   80
108 Tory Street, Wellington.
Telephone 857-496. Licensed.

Korean Barbecue   82
27 High Street, Auckland.
Telephone 33-382. BYO.

Kurashiki   84
Gloucester and Colombo Streets, Christchurch.
Telephone 67-092. Licensed.

La Bonne Auberge   86
Moana Court, Orewa.
Telephone 65-379. BYO.

Landmark   88
1 Meade Street, Rotorua.
Telephone 89-376. Licensed.

Last and First Cafe   90
192 Symonds Street, Auckland.
Telephone 792-877. BYO.

Le Petit Café   98
8 Bannister Street, Masterton.
Telephone 85-776. BYO.

Louis'   100
139 Worcester Street, Christchurch.
Telephone 61-969. BYO.

Maggie's Farm 102
303 Dominion Road, Auckland.
Telephone 602-714. BYO.

Martini's 104
128A Oxford Terrace, Christchurch.
Telephone 69-363. BYO.

Mekong 106
12 Victoria Street West, Auckland.
Telephone 797-591. BYO.

Meridian 108
The Parade, Bucklands Beach, Auckland.
Telephone 534-4943. BYO.

Orsini's 110
50 Ponsonby Road, Auckland.
Telephone 764-563. Licensed.

Packer's Arms 112
Queenstown.
Telephone 929. Licensed.

Papillon 114
286 Jervois Road, Herne Bay, Auckland.
Telephone 765-367. BYO.

Pedro's 116
143 Worcester Street, Christchurch.
Telephone 797-668. BYO.

Penguin's Nest 118
174 Hurstmere Road, Takapuna, Auckland.
Telephone 499-574. Licensed.

Penmarric 120
50 Hamilton Road, Cambridge.
Telephone 4610. BYO.

Pierre's 122
342 Tinakori Road, Wellington.
Telephone 726-238. BYO.

Portobello 126
270 Victoria Street, Hamilton.
Telephone 82-305. BYO.

Plusone 124
63 Bank Street, Whangarei.
Telephone 89-993. BYO.

Roaring Meg's 134
57 Shotover Street, Queenstown.
Telephone 968. BYO.

Rogann's 136
12 Wyndham Street, Auckland.
Telephone 398-689. Licensed.

Seddon House 138
67 Seddon Street, Hamilton.
Telephone 78-294. BYO.

Sheraton 140
107 Milson Line, Palmerston North.
Telephone 77-686. Licensed.

Shiraz 142
470 Richmond Road, Grey Lynn, Auckland.
Telephone 766-276. BYO.

Stanmore Cottage 144
201 Brightside Road, Stanmore Bay,
Whangaparaoa.
Telephone HBC-7074. BYO.

Upstairs Downstairs 146
66 Shotover Street, Queenstown.
Telephone 2203. BYO.

Vesuvio's 154
16 Swanson Street, Auckland.
Telephone 794-769. BYO.

Westy's 156
The Mall, Queenstown.
Telephone 609. BYO.